More Praise for *Goin*

"A great book on civic enterprise . . . an es
urban bookshelf."
—**Sam Smith, author of the** *Great American Political*
Repair Manual

"*Going Local* is on the short list of books for people serious about creating a positive future in their community. Easy to read, it offers ideas both inspiring and practical."
—**Michael Kinsley, Rocky Mountain Institute**

"If any community desired a handbook and a theoretical resource to support itself in its self-reliance vision, this is it."
—**Diane Fassel, in** *Social Policy*

"An impressive synthesis of current trends, policies, and initiatives into a rational agenda for building more sustainable local economies."
—**Robert Jaquay, in** *The Neighborhood Works*

"In this lively and fact-filled volume . . . Shuman inspires us to envision a world in which what we buy supports rather than undermines our goals for a just, sustainable, and compassionate future."
—**Fran Korten, President, Positive Future Networks**
and *Yes! Magazine*

"Thoughtful and imaginative proposals for making communities more economically and environmentally sustainable in the global marketplace."
—**Marc Weiss, Senior Fellow, Center for National Policy and**
former Special Assistant to the Secretary of HUD
Henry Cisneros

"Exciting, practical steps every city can take to nurture community-friendly businesses that enhance prosperity and security."
—**Larry Agran, former Mayor of Irvine, California**

GOING
LOCAL

Creating
Self-Reliant
Communities
in a
Global Age

MICHAEL H. SHUMAN

Routledge
New York

Published in 2000 by
Routledge
29 West 35th Street
New York, NY 10001

First published in hardcover in 1998 by The Free Press
and reprinted by arrangement with The Free Press.
First Routledge paperback edition, 2000

Routledge is an imprint of the Taylor & Francis Group.

Printed in the United States of America on acid-free paper.

Library of Congress Cataloging-in-Publication Data

Shuman, Michael
Going local : creating self-reliant communities in a global age /
    Michael H. Shuman.
        p.   cm.
    ISBN 0-415-92768-4
    1. Sustainable development—United States—Case Studies.   2. Free enterprise—
    United States—Case Studies.   3. Community development—United States—
    Case Studies.   I. Title.
    HC110.E5S49 1998
    338.973—dc21   97-27339
                                                                             CIP

10   9   8   7   6   5

FOR DEBORAH

The real work of planet-saving will be small, humble, and humbling, and (insofar as it involves love) pleasing and rewarding. Its jobs will be too many to count, too many to report, too many to be publicly noticed or rewarded, too small to make anyone rich or famous.

—WENDELL BERRY

C O N T E N T S

Acknowledgments   xi

INTRODUCTION   1
  No Place Like Home   6
  The Perils of Mobility   8
  The Triumph of Economists   15
  An Emerging Countermovement   20
  A Way Forward   26

1. PLACE MATTERS   31
  Bad People and Bad Civics   33
  The Science of Efficiency   37
  Free Trade vs. Community   39
  A New Economics of Place   45

2. NEEDS-DRIVEN INDUSTRIES   51
  Import Replacement   52
  Food Industries   58
  Energy Industries   64
  Natural-Resources Industries   71
  Materials Industries   74
  Beyond Necessities   77

3. COMMUNITY CORPORATIONS   83
  A Taxonomy of American Business   85
  Engines of Self-Reliance   88
  New Models   98
  Empowerment Through Ownership   104

4. FINANCING THE FUTURE   106
  Bankers vs. Communities   107
  Community-Development Financial Institutions   111
  Unconventional Loans   115

Locally Owned Equity ... 117
Pension Reinvestment ... 120
The Role of Public Policy ... 121

5. **PRO-COMMUNITY LOCAL GOVERNANCE** ... 123
The Virtues of Localism ... 124
Local Reinvestment ... 128
Local Purchasing ... 132
Selective Privatization ... 138
Local Hiring ... 140
Local Taxes ... 144
A Question of Power ... 149

6. **BRINGING HOME POWER, NOT BACON** ... 152
Real Home Rule ... 155
A New Approach to Trade ... 158
Rethinking Corporations ... 167
Neighborhood Banking ... 171
Community Lobbying ... 174

7. **MAKING HISTORY** ... 177
Ten Steps Toward Community Self-Reliance ... 180
The New Global Village ... 198
The Lilliputian Strategy ... 200

Appendix: Around the World Economy in 80 Ways ... 205
Notes ... 285
Index ... 307

A c k n o w l e d g m e n t s

Going Local came about from what might be called an unexpected pregnancy. In July 1995, I sent Adam Bellow and Mitch Horowitz, editors at The Free Press, a book proposal concerning the emerging overlap between what many refer to, politically speaking, as left and right policies. They were particularly intrigued by a single paragraph of the proposal in which I suggested that progressives ought to transform their antipathy toward corporations into a principled commitment to create community-friendly businesses. Ultimately, Adam and Mitch offered a *two*-book deal—one based on the proposal and the other on the paragraph—and insisted I write the second first. Aware that my bargaining power as an author was negligible, I only halfheartedly signed the contract. But whatever reservations I had about proceeding evaporated quickly when I realized that this project could enable me to pull together 15 years of organizing, thinking, and writing about community economics.

My involvement in local politics began shortly after I graduated from Stanford Law School in 1982, when I cofounded and then directed the Center for Innovative Diplomacy (CID). For nine years, CID built up a network of several thousand mayors and council members who were eager to influence international relations through initiatives like antiapartheid divestment, nuclear-free zones, sister cities with war-torn villages in Nicaragua and El Salvador, and stratospheric ozone-protection ordinances.

With a fellowship from the W. K. Kellogg Foundation in 1987, I tried to map out how these practitioners of municipal foreign policy could move beyond arms control and human rights, and into economic development. How, I wondered, could wealthier communities in the First World alleviate the poverty in most Third World megacities and villages? The best answers to this question were coming from a group called Towns and Development, a coalition of citizen groups, nongovernmental organizations, and elected officials based in The Hague, which was overseeing creative sister-city links among more than 4,000 communities worldwide. Towns and Development commissioned me to write an evaluation of their programs, and I put my findings in a book titled *Towards a Global Village* (London: Pluto, 1993). While generally enthusiastic about municipal North–South relationships, I also voiced reservations. I was particularly concerned that participants professed their dedication to creating "sustainable communities," yet had no coherent vision of what the term meant.

The more that criticism sank in, the more I worried about continuing to work abroad. Were sister-city programs pushing southern partners down a path of free trade, economic growth, and modernization that would ultimately destroy their ecosystems, communities, and families? Did it make sense to promote programs to alleviate poverty abroad while we still had no coherent program for doing so at home?

And so began my search for the meaning of sustainable communities in the United States. In 1994, I wrote a paper on "Reclaiming the Inner City" for the Kellogg Foundation's Task Force on African-American Men and Boys, with supervision by and much encouragement from Bobby Austin. I began to collect stories about communities making strides toward economic self-reliance. Little of this good news, I discovered, reaches the mainstream press, and even the most innovative communities haven't a clue about what others may be doing down the road.

This book aims to weave these anecdotes into a larger story of how community development can succeed in an era of globalization. I promised myself at the outset not to shy away from taking positions that would challenge and shake up more than a few friends and colleagues, so let me assure readers that indeed few (if any) of the people listed below agree with all the ideas presented. However, nothing is better for sharpening a manuscript than tough critics, and in that spirit I'd like to thank:

—Mitch Horowitz, the book's editor and father, who continually offered helpful editorial suggestions and encouragement;

—Ron Goldfarb, agent extraordinaire;

—various interns (Neil Allison, Meg Moga, and Rachel Gilliar) and research assistants (Marc Norman and Jenny Kassan), who have been true intellectual partners in the development of the ideas that follow;

—the fellows of the Institute for Policy Studies (Gar Alperovitz, Sarah Anderson, Richard Barnet, Phyllis Bennis, Robert Borosage, John Cavanagh, Martha Honey, Saul Landau, and especially Marcus Raskin, whose project on Paths for the 21st Century sponsored this work);

—my colleagues at the Institute for Local-Self Reliance, on whose board I now sit, who have pioneered the theory and practice of sustainable community economics (notably Harriet Barlow, Margie Harris, Richard Kazis, Kirk Marckwald, David Morris, Brenda Platt, Rachel Pohl, Ronni Posner, Neil Seldman, and Leslie Tolf);

—the Jennifer Altman, Dorot, HKH, and New Land Foundations, Andre Carothers, and Peter Ungerleider for underwriting parts of this work;

—the members of my "econ salon" reading group who brought wonderfully diverse perspectives to two years of discussions about community economics (Naomi Friedman, Marty Gelfand, Tom Hilliard, Larry Martin, Margie Suozzo, Andrea Torrice, and Michael Wood-Lewis);

—the students who have taken my course on sustainable communities at the IPS Social Action and Leadership School for Activists (SALSA), who are among my most important teachers; and

—the people who generously provided comments on early drafts, including David Anderson, John J. Berger, Don Brake, Peter Brown, Edgar Cahn, Scott Campbell, Robert Lolo-Charbonneau, Kate Clancy, Don Edwards, Olaf Egeberg, Ellen Furnari, Hal Harvey, Colin Hines, Jenny Kassan, Gregory Kats, Terry Kistler, Larry Martin, John McClaughry, Russell Mechem, Toni Nelson, Dave Ranney, Jan Reiner, Mark Ritchie, Tom Schlesinger, Trent Schroyer, Richard Sclove, Jack Shuman, Sam Smith, Anja Speerforck, Charlie Spencer, Shann Turnbull, Stephen Viederman, Thad Williamson, Susan Witt, and Michael Wood-Lewis.

Finally, I would like to thank Deborah Epstein, to whom I've dedicated this book. She has been everything a writer could ever hope a spouse would be: tolerant of inexcusably long working hours; supportive during hard times and unabashedly critical during the rest; patient with a stream of bizarre thoughts at 4:00 A.M.; and, above all, fun to work alongside in a household with dueling word processors.

I have written this book for anyone and everyone committed to reviving his, her, or their own community. Since most community-change agents do not have a lot of time on their hands, I've tried to keep this volume short, and free of economic jargon. I leave the in-depth case studies, city-by-city blueprints, and econometric modeling to others.

Given my long-time association with progressive political causes, many readers will be surprised—and some annoyed—to find that I'm also a strong believer in economic growth, weak central government, private ownership, and the profit motive. How all these views can exist within the same person is the story of this book. I believe that they not only are consistent but also have the potential to revive an all-but-dead progressive movement in America. *This* thesis, however, must await completion of the book I initially proposed to Mitch and Adam.

Michael Shuman
August 1997

Introduction

Nearly every state, county, city, town, and village in America is hitching its future to globe-trotting corporations. Most communities have become convinced that by creating a favorable business environment to attract multinational, export-oriented firms, they can compete in the new global economy and ensure "good jobs at good wages." Local elected officials shuttle across oceans to offer up lavish financing, tax breaks, and deals to lure foreign investors. "I strongly believe that if cities are to be competitive in the twenty-first century, they need to be international," says Mayor Kurt Schmoke of Baltimore.[1] By this he means not only finding global sales opportunities for Baltimore firms but also "creating an environment that will enable international companies to use Baltimore as a gateway to the United States."[2] The actual results of going global may not be known for years, but even some of the winners in this competition are beginning to have second thoughts. Just ask the residents of Cleveland, Ohio.

Cleveland is widely considered the comeback kid of American cities. A generation ago, this jurisdiction of rusting smokestacks was the butt of national jokes. The main river running through town had become so polluted that it spontaneously combusted, inspiring the folk lyrics "Burn On, Cuyahoga." Today Cleveland is thought to be one of the better places to live in the United States. The Flats, an area where smokestack industry once blackened the sky, has been rehabilitated into a popular nightspot

with restaurants, bars, and discos. The locals brag about the new downtown stadium (Jacobs Field) and the basketball arena next to it. Tourists
flock to the recently opened Rock and Roll Hall of Fame. Residents and
outsiders praise Mayor Michael White for revitalizing downtown with
freshly constructed indoor malls, hotels, and office buildings.

Many believe that the rebirth of Cleveland was catalyzed by the city's
aggressive participation in the global economy. In 1993, *World Trade* magazine rated Cleveland number one in its review of "Best Cities for
International Companies."[3] Harvard business professor Rosabeth Moss
Kanter, in her book *World Class: Thriving Locally in the Global Economy,*
congratulates Mayor White and his associates on opening up his municipal economy to foreigners:

> [O]wnership of major Cleveland companies moved outside of
> Cleveland and even outside of the United States; Nestlé bought
> Stouffer's and BP (British Petroleum) bought Sohio. A Cleveland com-
> pany featured at a U.S. Labor Department conference on exemplary
> workplaces was a joint venture with a Japanese company. Local leader-
> ship grew after foreign ownership increased.[4]

The Cleveland World Trade Association, founded in 1915, holds 40
events a year to help 1,400 local manufacturers sell goods overseas. In
1991, William Butler, head of the Eaton Corporation, persuaded a number of local CEOs, city and county officials, and the port authority to
form the Greater Cleveland International Trade Alliance, which in turn
built a World Trade Center in 1993. Other initiatives taken through
public–private partnerships include a $1 billion expansion of the air-
port's international hub, deep discounts in container shipping in the
local port, and new foreign-trade zones with reduced taxes and suspended regulations. Mayor White is not shy about articulating his vision:
"There's a whole world waiting to buy what we make in Cleveland. We
live in a global village; cities like Cleveland must reach out to the world
and market our strengths."[5]

Two successive Ohio governors, Democrat Richard Celeste and
Republican George Voinovich, have assisted Cleveland's trade efforts. The
state rewards its corporations with an export tax credit and provides computerized catalogs to facilitate exports. Regular listeners to National Public

Radio hear an enhanced-underwriting jingle in which the state of Ohio boasts that it is "number one" in corporate site selection.

Beyond the hype about the new Cleveland, however, are some disquieting facts. Over the past 35 years, nearly half the city's population has moved to the wealthier suburbs, creating an explosive level of economic and racial segregation: Three out of four poor African-Americans live in impoverished neighborhoods in Cleveland; three out of four poor whites, in contrast, live in more affluent areas. A quarter of a million people—42 percent of its residents—live below the poverty line (which the federal government now defines as $15,150 per year for a family of four).[6] Two out of three kids never graduate from high school.[7] Stores and shops run for generations by families are shutting down because of the proliferation of chain stores like Wal-Mart, Barnes & Noble, and Home Depot, which offer less expensive products. In the quest to find lower-wage venues elsewhere in the world, local industries have taken 96,000 high-paying manufacturing jobs out of the city since 1979, with offsetting job growth occurring primarily in low-pay professions like sales and clerking.

And then there's the matter of the Browns. If there's any sport that Clevelanders take seriously, it's football. "The Browns Are Cleveland" is what signs throughout the city used to say. For 45 years, loyalists endured rain, snow, and bitter cold to root for the home team. In November 1995, however, a week after the city's baseball team narrowly lost the World Series, fans were stunned to learn that Browns owner Art Modell planned to move the football team to Baltimore. After failing to strong-arm Cleveland officials to build a new stadium, Modell decided to skip town. Clevelanders were livid and felt betrayed, cheated, abandoned. Some told Modell to go to hell; others begged him to stay. Either way, the decision was out of their hands.

A few hundred miles across the Great Lakes was a community with a football franchise that had no such worries. To much of the world Green Bay, Wisconsin—a smallish town with 97,000 people—is known for one thing: the Packers. In 1922, three years into their existence, the Packers were teetering on bankruptcy. The team's original owners had invested very little at the outset, and gate receipts were lower than expected. But then four fans decided to help. They reorganized the franchise into a nonprofit corporation whose 15 directors would be elected by local shareholders. With the help of the city and the school board, the nonprofit built the team's first stadium. During the Depression the team stumbled again, and went into receivership, but now the nonprofit leadership came up with a novel idea. Pointing out how vital the team was for local business and tourism, the Packers' Executive Committee convinced the Green Bay Association of Commerce to organize its members into neighborhood teams and sell $25 shares, door-to-door. As of this writing, 1,915 shareholders owned 4,634 shares of the team, and 60 percent lived in Green Bay.[8] Shareholders can trade shares within their families, or sell them back to the corporation for $25. But nobody can own more than 20 shares.

Because the Green Bay Packers are a nonprofit corporation, shareholders receive neither annual dividends nor capital gains upon resale, though they do exercise control over the franchise by voting for the board of directors (currently numbering 45 members). The team's general counsel, Lance Lopes, proudly says that the corporation's mission is "to field a competitive team and maintain the team in Green Bay in perpetuity. You might have noticed, I never mentioned the word 'profit.'"[9] When the team runs a financial surplus, as it has in recent years, net revenues are reinvested either in the stadium or in the players, or in both. If the team were ever to run a loss (it hasn't, however, failed to sell out a local game since 1958), the corporation could sell additional stock to members of the community to rejuvenate finances. The bylaws stipulate that, in the event of dissolution, the proceeds are to be donated to the local chapter of the American Legion. Green Bay will never be run by an Art Modell, and Baltimore will never have a team called the Packers.

Sports teams and stadiums may be overrated tools for community economic development, but the Packers have proven to be a remarkable exception. A recent study by the conservative Wisconsin Policy Research Institute calculates:

> *The direct economic benefits to Green Bay from the Packers are about $60 million a year from an asset that would cost roughly $200 million to replicate, if it were even possible to do so. The indirect economic effects of the Packers as part of the area's magnet are almost impossible to measure, but locals believe the team is important for their long-term well-being. Local charities will earn about $400,000 this year operating the Lambeau Field concession stands.*[10]

The team's victory in the 1997 Super Bowl undoubtedly will boost these numbers.

Liberals and conservatives alike are impressed by the structure of the Green Bay Packers. "Essentially public property," argue Harvey Kaye and Isaac Kramnick, two liberal social scientists, "the Packers have been secured for the generations and to the city. If the corporate types who dominate the NFL had their way, the Packers would have long ago been transferred to a bigger city with a larger population and media market. In the fashionable language of the day, the Pack would have been 'privatized.' "[11] Paul Gigot, a right-leaning columnist on the op-ed page of the *Wall Street Journal,* says: "If any team can be called conservative, it is the one that embodies tradition and communal loyalties the way [the Packers] does."[12]

Two Midwestern cities, two football teams, two parables about the relationship between ownership and community well-being. It's easy to miss the significance of these stories by focusing on the subject matter—which is, after all, only fun and games. Most of us expect a city to be possessive of such cultural icons as sports teams, as Seattle was when it fought off Japanese plans to buy its baseball team, the Mariners. But does it make sense to be any less concerned about losing factories, offices, shops, and farms? Those enterprises are the lifeblood of a community. They provide the jobs that keep families alive. They pump up the local economy through sales, savings, and investments. They pay the income-, property-, and sales taxes that finance schools, hospitals, police, and street repairs.

The Green Bay Packers Corporation, it needs to be said, is not a model that other communities can copy. The National Football League dominates the professional market and imposes rules on its 30 franchises. Revenues from the sales of television rights, tickets, T-shirts, and nicknacks are shared among all NFL teams, and "caps" (limits) are placed on the sum of the salaries a team can pay. Without these rules, the Packers would have lower revenues and be less able to compete for top players. The NFL also has made it impossible for other teams to follow Green Bay's example: Every franchise, with an exception carved for the Packers, now must be at least 51 percent owned by a single individual.

Still, there is a valuable lesson for other communities in what Green Bay did: Ownership matters. When residents of a community own a thriving business, they are reluctant to let go of it; they naturally want to reap the benefits indefinitely. Community ownership, of course, can come in many forms. The citizens of Green Bay own the corporation running the Packers, whereas the municipality of Green Bay owns Lambeau Field, and uses taxes and fees from the Packers to pay for stadium upkeep and upgrades. Whatever the precise form, however, local ownership boosts local loyalty. It diminishes the chances of a community's receiving the kind of traitorous blow that Art Modell dealt Cleveland. It means that such difficult-to-quantify factors as community stability, cultural preservation, and civic pride enter business decisions along with traditional measures of profitability. And it gives a community the chance, even in an increasingly powerful global economy, to regain control over its own destiny.

NO PLACE LIKE HOME

This book is about how communities can reinvigorate their economies by "going local." For more than a generation, theorists like Leopold Kohr, Ivan Illych, E. F. Schumacher, Jane Jacobs, Paul Goodman, and David Morris have offered provocative ideas for a new economics sensitive to place. Think tanks have sprung up around the world to elaborate and apply these ideas, including the Institute for Local Self-Reliance in Washington, D.C. and St. Paul, Minnesota; the E. F. Schumacher Society in Great Barrington, Massachusetts; the Institute for Community Economics in Springfield, Massachusetts; the Rocky Mountain Institute in Snowmass, Colorado; and the New Economics Foundation in London. While these thinkers and institutions have diverse perspectives, they share one core belief: A community can best strengthen its economy when it builds on its internal strengths.

Going local does *not* mean walling off the outside world. It means nurturing locally owned businesses which use local resources sustainably, employ local workers at decent wages, and serve primarily local consumers. It means becoming more self-sufficient, and less dependent on imports. Control moves from the boardrooms of distant corporations and back to the community, where it belongs.

The key player in this transformation is an entity I will call a *community corporation*—any business anchored to the community through ownership. Some community corporations are small for-profits, with stock held by residents of the community. Others are public enterprises owned by the local government, or nonprofits effectively owned by the community as a whole. The term includes corporate "forms" that already exist, but also anticipates new kinds of business structures.

The focus is deliberately on a broad range of possibilities, because any given model is less important than the overall argument. And that argument is this: The only way communities can ensure their economic well-being is to stop chasing multinational firms with no community loyalties, and to start investing in community corporations. Prosperity follows when ownership, production, and consumption become intimately connected with place.

Most economists regard this argument as heresy. They believe that privately owned firms should be free to move anywhere, anytime, for any reason. As Milton Friedman argued in the *New York Times Magazine* in 1970, "There is one and only one social responsibility of business—to use its resources and engage in activities designed to increase its profits. . . ."[13] Community ownership, by this logic, only impedes the ability of business to move to more profitable locations.

Before becoming Secretary of Labor, Harvard political economist Robert Reich implored national decisionmakers to "get global managers to site good jobs in the United States. Our best interests are served by making it easy, attractive, and productive for them to do so, regardless of the nationality of the company they represent."[14] Reich did not even consider the possibility—let alone the desirability—of communities developing their own enterprises rather than luring outsiders. "Gone," Reich wrote, "is the tight connection between the company, its community, even its country. Vanishing too are the paternalistic corporate heads who used to feel a sense of responsibility for their local community."[15] The global economy in which businesses move freely and quickly is a given, so communities should not waste their time even trying to reclaim control. The goal is to win the worldwide competition for capital, not to tinker with the rules of the game.

Economists believe that if General Motors can manufacture a car at a lower cost in Mexico than in Detroit, the company would be foolish not to move south. Why deprive GM shareholders the benefits of higher profits, or U.S. consumers the benefits of cheaper cars? If workers in Detroit cannot produce the cheapest cars in the world, then they should enter another line of work that *is* globally competitive. Constraints on corporate mobility are ultimately self-destructive, since they make it less likely that a globally competitive business will set up shop in the jurisdiction in the first place.

It's fair to say that political leaders across America, whether liberal or conservative, Democrat or Republican, embrace this catechism. Politicians and planners only quibble about what a business-friendly environment should look like. Liberals like Robert Reich argue that a well-paid, well-educated, and well-organized labor force can improve the profitability of business, that environmentally sound production can be cost-effective, and that both require government intervention and corporate self-policing. They point out that smart regulations can prevent corporations from generating toxic wastes or marketing dangerous drugs like thalidomide, and thereby save them massive legal liabilities down the road. Conservatives like the editorialists of the *Wall Street Journal* have less sympathy for unions, ecosystems, and litigious consumers, as well as for government interventions to protect them, because they believe that market regulations of *any* type are a drag on business profits. Both camps agree, however, that prosperity for the nation as a whole necessitates that every community become an attractive place for mobile corporations to park themselves.

THE PERILS OF MOBILITY

No word better captures the new world economy than *mobility*. Millions of workers migrate across national boundaries to temporary jobs, to send small wads of cash back home to their families. The falling price of transportation has enabled technology, machinery, and natural resources to be affordably shipped to factories worldwide. Information, an increasingly important part of production, moves through the Internet at the speed of light and allows people thousands of miles from each other to work closely together. With global financial transactions now topping $3 trillion a day, few companies committed to maximizing profits can afford not to scour the planet for exciting new business deals.

The only part of the production process that cannot move is land. Parcels of real estate are where consumers live, farmers grow food, producers operate factories, and workers clock-in their time. And around these stationary islands emerge the networks of people, art, music, crafts, religion, and politics we call *community*.

Americans have mixed feelings about mobility. As a nation of immigrants, we celebrate people who have moved to greener pastures. Our national heroes include Columbus, the Pilgrims, Lewis and Clark, frontiersmen, cowboys, and astronauts. Seeing ourselves as transcending history, we are unusually open to packing our bags and exploring new horizons. Yet we also maintain profound attachments to place. Alexis de Tocqueville, writing about America in the 1830s, observed that the "New England township is shaped to form the nucleus of strong attachments, and there is meanwhile no rival center close by to attract the hot hearts of ambitious men."[16]

Perhaps it is our historic love–hate relationship with mobility that enables us to appreciate the double-edged nature of the new global economy. We welcome the influx of new ideas, cultures, technologies, and products that enrich our communities. Yet we also worry about the accelerating global circulation of guns, nuclear-bomb materials, AIDS, insect vectors, drugs, pornography, and crime syndicates. And more and more of us recognize that, despite assurances from economists, the increasing mobility of our economic assets carries enormous risks.

The growing power and will of corporations to move without notice or warning has presented many communities with a terrible dilemma: Either cut wages and benefits, gut environmental standards, and offer tax breaks to attract and retain corporations, or become a ghost town. Almost every U.S. town or city has learned that capital flight is not just a hypothetical danger. According to estimates by Barry Bluestone of the University of Massachusetts, decisions by corporations to move to other states or overseas resulted in the loss of between 32 million and 38 million jobs in the 1970s.[17] A recent analysis by the U.S. Department of Labor documents that 43 million jobs have been eliminated since 1979.[18] Most of these displaced workers found new jobs, but they typically had to accept pay cuts and lower-quality work.[19] More than a third of American households during this period went through the agony of having at least one family member laid off.[20]

How have states and cities responded to this dilemma? By offering ever-larger incentives for corporations to come in and set up shop. Public authorities have convinced themselves that modest investments in new firms will generate huge benefits in the form of greater consumer expenditures, new ancillary business, and increased tax revenues. A decade ago, both Illinois and the in-state town of Bloomington tried to induce Diamond Star Motors, a joint venture between Mitsubishi and Chrysler, to build an automobile assembly plant in Bloomington. The state ponied up $276 million in aid and tax breaks, and the city offered $10 million worth of land and $20 million in local tax abatements—a total of almost $28,000 per new job.[21] In 1985, Kentucky gave incentives to Toyota in the same range, as did Tennessee to General Motors Saturn.[22] In 1986, Indiana paid $50,000 per job to convince Subaru-Isuzu to open a factory in Lafayette.[23] By the 1990s, Alabama was agreeing to pay between $150,000 and $200,000 per job to convince Mercedes-Benz to build a new plant, and Kentucky was doling out $350,000 a job for Canadian steelmakers Dofasco, Inc., and Co-Steel, Inc.[24] To make good on its promises, Alabama officials tried unsuccessfully to snatch money away from public education (even though the state already ranked last in elementary- and secondary-school spending), and then resorted to borrowing from the state's pension fund.

Multinational corporations have become increasingly adept at pitting locales against one another.[25] In 1992, the German automaker BMW simultaneously courted South Carolina and Nebraska as possible locations for a new assembly plant that would cost $250 million to $300 million and produce 2,000 jobs.[26] Nebraska offered a benefits package worth $100 million; South Carolina countered with a $150 million package and won the deal. Two additional reasons why BMW chose South Carolina were the state's low wages and its historic hostility to unions. The average manufacturing wage in South Carolina, which BMW ultimately paid, was $10 per hour— $7 less than that received by the average U.S. auto worker, and $13 less than that earned by his or her German counterpart.

Old jobs have been put on the auction block alongside new ones. In 1982, Hyster warned all the locales where its factories assembled forklift trucks that the least profitable operations would be shut down.[27] Public officials in five U.S. states and three other countries were asked to make offerings from the public till to convince the company to keep plants open. The United Kingdom pumped $20 million into a Hyster plant employing 1,500 in Scotland, more than $13,000 a job. Towns in Alabama, Illinois, and Kentucky offered $28 million in grants and subsidized loans to protect their factories. In the end, Hyster managed to extort virtually $72.5 million from governments around the world. Other companies have exacted similar payoffs by threatening to move, including Raytheon (which bagged $20 million in tax breaks from Massachusetts),

Morgan Stanley and Kidder, Peabody & Company ($30 million each from New York City), and the Walt Disney Company ($800 million in highway and other infrastructure improvements from California and the city of Anaheim combined).[28] Today, more than 40 states offer property-tax abatements, loans for machinery and equipment, state revenue bond financing, accelerated depreciation, and special funds as incentives to help cities make deals.[29]

Politicians, of course, condemn these tactics even while they're signing the checks. Jim Edgar, Governor of Illinois, told his colleagues in the Council of State Governments that they can meet their economic responsibilities to the state only "by calling a truce to the bidding wars."[30] But, he added, "In Illinois, we are not disengaging unilaterally." The National Governors Association passed a resolution in 1993 declaring that "the public and private sectors should undertake cooperative efforts that result in improvements to the general economic climate rather than focus on subsidies for individual projects or companies."[31] During the two years in which the resolution was in effect, subsidies were still permissible, provided, among other things, they would "be used to encourage and foster development that otherwise would not occur, not merely to influence the location of private investment." Senators as ideologically far apart as Democrat Edward Kennedy of Massachusetts and Republican Alfonse D'Amato of New York have requested a congressional investigation into improper uses of federal money for corporate packages.

The most powerful influence that corporations wield over states and localities, however, is rather more abstract and insidious. State legislators and city-council members, under a steady barrage by corporate-supported think tanks and economists, are convinced that the key to global competitiveness is to "get government off the backs of private enterprise." This translates into fewer legal protections for union activities, wider tolerance for child labor and 60-hour work weeks, looser environmental standards, and greater obstacles to lawsuits against manufacturers of defective products.

No piece of legislation protecting workers, consumers, or ecosystems can proceed very far without opponents warning about the dire consequences for the business climate. Even if, as liberals argue, businesses benefit in the long run from well-paid workers and decent environmental regulations, few CEOs today actually believe this. Consequently, most com-

munity efforts to improve the quality of life weaken their ability to attract
or hold on to footloose corporations.

Corporate mobility today poses four fundamental threats to U.S. communities. First, it guarantees that U.S. communities will continue to experience declines in both the quantity and the quality of jobs, as indeed they
have for the past generation. As long as 700 million people in the world are
unemployed or underemployed (with another 700 million expected to join
their ranks in the next 20 years), firms that depend on large, uneducated
labor forces will have the attractive option of moving to places where they
are able to hire a new work force for $5 to $10 a day—or substantially less.[32]

Economists reply that what lures firms is not low labor costs per se, but
high worker productivity. The right question, they contend, is this: How
much production is coming from every dollar expended on labor?
American workers can compete with Third World workers, the argument
goes, because their better education and superior technology make them
far more productive. Even if an American steelworker is paid 10 times
more than a Brazilian steelworker, a plant will stay north if an American
worker has the skills and machinery to generate 20 times as much output.

The problem for the American worker, however, is that in many of the
most dynamic developing world economies where basic industrial infrastructure is now in place (such countries as Brazil, China, India, Indonesia,
and Mexico), labor productivity is rising much faster than our own. As
state-of-the-art technology proliferates around the world and becomes
more user-friendly, it is increasingly being used to raise the productivity of
poorly-paid workers in São Paulo, not well-paid workers in Pittsburgh.
And if USX is more loyal to its bottom line than to its workforce in
Pittsburgh, it will train workers in Brazil, and send machinery there that
will increase their labor productivity at much lower wages. In fact, it turns
out that steelworkers in Brazil are 58 percent as productive as their
American counterparts, but paid only one-tenth the wages.[33]

Harley Shaiken, a professor at the University of California at San Diego,
has shown that since the signing of the North American Free Trade
Agreement (NAFTA) in 1993, Mexican workers' wages have fallen to 1980
levels, despite a 65 percent increase in direct foreign investment in the
country's industrial sector.[34] In the *maquiladoras* near the U.S. border,
where U.S. companies can operate with virtual impugnity from regulation
by Mexican authorities, employment has practically doubled while wages

have hovered at about 91 cents an hour. Other studies prepared by the International Trade Commission, the United Nations, and the World Bank confirm that productivity differentials between and among developed and developing countries are much narrower than wage differentials,[35] which explains why corporate departures are so lucrative.

The productivity argument falls apart entirely when environmental protection enters the picture. Legal mandates to reduce pollution or protect endangered species typically require a firm to adopt more expensive methods of production, which in turn reduce labor productivity. This underscores why "business-friendly" environmental regulation typically means greater toleration of smokestacks spewing poisonous sulfur dioxides and carbon monoxides, drainpipes dumping sewage and chemicals into rivers, and nearby ditches holding piles of unprocessed toxic wastes. It also explains why most developing countries, with fewer and weakly enforced environmental measures, are becoming increasingly attractive sites for northern companies. When Lawrence Summers was serving as the chief economist for the World Bank in 1992, he wrote in a confidential memo to his staff: "Just between you and me, shouldn't the World Bank be encouraging more migration of dirty industries to the [less developed countries]?"[36] He added that the "underpopulated countries are vastly underpolluted." Little wonder that critics of globalization call it "the race to the bottom."

In the new global economy, *any* community that attempts to hold onto a corporation may have to pay a steep price. Notwithstanding the subsidies and tax abatements that fleece the local treasury, it must cope with the deterioration of the local quality of life, as unions are busted and pollution laws are suspended to keep jobs in town. To be sure, the departure of environmentally damaging facilities like nuclear-power plants or cattle slaughterhouses might bring a measure of relief to some. But those thrown out of work will never cheer the departure of a business. Furthermore, their economic insecurity usually is accompanied by such serious social costs as increased suicide rates, domestic violence, crime, and despair.[37] Analyzing unemployment data between 1940 and 1973, Dr. Harvey Brenner of Johns Hopkins University found that every additional percentage point of unemployment over a six-year period was correlated with the addition of 3,300 state-prison incarcerations, 4,000 mental-hospital admissions, 500 deaths from cirrhosis of the liver, 650 homicides, 920 suicides, and 37,000 early deaths.[38]

A second way in which corporate mobility harms a community is that sudden departures impose huge costs on *all* levels of government. A company that abandons a community rarely has to contribute to unemployment compensation and welfare benefits. Nor does it have to figure out how ancillary businesses will be kept alive when more residents don't have jobs, and thus have little or no disposable income to spend. Once gone, the firm leaves behind plummeting property values, foreclosed mortgages, defaulted loans, and a depleted tax base that no longer can support basic services like schools, hospitals, street repairs, electric utilities, and police. The layoff of thousands of steel workers in Youngstown, Ohio, in 1977 hit up the federal government for $70 million over the following three years in unemployment compensation, welfare payments, lost taxes, and other costs.[39]

A third problem that mobile corporations pose for communities is the gradual destruction of local culture. The global rush to free trade through such treaties as NAFTA and the General Agreement on Tariffs and Trade (GATT) not only has lowered the quality of life everywhere but also has blurred distinctions between communities. Only with extraordinary zoning or planning measures can communities resist the onslaught of national and international chain stores, and even these legal limitations might be overturned by courts as property-right takings without just compensation.

The spread of the same brands, the same stores, and the same institutions has homogenized communities and dulled people's sense of place. Community life simply becomes less interesting if the streets in Encinitas, California, look identical to those in Portsmouth, New Hampshire—or, for that matter, to the canals of Venice, where McDonald's now appears alongside the gelato stands.

A final problem posed by mobile corporations is that they undermine the capacity of communities to plan for the future. The standard tools of regulation and taxation that communities once used to establish a balanced, give-and-take relationship with private firms are now branded as bad for business. Special interests dictate the public interest. Increasingly, governance is driven not by any consensus among the myriad constituencies within a community, but by its most powerful corporations. The city of Atlanta follows the lead of Coca-Cola, Turner Broadcasting, and Delta Airlines. Houston accommodates Exxon, Shell, and Arco. Seattle is beholden to Microsoft and Boeing. New York bends over backwards to assist the development plans of Donald Trump. More and more communities in America have become Company Towns. It's just a matter of degree.

THE TRIUMPH OF ECONOMISTS

How have America's politicians reacted to the acceleration of corporate mobility and its impact on communities? In 1996, only the marginal candidates for president—Patrick Buchanan on the right, Ross Perot in the "radical middle," and Ralph Nader on the left—spoke to the problem. And indeed, their challenge to economic orthodoxy contributed to most journalists' and pundits' ridiculing them as kooks.

Free-marketeers dismiss the costs imposed on communities by mobile corporations as irrelevant. The "gales of creative destruction," as economist Joseph Schumpeter put it two generations ago, are what capitalist competition is all about. If agribusiness conglomerates operate more efficiently than family farmers, then it's time for the latter to pack up their bags and move to the cities; nostalgia for rural America should never stand in the way of cheaper food. If some communities lose factories while others gain them, don't bail out the losers; move unemployed workers from decaying communities to vibrant ones.

In his widely read *Newsweek* column, economist Robert J. Samuelson tells readers to stop whining about the downsizing of companies: "[W]hat's bad for individual workers and firms—job insecurity, bankruptcy—may be good for society."[40] Recent economic history, Samuelson implores, teaches that insecurity is the necessary price of a healthy economy:

> *From the 1960s to the early 1980s, government officials and corporate managers consciously strove to expand employment, eliminate recessions and enhance job security. Keynesian economics dominated; "responsible" companies promised, implicitly or explicitly, lifetime jobs.*
>
> *The experiment failed: the concerted pursuit of these worthwhile goals—total job security and economic stability—gave us higher unemployment as well as higher inflation.*[41]

Certainly the vast majority of Americans who enjoyed improved incomes and job security for nearly 50 years after the inauguration of the New Deal, despite periodic episodes of inflation, would dispute Samuelson's version of history. But it does accurately represent the consensus among free-marketeers that stability for workers—and, implicitly, stability for communities—is ultimately self-destructive.

Many economists worry about job security because they believe it causes inflation. In their view, a certain "natural" rate of unemployment (the so-called NAIRU, or Non-Accelerating Inflation Rate of Unemployment), in the range of 5 to 6 percent, is necessary to keep down inflation and protect national well-being. If too many workers are employed, they'll start demanding higher wages, which in turn will trigger inflation. This explains why a *New York Times* headline can indicate that the head of the Federal Reserve Board, Alan Greenspan, "*Warns* of Wage Rises."[42] NAIRU, a theory originally articulated by conservative economist Milton Friedman, ironically resurrects Karl Marx's argument that capitalists strive to keep wages down by having a "reserve army of the unemployed."

The actual data underlying the hypothesized linkage between inflation and employment turn out to be weak, and even some traditional economists concede that the NAIRU appears to be—miraculously—falling.[43] But think about the underlying logic for a moment. If the government stepped in and taxed corporate managers, then redistributed their eight-figure salaries to their workers, wages could go up and product prices could stay even. That the planet's 447 billionaires now have more money than the poorest half of the people in the world combined suggests how much room for redistribution there is. Alternatively, if shareholders turned some of their profits back into paying workers higher wages, prices also could remain stable. Inflation, in other words, could be said to reflect not a failure to keep a certain number of people out of work, but a refusal of corporate heads and shareholders to redistribute more fairly the gains from production. A rigorous national anti-inflation policy might better focus on placing upper limits on incomes and profits, rather than lower limits on unemployment. What the popularity of NAIRU theory among economists really demonstrates is a *moral* posture: They would prefer to throw 5 percent of the workforce onto the streets than to shrink the rewards to managers or shareholders.

The same economists who worry about stable jobs also worry about stable communities. While it is virtually impossible to find an economist who will say this outright, an implicit precept of prevailing economic theory is that a certain degree of community instability is good for the national economy. As long as communities compete with one another for mobile business, they will be forced to maintain a good business climate. The movement of firms from cities in the rustbelt to those in the sunbelt, or from big cities to edge cities, is good for us, because it sets a limit on how far communities can go in protecting labor and the environment.

A favorite whipping boy of national politicians over the past generation has been the free-wheeling, free-spending, overregulating big city. When Gerald Ford refused to rescue New York City from bankruptcy in 1975, a *Daily News* headline read: "Ford to City: Drop Dead." That's a fair description of the federal government's approach to America's big cities ever since. Budget-cutters throughout the 1980s reduced federal grants to state and local governments by $78 billion.[44] Factor out increases in federal dollars earmarked for medical care and housing, and reductions in other federal programs are even more dramatic. By 1990, states and cities were receiving $1 billion less each year for Economic Development Assistance and Social Service Block Grants than they were in 1980; $2 billion less for Community Service Block Grants, Community Development Block Grants, and Small Business Assistance; $4 billion less for wastewater treatment; $7 billion less for job training; and $10 billion less for General Revenue Sharing. Despite some refreshing city-friendly rhetoric, and several low-cost initiatives regarding housing and community banking, President Clinton has not reversed this trend. His single-minded pursuit of deficit reduction has effected a continued decline (in real terms) in federal money to the cities, and many local officials fear that his welfare reforms soon will impose huge new burdens on overstretched local budgets.[45]

The ranks of the free-marketeers who are willing to write off sizable parts of America's cities include not only libertarians and Fortune 500 CEOs but also many self-identified liberals. Nicholas Lemann, one of the nation's most eloquent historians on LBJ's War Against Poverty, wrote a widely discussed piece in the *New York Times Magazine* in early 1994 entitled "The Myth of Community Development."[46] Lemann reviewed the disappointing results of programs like Urban Renewal, Economic Revitalization, and Model Cities, and concluded that such initiatives are inevitably doomed to failure:

The problem is that on the whole, urban slums have never been home to many businesses except for sweatshops and minor neighborhood provisioners. The slums are usually near downtown, and the residents,

*when they can find work, have usually found it downtown. Also, poor
neighborhoods are usually transitional: rather than being stable, self-
sufficient communities on the model of a village in Vermont, they tend
to be home to people who plan to move out as soon as they make a little money. The standard model of progress for poor people living in
urban slums, repeated millions and millions of times over the decades,
is to get a good job outside the neighborhood and then decamp for a
nicer part of town.*[47]

The logical next step, of course, is to force poor people to decamp, if
they don't want to leave. Polite musings toward this end have crept into
such respectable periodicals as the *Atlantic Monthly*. In the October 1995
issue, Witold Rybczynski, a professor of urbanism at the University of
Pennsylvania, suggests that it's time to downsize cities:

*Rather than mounting an ineffectual rearguard action and trying to pre-
serve all neighborhoods, as is done now, the de facto abandonment that
is already in progress should be encouraged. Housing alternatives should
be offered in other parts of the city, partly occupied public housing vacat-
ed and demolished, and private landowners offered land swaps. Finally,
zoning for depopulated neighborhoods should be changed to a new category—zero occupancy—and all municipal services cut off.*[48]

What gives this proposal the chill of ethnic cleansing is that Dr. Rybczynski
understands that "since the poorest city inhabitants are predominantly
black and Hispanic, relocation would undoubtedly affect members of
these groups more than others."[49] Moreover, even though residents might
be asked to go quietly, if they don't, they will be removed. "Inevitably con-
solidation would involve the movement of individuals and families from
one part of the city to another. It is true that private freedoms would be
sacrificed for the common good. . . ."[50]

Not all economists, of course, are so callous to people's attachments to
place. Within the economics profession is a minority who resist cheering
about the new global economy but nevertheless believe that nothing can
be done about it—except to compete and win. Harvard Business School's
Rosabeth Moss Kanter laments the recent layoffs by AT&T, Lockheed
Marietta, Boeing, and countless other firms that have devastated commu-

nities across America: "[I]t is a grim but inevitable reality of our world economy that companies no longer have the same kind of civic attachment to communities that they once did."⁵¹ It is indeed an inevitable reality in the new global economy that privately owned firms, seeking to maximize profits, will relocate production facilities to the most business-friendly areas in the world. Yet Kanter reminds communities of the imperatives of operating a successful business:

> *In today's economy, if a company is to survive, it cannot always afford to employ people it doesn't need or to keep operations open in one city if it makes strategic sense to move them to another. Global competitors like AT&T need the flexibility to pursue resources and markets anywhere they can. In the short run, this may seem uncompassionate, but a corporation that doesn't behave this way risks failure, jeopardizing many more jobs in the long run.⁵²*

Her advice to localities? "Mold [yourselves] into regions that help companies become more globally competitive."⁵³ Think globally, act globally. "The route to success for people, companies, and localities is to become links in these global chains and to ensure that local activities meet world standards of excellence. Thus, cities and states—local and regional economies—will flourish to the extent that they provide linkage to global activities and networks."⁵⁴

And how can communities do this? Kanter urges municipalities to inventory their resources and decide whether they are Thinkers, Makers, or Traders. *Thinkers,* like Silicon Valley in northern California or Route 128 in Boston, thrive on computer hardware and software and other knowledge industries. *Makers,* like Cleveland, specialize in high-quality manufacturing. *Traders,* like Miami, take advantage of the confluence of nearby countries and cultures to focus on international deal-making. Once a community decides which identity to assume, it will be able to choose strategically which companies to court.

Even if one accepts the assumption that a community can prosper only if it competes more effectively in the national and global economies, the question remains concerning the best means to do so. Kanter does not differentiate locally-owned and -operated corporations, which have a long-term commitment to a community, from multinational corporations with no local commitment whatsoever. In her view, *any* firm that can contribute to the chosen development strategy—Thinker, Maker, or Trader—should be chased and seduced. But urging cities to be equally friendly with rootless corporations is like telling a loyal wife to accept the inevitability of philandering by her husband, and to appease him by buying more sexy lingerie and cooking nicer dinners. If a community is reduced to a link in a global chain, it will be dragged to wherever the corporation controlling the chain wants.

AN EMERGING COUNTERMOVEMENT

Are low wages or no wages the only choices available to communities? Must they decide whether they prefer depression of the local economy or exhaustion of local ecosystems? A small but growing number of dissidents throughout the world (mostly activists but also academics, philosophers, businesspeople, politicians, and even a few heretical economists) refuse to accept these grim options. They question some of the fundamental assumptions underlying the "dismal science" of free-market economics, and are reinventing the field so that the well-being of workers, ecosystems, and communities is the central objective, rather than an afterthought. Whatever their disagreements, they aim to develop a new economics which is more prescriptive about *what* is being produced, *how* it's being produced, and *where* it's being produced—questions toward which traditional economists have shown astonishing indifference.

Those concerned about *what's* being produced raise the following question: Why are we producing so little of what we really need, and so much of what we don't need? Thirty-six million Americans, one in seven, live below the official poverty line; 14 million are children, nearly half under the age of six.[55] Three hundred thousand Americans are estimated to be homeless, 27 million functionally illiterate, and 40 million without health insurance.[56] Among industrialized countries we have the highest rates of teenage pregnancy, abortion, infant mortality, divorce, single-parent families, murder and rape, drug consumption, imprisonment, air pollution, and toxic-waste production.[57] An economy that fails to provide such basic standards of decency to its citizens can hardly be considered an unequivocal success.

A growing number of think tanks and scholars argue that the economy's inability to provide so many necessities is inexcusable when so many industries are churning out products that are deadly (like handguns and land mines), addictive (like tobacco and alcohol), ecologically harmful (like hormone-disrupting chemicals), or essentially useless (like Pet Rocks). Redefining Progress, a new institute in San Francisco, is pressing to change economic indicators like the Gross Domestic Product, to ensure that bads are no longer counted as goods. The Center for a New American Dream raises tough philosophical questions, as every major religion has throughout human civilization, relating to whether greater consumption is really the road to personal and social Nirvana. Juliet Schor, an economist at Harvard, has documented that even though American workers have doubled their productivity since 1948, the expanding gap between declining wages and rising costs has forced them to reduce their leisure time by about 30 percent.[58]

In a 1995 survey conducted by the Harwood Group, an astounding 91 percent of respondents agreed that "we focus too much on getting what we want now and not enough on future generations."[59] A large majority said they had more possessions than their parents did, and are more financially secure, yet less than half said they were happier. Eight out of 10 respondents said that "most of us buy and consume far more than we need; it's wasteful."[60] Nearly as many agreed with the statement "If I wanted to, I could choose to buy and consume less than I do." Most would like to "spend more time with their friends and family" rather than to work more hours for "more nice things in my home."

It's hard to imagine a vision of the future more out of sync with these views than the traditional economists' model in which people with ever-expanding desires become economic nomads who move from job to job without any roots to place. If the world's population doubles in the next century, as expected, our ability to survive as a species may depend on our ability to *reduce* per capita consumption of energy, water, wood, and other natural resources.

Over the past century, social movements in America have struggled to change the *how* of production. They have insisted that business treat workers, consumers, and ecosystems better. The U.S. labor movement successfully lobbied for enactment of a minimum wage, an eight-hour work day, a ban on child labor, and the rights to unionize, strike, and engage in collective bargaining. Consumers, farmers, and populists joined labor organizers to challenge the business practices of commercial banks, railway robber barons, oil trusts, and private utilities, leaving a legacy of antitrust and consumer-protection laws. Environmentalists placed legislative limits on corporations' former freedom to dump pollutants into the air or water, wipe out wildlife species, and generate toxic wastes.

In recent years these diverse constituencies have begun to come together to advocate "sustainable development." This term entered the popular vernacular in 1987 when the World Commission on Environment and Development, chaired by Gro Harlem Brundtland, Prime Minister of Norway, proclaimed it the new global goal for economic progress. The Commission defined sustainable development as "development that meets the needs of the present without compromising the ability of future generations to meet their own needs."[61] This definition, however, has several obvious defects: It overlooks the ecological damage—inflicted by previous generations—which must be repaired; ignores inequalities imposed by development within each generation; and assumes that development can be rendered consistent with ecological well-being. Despite these problems (or perhaps because of them), the term is now regularly used by the nuclear-power industry, Monsanto Chemical, and the World Bank, and is the password that must be used by any ecologist aspiring to have access to mainstream decisionmakers.

Artful phraseology alone, however, cannot resolve the deep contradictions between "sustainability" and "development." It's easy to protect the environment: Declare a parcel of land protected, ban economic activity, prohibit human habitation, and *voilà!*—instant wilderness. It's equally easy to create short-term jobs, as countless miners, loggers, fishing fleet managers, and manufacturers know: Plunder natural resources, wreck the environment, and move on before someone sends the bill. The real challenge is how to create decent, long-term jobs *without* compromising the long-term health of surrounding ecosystems.

This challenge can be met only if the *where* of production is considered. As long as corporations are free to move from place to place, no jurisdiction's efforts to target production toward basic needs, or protect its workforce or environment, can succeed. Once regulations become onerous, a profit-maximizing firm will move on. Too many advocates of sustainable development and sustainable communities seem unwilling to face the problem of corporate mobility squarely.

An officer of the U.S. Environmental Protection Agency recently came to my office to discuss a sustainable-communities home page he was underwriting on the World Wide Web. When I suggested that this electronic library should include resources on how communities are addressing capital mobility, he shifted in his seat uncomfortably. "I'm not sure we can do that," he explained. "We're trying to be nonpartisan; we don't endorse any agenda." Upon a little prodding, he conceded that well, yes, promotion of environmental cleanup, recycling, energy conservation, green products, and the like did constitute an agenda. What he really meant was that criticizing corporations was off limits.

Similar political gymnastics can be observed in the report of the President's Council on Sustainable Development.[62] With a board including the top brass of Ciba-Geigy, Pacific Gas & Electric, Georgia-Pacific, Chevron, General Motors, Enron, Browning-Ferris Industries, and Dow Chemical, as well as the heads of such corporate-friendly national environmental groups as the Nature Conservancy and the Environmental Defense Fund (and a token representative from the old guard of the AFL–CIO), no one should be surprised that the Council's report contains no criticism whatsoever of corporate mobility. The report waxes enthusiastic about the opportunities of the global economy: "U.S. enterprises can no longer thrive by looking only to domestic markets and domestic competitors. The fastest growing markets are not in the industrialized countries, but in those countries whose economies are in the process of becoming industrialized."[63] Only after a hundred pages or so does the reader learn that globalization is a mixed blessing:

> In recent years, dramatic changes in the global economy have resulted in major shifts in local economies as both national and local markets adjusted to the trends. In some cases, the nation became more competitive. In the process, however, many local economies lost jobs and/or income; for some, the future of the communities was endangered. Government has, in some cases, an obligation to address the human consequences of policy decisions on environmental, trade, or defense issues that result in job losses in a community.[64]

The problems identified are vague "changes in the global economy." Without fingering capital mobility as the culprit, the report need not hold business responsible for the solution. Government has an obligation, though only in "some cases," to offer charity to the losers of trade and military-base closures, but not to rein in private corporations causing economic havoc.

The chapter in the report on "Strengthening Communities" studiously tiptoes around the fundamental dilemmas. Look at how it defines sustainable communities:

> [W]hile there is no single template for a sustainable community, cities and towns pursuing sustainable development often have characteristics in common. In communities that sustain themselves, all people have access to educational opportunities that prepare them for jobs to support themselves and their families in a dynamic local economy that is prepared to cope with changes in the national and global economy. People are involved in making decisions that affect their lives. Businesses, households, and government make efficient use of land, energy, and other resources, allowing the area to achieve a high quality of life with minimal waste and environmental damage. These communities are healthy and secure, and provide people with clean air to breathe and safe water to drink.[65]

The recommendations that flow from this milquetoast definition are straightforward: Cities should be redesigned to "promote accessibility, decrease sprawl, reduce energy costs, and foster the creation of built environments on a human scale."[66] They should incorporate "environmentally superior technologies for transportation, industry, buildings, and agriculture" to reduce pollution and lower costs. "[P]artnerships involving business, government, labor, and employees" should discuss how to measure sustainability and how to move the community onto a sustainable pathway. Better design, better technology, better discourse—few could dispute this agenda. Yet it says nothing about the products, behavior, and ownership of business.

Within the environmental movement itself is a more heartening commitment to address these questions. True, major corporations have co-opted some of the traditional environmental groups. As several journalists have documented, organizations like the Audubon Society, Environmental Defense Fund, Izaak Walton League, National Parks and Conservation Association, National Wildlife Federation, Natural Resources Defense Council, Nature Conservancy, Sierra Club, Wilderness Society, and World

Wildlife Fund are increasingly represented by corporate executives on their board, and funded by corporate donations.[67] All these groups but the Sierra Club supported NAFTA, to the dismay of grassroots activists who saw the agreement as helping U.S. firms to move to Mexico to exploit lower wages and unenforced environmental rules. But the NAFTA debate did force many to air their views on free trade, and by the time GATT came up for a congressional vote a year later, most were in opposition. More importantly, literally hundreds of local environmental groups are blending economic and environmental goals under the banners of bioregionalism, environmental justice, green politics, sustainable jobs, voluntary simplicity, permaculture, industrial ecology, and sustainable agriculture.

The unions and their progressive supporters have long appreciated the problem of capital mobility. The tendency of big business to move from place to place in order to exploit cheap labor and natural resources has long been a basic tenet of the critique of capitalism by Karl Marx and his progeny. Labor's solutions to capital mobility have varied considerably. Radicals urged nationalization of the means of production. Today, however, the disappointing record of state socialism and state-run industries has caused many progressives to call for small-scale public enterprises and public–private partnerships. The more common strategy of labor in the United States and Western Europe is to exact from management (along with concessions on wages and working conditions) a commitment to keep a plant operating in a given community. Sometimes labor even teams up with management to prevent capital mobility by pushing for tariffs and other trade barriers meant to protect industries. Textbook protectionism, however, has become more politically difficult to support as more Americans perceive it as saving a few special industries at the expense of the public good.

A sign of the maturity of the labor movement since coming under the leadership of John Sweeney in 1996 is the replacement of old protectionist arguments, which play American workers against foreign workers, with a new language advocating labor solidarity worldwide. By seeking to raise working standards at home and abroad for all industries, labor has been able to work closely with prominent consumer, environmental, and farm groups in its fights against NAFTA and GATT. But this loose-knit coalition remains more comfortable critiquing free trade than developing a coherent model of ecological economics.[68] A long laundry list of proposals for controlling corporate behavior says little about the kinds of businesses that should be supported.

It has become almost axiomatic in this country that to be engaged in commercial activity means to be conservative. To use the term "left business" is to elicit responses of raised eyebrows and belly laughter. The social movements that aspire to represent the interests of the working class have remarkably little to offer in the way of jobs and economic development. The absence of a clear progressive vision of business has ensured the dominance of the conservative vision.

A few progressive entrepreneurs have risen to this challenge by attempting to create socially responsible businesses. Some have focused on what's being produced. Investment houses like Working Assets lure the money of progressives by promising not to invest in nasty industries like nuclear power, defense contracting, or tobacco. Others stress their production methods. The Body Shop doesn't sell products developed through cruel animal experiments. Ben & Jerry's won't exploit nut growers in Brazil. The Gap is committed to eliminating sweatshop conditions in El Salvador. An expanding network of community banks and community-development corporations aim to root their business in a specific area. Back in the late 1960s, a group of activists—one of whom later founded and became the President of Patagonia Inc.—even formed an alternative business school called the New School for Democratic Management that featured classes on how to run cooperatives, credit unions, and other community-friendly businesses. These are all positive innovations—though as we will see, many of these socially responsible firms have a mixed track record fulfilling their own goals.

Clearly, there is much ferment throughout American society aimed at rethinking economics and business. Despite the false starts, the contradictions, the political struggles, and the untested ideas, a growing number of social critics, environmentalists, labor organizers, and progressive entrepreneurs seem to be moving toward a new philosophy of business that meets people's basic needs with responsible production methods, and nurtures the well-being of communities.

A WAY FORWARD

This book provides the outlines of both a new economics and a new business philosophy, both based on the conservation of communities. The imperatives for activists, businesspeople, politicians, and planners are simple:

• Stop destroying the quality of local life to accommodate mobile corporations, and instead nurture community corporations that are dedicated to raising the quality of local life.
• Stop trying to expand economic activity through exports, and instead strive to eliminate dangerous dependencies by creating new import-replacing businesses that meet people's basic needs.
• Stop lobbying Washington for new dollops of federal pork, and instead insist on the legal and political power necessary to create a rich soil for homegrown enterprises.

The vision that follows is a modest one. Communities should increase their self-reliance on local resources, workers, and capital, fully appreciating that they cannot unplug from the global economy altogether. Even as community corporations meet more needs of a community, it's likely that multinational firms will operate alongside for a very long time to come. And even though there's much that communities can do to reclaim control over their economic destiny (from national government, from international agencies, and from global businesses), these powerful actors will still exert a powerful influence upon the structure, rules, and operation of the international economy. It is essential, therefore, for a community pursuing localism to ally itself with *simpatico* communities and popular movements throughout the world. To succeed in a world of shifting loyalties, a community going local must simultaneously retain a global perspective.

Communities have many more choices for securing prosperity than ideologues on either the right or the left would have them believe. Conservatives insist that communities align themselves with privately owned corporations, despite overwhelming evidence that fixation on just the bottom line bodes ill for workers, families, ecosystems, and communities. Progressives remain romantic about state-controlled business, despite overwhelming evidence that such modes of organization lead to bureaucracy, inefficiency, and corruption. Community corporations hold out the possibility that the benefits of each sphere—the efficiency of the market and the social-mindedness of the public sector—can be realized without the liabilities of either.

A new commitment to going local would mark a dramatic shift in the economic-development strategy of almost every city in America. It's a strategy that will unify people of many political stripes. Talk with the heads of Chambers of Commerce and the leaders of progressive social movements, and you find that both are livid about being misled and sold out by the promises of disloyal corporations. The examples in this book suggest how these groups, and many others, can find common cause in creating home-grown businesses.

Chapter 1 presents an argument for addressing Americans' yearning to renew their communities with a new economics that takes into account the critical importance of place. Given the pressing problem of mobile capital, efforts to strengthen communities by focusing exclusively on social pathologies (as conservatives do) or on civil society (as communitarians do) are way off the mark. So are the prescriptions of mainstream economists who have long urged severing the links between business and community in the name of efficiency. An economics of place would shift the development policies of every American city and town to a new goal: community self-reliance.

The following chapters explore three different features of self-reliance: producing locally for local needs, owning business locally, and recycling finance locally. The discussion of community industries precedes that of community corporations to help the reader visualize what a self-reliant economy might look like. Chapter 2 gives numerous examples of how communities are increasingly producing for themselves necessities like food, energy, water, and materials. Contrary to arguments made by economists about the efficiencies of global corporations, a growing number of businesses *are* finding it profitable to go local—using local labor, land, capital, and technology to serve local markets. Chapter 3 looks at the issue of ownership, and concludes that the most common type of corporate structure, with private owners living far away from the business, is the least likely to benefit a community. Nonprofits, cooperatives, and public enterprises are inherently more loyal to their home base, but the best alternative of all may be a for-profit whose shareholders are exclusively residents. Since it's inconceivable that such corporations can be formed without new infusions of capital, Chapter 4 suggests that the starting place for restructuring the local economy needs to be the financial sector. Community banks, thrifts, credit unions, and pension funds can help place even a relatively poor economy on a stronger economic footing.

All these initiatives—local production, ownership, and finance—can proceed entirely in the private sector, but smart government policies certainly can accelerate them. Chapter 5 explores how a municipality can boost the economy by awarding subsidies, investments, contracts, and purchases primarily to community corporations. It also can help the economy to go local through such novel tools as community currencies, Time Dollars, barter directories, and green taxes. Chapter 6 shows the critical role that the federal government has to play, primarily by removing the enormous number of anticommunity subsidies, tax breaks, and regulations that govern trade, corporations, and banks.

The book concludes in Chapter 7 with a 10-step plan for how you can help your own economy go local. An appendix follows which lists organizational contacts, addresses, telephone numbers, and Web sites that can help you get started.

A basic precept of community economics is that generalization is dangerous. Every locality must find its own way. The arguments here can be nothing more than a framework for a community to retake control of its own economic destiny. But the prescriptions and examples that follow suggest possibilities for considerably more detailed economic planning. Any community—whether rich or poor, urban or rural, big or small, old or new—now finds itself, like Pogo, confronted by insurmountable opportunities. And—to exploit these opportunities—a community needs to start in its own backyard.

Place Matters 1

Ask your family, friends, and neighbors what matters most to them, and you're likely to hear words like love, security, spirituality, beauty, good health, even fun. Americans wax eloquent about their children and grandchildren having a decent education, safe neighborhoods, humane values. They reflect on the importance of their church or synagogue, their favorite sports teams or television show, or their latest political cause. Coloradans brag about the snow-capped Rockies, Midwesterners about the muddy Mississippi River, and Californians about the breathtaking coastline. Even the most business-minded mention families and passions before they turn to shopping, mortgages, wages, and material possessions that are the preoccupation of economists.

Our deepest yearnings are linked to a sense of place. We care especially about our neighbors, our community institutions, and our ecological heritage. Even post-modern nomads who crisscross the globe for pleasure or profit carry loyalty to somewhere. Why else do you get excited when you're driving down a highway, a thousand miles from home, and see a car with your state's license plate or with your university's name prominently displayed on the back windshield? Why, when you're in a foreign airport and discover that the person standing next to you grew up in your hometown, is there an odd sense of connection, familiarity, and comfort with someone who is otherwise a total stranger? Our politicians, keenly aware of this phenomenon, declare their loyalty to place at every opportunity. (In the 1992 and 1996 presidential elections, Bill Clinton grew misty-eyed whenever he spoke of his hometown, "a place called Hope.")

Between 1990 and 1991, pollster Richard Harwood conducted focus groups for the Kettering Foundation in 10 cities across America. The topic was "Citizens and Politics." Participants expressed deep cynicism about national political discourse, and it was clear that both a cause and an effect of this trend was the collapse of community. According to Harwood's published report:

> *It is no secret today that citizens feel a loss of community; and many citizens remarked that this loss undermined people's desire to participate in politics. Consider these comments by a Richmond woman: "We no longer have neighbors. You say 'hello' but you don't really know them. We lost that togetherness to share and reach out. We don't live like people should in America." And a Los Angeles man, who said, "We lead such factious lives—our work, our homes—[and] technology makes it all so impersonal." A Philadelphia man observed, "I know my neighbors, but I don't know the people on the next street." Now . . . neighbors change regularly, people do not answer their doors after dark, citizens increasingly take less of an interest in each other and in each other's concerns.[1]*

Politicians and political organizers across the ideological spectrum decry the loss of community. During the 1996 presidential campaign, both Bill Clinton and Bob Dole were for reviving communities. Conservative moralist Bill Bennett regularly preaches the importance of community as fervently as does progressive moralist Reverend Jesse Jackson. The word "community" has become such a familiar mantra, recited by the advocates of such radically different agendas, that it's worth pausing for a moment to ask what it really means.

Some people use the term to refer to a social network, such as the Catholic community or the business community. But most Americans also mean a specific *place*—one where they have deep attachments to the people, culture, aesthetics, and nature. The term will be used this way throughout this book. A community is a geographically contiguous area with political and legal power that is closest to its own citizens. The concept applies to municipalities of all sizes, including big cities, suburban towns, and rural villages. But even if Americans can agree on what community is, and how much it's missing from their lives, they have *no* common view on how to restore it.

BAD PEOPLE AND BAD CIVICS

One popular view is that communities have broken down, not for economic reasons, but for social reasons. Prominent conservative thinkers such as Charles Murray, Norman Podhoretz, and Thomas Sowell put the blame on the proliferation of people with bad habits: sixties hippies, women's libbers, gays and lesbians, immigrants, and—of course—the poor. These groups, the argument goes, have lost the family structures, religious values, and basic work ethic necessary for a community to thrive. Another group of influential intellectuals with more progressive leanings, who call themselves communitarians, blame modern liberalism for overemphasizing individual liberties at the expense of communitarian values. The group, which includes Benjamin Barber, Robert Bellah, William Galston, Mary Ann Glendon, Alasdair MacIntyre, Michael Sandel, Charles Taylor, and Roberto Unger,[2] explores the implications of communitarianism in policy areas like crime, education, affirmative action, and welfare, in a quarterly journal called *The Responsive Community.*

The conservative position is nicely summarized by Joe Klein, the *New York* magazine columnist and confessed author of the novel *Primary Colors,* who argues that "businesses began to flee the inner cities in the early 1970s—along with many of the remaining middle-class residents, black and white—as a *consequence* of higher crime, a declining pool of educated or disciplined workers and higher taxes (which were themselves caused by the increased cost of dealing with all these disasters)."[3] The real causes of community decline, Klein believes, are laziness, promiscuity, stupidity, and antisocial behavior. "The 'truly disadvantaged,'" he writes, "represent the demographic sliver that is not ready, willing or able [to work]. . . . [T]heir behavior—their social and educational limitations, the psychological and cultural signals that they send prospective employers—is what keeps them out of the workforce."[4]

Blaming the breakdown of community on the bad work habits of the underclass, however, overlooks one contradictory piece of evidence: Most American communities (and not just inner cities) are struggling today.

Footloose corporations are deserting urban, suburban, and rural areas alike to relocate in the *maquiladoras* of Mexico or the sweatshops of Malaysia. Most Americans, and not just the poor in the ghetto, are facing lives characterized by growing economic insecurity. Real wages have been going down since 1973; four out of five American workers have seen their wallets shrink.[5] Corporate pensions are increasingly being swallowed up in mergers and acquisitions. And social-security reform, if it occurs, is as likely to improve the lot of retirees as welfare reform did for the estimated one million children about to be thrown into poverty.

Yes, we need better education; we need better crime control; we need healthier families; we need a stronger work ethic. But without a thriving local economy, *none* of these goals is possible. Without a strong tax base, a community cannot possibly hire decent teachers, social workers, or police. Without decent incomes, even families committed to good parenting must struggle as both spouses work overtime to pay the bills. Without the availability of decent-paying jobs, even motivated workers earning a minimum wage can be destitute. (Today's minimum wage, despite its recent increase, is one-fifth smaller than it was in the late 1960s, once inflation is factored out.[6])

The first communitarians acknowledged the central role of economic change. In 1984, Michael Sandel of Harvard University expressed concern "about the concentration of power in both the corporate economy and the bureaucratic state, and the erosion of those intermediate forms of community that have at times sustained a more vital public life."[7] He recommended, among other things, that states committed to communitarian values should "enact laws regulating plant closings, to protect their communities from the disruptive effects of capital mobility and sudden industrial change."[8] Yet, in the decade since, communitarian writers have offered remarkably little in the way of an economic program.

The bible of the communitarian movement has become *The Spirit of Community*, written by George Washington University professor Amitai Etzioni, who argues that American communities have been decimated by the steady expansion of personal rights without concomitant social responsibilities.[9] The book contains myriad prescriptions for strengthening families, schools, and civic institutions, and deciding the proper level of government intervention to fight crime, AIDS, and "hate speech," but the attentive reader strains to find even a sentence or two about the responsibilities and betrayals of globe-trotting business. The same can be said about the articles published in *The Responsive Community* over the past five years. Fewer than a half-dozen even remotely touch on economics, and even these tend to focus on economic incentives for getting the poor off welfare, increasing volunteerism and voting-participation rates, and otherwise inducing higher moral standards in wayward community residents.

The scholar with communitarian inclinations who has probably attracted the widest popular audience is Harvard political scientist Robert Putnam. His 1993 book, *Making Democracy Work,* examined 20 regional governments in Italy, and concluded that the administrations with the highest levels of civic engagement were most successful at "creating innovative day care programs and job-training centers, promoting investment and economic development, pioneering environmental standards and family clinics."[10] Among the best indicators of civic engagement were "voter turnout, newspaper readership, membership in choral societies and literary circles, Lions Clubs, and soccer clubs."[11] Social networks within churches, cooperatives, neighborhood associations, and guilds provided "organized reciprocity and civic solidarity."[12] And these provided a foundation for economic development:

These communities did not become civic simply because they were rich. The historical record strongly suggests precisely the opposite: They have become rich because they were civic. The social capital embodied in norms and networks of civic engagement seems to be a precondition for economic development, as well as for effective government. Development economists take note: Civics matter.[13]

Putnam popularized his findings in the United States in an article in *The Journal of Democracy* cleverly entitled "Bowling Alone."[14] (Other versions subsequently appeared in *The Responsive Community* and elsewhere.)[15] Between 1980 and 1993, he noted, even as the number of Americans bowling increased, participation in league bowling declined by 40 percent. "The broader significance," he wrote, "lies in the social interaction and even occasionally civic conversations over beer and pizza the solo bowlers forgo."[16] Putnam gave other examples of weakening civic ties in the country. Since 1973, one-third fewer Americans report attending a school board or city council meeting over the course of the year. There also is evidence of decreasing attendance of church, membership in labor unions, or participation in Parent–Teacher Associations.

Critics of Putnam's work cite other data that suggest that civic participation may be holding steady, or perhaps even increasing. Nicholas Lemann notes the spectacular growth of soccer leagues, restaurants, small businesses, charitable contributions, and advocacy groups like the American Association of Retired People.[17] Katha Pollitt, a columnist in *The Nation,* calls Putnam's view of civic life "remarkably, well, square":

I've been a woman all my life, but I've never heard of the Federation of Women's Clubs. And what politically minded female, in 1996, would join the bland and matronly League of Women Voters, when she could volunteer with Planned Parenthood or NOW or Concerned Women of America, and shape the debate instead of merely keeping it polite? It's probably going too far to argue that the decline of the Boy Scouts is directly related to its barring of gay and nonbelieving lads. But should it really surprise us that such a stodgy organization has a hard time finding volunteers?[18]

Perhaps the deepest flaw in Putnam's work—and in the communitarian approach in general—is the assertion (little more) that civics trumps economics. Strong civic ties may create the foundation for a strong local economy, as they did in northern Italy, but they cannot save a dying community. What can civic ties possibly accomplish if residents of a community have declining incomes and no jobs? One reason adults no longer bowl in family-style leagues or participate in PTAs is that both parents now have to work to make ends meet. They come home, cook dinner, put the kids to bed, and collapse from exhaustion. As Washington pundit Sam Smith observes, "In a corporatist world there is no time for bowling, period. Someone else would be glad to take your job if you really prefer ten pins to working late."[19]

Civic ties are undoubtedly valuable for economic development. But without a viable economic base, even a strong civil society faces only three options: migrate, rebel, or collapse. To focus on political reform, social policy, and civic culture, while giving only minor lip service to economic policy, puts cause and effect backwards. Communitarians, like their conservative counterparts, effectively distract attention from the real roots of the collapse of community, and from the real solutions.

THE SCIENCE OF EFFICIENCY

Communities cannot simply tinker with personal and civic morality and expect a dying local economy to bounce back to life. But the advice offered by mainstream economists also is of limited use. As we saw in the Introduction, economics, like ancient religions, now requires periodic public sacrifice to appease the gods of prosperity. Onto the altar of steady growth must be tossed one out of twenty workers to achieve a "natural" rate of unemployment and low inflation. Environmental tribute must be paid in the form of endangered species, sacred canyons, the stratospheric ozone layer, clean air and water, whatever it takes to keep the economy growing. The willingness of economists to write off certain workers and ecological assets suggests the low value they assign to community.

Economics was originally touted as a scientific tool to help a society reach the goals it really cares about. Paul A. Samuelson, a professor at the Massachusetts Institute of Technology, has been writing the most widely used introductory text on economics since 1948. The twelfth edition, published in 1985 and cowritten by William D. Nordhaus of Yale University, defines economics as "the study of how people and society choose to employ scarce resources that could have alternative uses in order to produce various commodities and to distribute them for consumption, now or in the future, among various persons and groups in society."[20]

Put another way, economics is the science of *efficiency*—the efficiency of consumption, production, and distribution. Economics cannot tell us which natural resources to consume and which to conserve; but it *can* tell us, once these decisions have been made, how to consume and conserve efficiently. It cannot tell us which commodities are socially useful and which are dangerous, addictive, or unimportant; but it *can* tell us how to make goods we choose to manufacture in the least costly way. It cannot tell us what constitutes a fair distribution of commodities; but it *can* pinpoint how best to achieve a socially desirable goal of equity. Applied creatively with democratic processes that set society's goals for consumption, production, and distribution, economics can be an indispensable tool for strengthening communities.

But an ambitious reader of the classics of the profession will be stunned to discover that community is barely mentioned at all. Adam Smith focused on the *Wealth of Nations,* not the wealth of communities. So did the other influential early writers on economics and political economy, like Jeremy Bentham, John Stuart Mill, and David Ricardo. Samuelson's and Nordhaus's *Economics* text, nearly a thousand pages long, says virtually nothing about communities setting goals and applying the tools of economics to achieve them.

Amazingly, the most influential critics of economics also paid little attention to community. John Maynard Keynes observed that during periods of slack aggregate demand, the *national* government could stimulate the economy and boost employment through public expenditures or tax cuts. Karl Marx, Friedrich Engels, and other radical economists also focused on the national government, arguing that it should collectivize the means of production and the distribution of goods (and relegating the dream of self-governing communes to some distant and utopian future). Advocates of the New Deal such as John Kenneth Galbraith, and their social-democratic contemporaries in Western Europe like Gunnar Myrdal, were committed to creating a safety net of national welfare programs that provided jobs, income security, education, and other benefits. Their passion was equity, not community.

For traditional economists and their critics, place was beside the point. The basic unit of analysis for microeconomics was the firm, and for macroeconomics the nation. Community, a level of organization somewhere in between, didn't really fit.

Today, the absence of concern about community among economists is clear in their consensus on trade. In 1994, virtually every nation on earth signed the Uruguay Round of the General Agreement on Tariffs and Trade (GATT). Since 1948, successive rounds and agreements under GATT have chopped tariffs, and over the next 25 years merchandise trade for industrial nations grew at an average rate of 8 percent per year, double the average growth rate of their gross national products.[21] Economists' contention that this accelerating exchange of goods and services is in the interests of all the world's people is now almost universally accepted gospel. Free trade was once a pet postwar project of the United States, but it is now being embraced by the communist party leaders of China, the welfare-state bureaucrats of Scandinavia, the conservative monetarists of Chile, the dictator of Indonesia, even the Prince of Monaco. Almost everyone loves free trade—despite the consequences for community.

FREE TRADE VS. COMMUNITY

Economists who rarely agree on anything believe that free trade is unambiguously beneficial. Why? The theory of comparative advantage says so. As MIT economist Paul Krugman writes:

> *Because comparative advantage is a beautiful idea that it seems only economists understand, economists cling to the idea even more strongly, as a kind of badge that defines their professional identity and ratifies their intellectual superiority. In effect, the statements, "I understand the principle of comparative advantage," and, "I support free trade," have become part of the economist's credo.*[22]

According to the theory of comparative advantage, a free-trade world enables every nation to take advantage of its natural strengths and share them with consumers globally.[23] Americans grow wheat, the French grapes for wine, the Cubans sugar, the Japanese rice, and so forth. As specialized industries expand and achieve greater efficiencies, trade increases and rewards everyone with cheaper, more variegated products. Samuelson and Nordhaus put in the following terms the catechism about who gains when two countries trade: "If each country specializes in the products in which it has comparative advantage (or greatest relative efficiency), trade will be mutually beneficial. Real wages and incomes will rise in both countries. And these statements are true whether or not one of the regions is absolutely more efficient than the other in the production of every good."[24]

Economists concede that freer trade may result in losers, but this, Samuelson and Nordhaus argue, is the necessary—and acceptable—price of progress:

> *Suppose an industry (say, steel) formerly has a comparative advantage but has lost it—because other industries have had greater technological improvements, because the domestic factors it uses have become more expensive through becoming more valuable elsewhere, or for any other reason. The theory of comparative advantage says that this industry*

*ought to be injured by imports. Indeed, it ought to be killed off by the
competition of our more productive industries.*

*This sounds ruthless indeed. No industry willingly dies. No region
gladly undergoes conversion to new industries. Often the shifting
between old and new industries involves considerable unemployment
and hardship. Moreover, a sector that is imperiled is probably already
sick, with a past history of suffering. So the weak industry and region
feel they are being singled out to carry the burden of progress.*

*A compromise that recognizes the force in both political and eco-
nomic arguments is to introduce tariff reductions gradually, so that
vested factors will have time to move; and, as has occurred since the
1962 Trade Act, to give "trade adjustment assistance," or federal aid to
dislocated factors of production.*[25]

Why *ought* an industry be killed off by cheaper imports? Because, as
another introductory textbook by economist George Leland Bach of Stanford University explains, an effort to protect an economy results in "a shift
of workers from relatively efficient export industries (where they would be
situated under free trade) into less-efficient protected industries."[26] Note
the very specific meaning given to the term efficiency—the ability of a firm
to maximize its profits. Because a foreign industry can sell a good at a
lower cost than ours can, ours is inefficient and ought to die. But suppose
our country wanted to have a network of strong, stable communities, without ruthless dislocations, without massive unemployment, without painful
changes in people's lives. Recall the example of Youngstown, Ohio, in
which the federal government shelled out $70 million in unemployment
and welfare assistance the first three years after a major steel mill closed.
From society's standpoint, it would have been more efficient for the federal government to have invested $69 million in Youngstown over the same
period to keep the plant running.

The point is not that governments ought to prop up money-losing ventures. But the bottom line for a community often differs dramatically from
that of a privately owned business. While a private owner is looking for the
highest rate of profit, a community might find any rate of return above
zero worthwhile. In 1975, Sperry Rand Corporation decided to shut down
a subsidiary called the Library Bureau in Herkimer, New York, because it
was not achieving a rate of return of 22 percent, the ambitious target the

parent company had set for its subsidiaries.[27] Closure of this plant, which employed 250 people, would have decimated the community. So the workers and local residents decided to buy the firm from Sperry Rand. A third of the money was raised by selling $1 and $2 shares of stock, and the rest came from loans from local banks and the U.S. Department of Commerce. In its first year of operation under new management, the firm earned a 17 percent rate of return—inadequate for Sperry Rand, but more than enough for Herkimer. It then continued to perform profitably for more than a decade.

Skeptics might reply that the community would have been smarter to invest its money in firms like Sperry Rand that were earning 22 percent or more elsewhere. But one rarely knows in advance what the rate of return on an investment will be. In a competitive economy the quest for higher returns means higher risks. It is certainly rational for a community to invest in a known enterprise in its own backyard, which it can improve through sweat equity and which will benefit the local economy for many years to come, than to risk money in an unknown enterprise hundreds or thousands of miles away.

Economists like Samuelson, Nordhaus, and Bach acknowledge the costs to communities that lose as trade doors swing open. If communities with new businesses compensate the less fortunate ones whose old businesses were destroyed by cheap imports, the losers still can develop new businesses and livelihoods. Meanwhile, consumers across the country can enjoy the benefits of cheaper goods. Everyone wins. And so economists, in the spirit of charity and fairness, propose "trade adjustment assistance."

The historical fact, however, is that redistribution in the United States has hardly occurred at all since 1962.[28] Throughout the 1980s, as the trade barriers were lowered, income and wealth were dramatically redistributed from the poor to the rich. Divide the population of the United States into five equal parts based on income, and the grim story of growing inequality between 1969 and 1988 becomes clear. The lowest-income group received less income over this period (dropping from 5.6 percent to 4.6 percent of all income), while the highest-income group received more (from 40.6 percent to 44.0 percent).[29] Between 1979 and 1989, the top 1 percent of all earners saw their incomes double.[30]

The regressive movement of distribution was even more dramatic with respect to wealth. The richest 1 percent of Americans expanded their wealth holdings between 1983 and 1992 from 31 percent to 37 percent.[31] That 1 percent now holds as much wealth as the poorest 40 percent of the American people. The causes of increased inequality go far beyond trade, but the point here is that without redistribution mechanisms that really work, adjustment assistance provides little more relief to the losers from free trade than does the Tooth Fairy.

Without redistribution, the best that free trade offers is the destruction of some communities for the benefit of others. It means that people thrown out of work, many of them poor single parents, must choose between going on unemployment and welfare or packing up their bags and moving to the winning communities. Prevailing social mores about public assistance suggest that the dignified approach is to move, even if it means pulling the kids from school, severing ties with friends and neighbors, leaving behind church and social-support networks, and so on. Each departure also means that the community loses part of its tax base, and that all kinds of community services—libraries, police, street repairs—must be cut, all of which encourages still more people to leave. The loser communities can easily plunge into a death spiral and become ghost towns.

A closer look at the theory of free trade, undertaken recently by economist Herman Daly and theologian John Cobb in their book *For the Common Good,* reveals that the possibilities for gains from trade for the winning communities and for consumers—even in principle—have been greatly exaggerated.[32] When the architect of free-trade theory, David Ricardo, first made the case for tearing down tariff walls in *Principles of Political Economy and Taxation* in 1817, he used the example of Britain and Portugal. British factories might specialize in making cloth, Portuguese factories in making wine. If each does what it can do best and pursues its comparative advantage, both will find that by trading they each can enjoy a cheaper combination of wine and cloth.

Ricardo's modern disciples, however, conveniently left out one critical assumption: For the theory to work, capital must be immobile. If British or Portuguese firms can move, they will naturally relocate to the country where wages are lowest. Ricardo hypothesized what might happen if English firms took advantage of less-expensive labor in Portugal:

It would undoubtedly be advantageous to the capitalists of England, and to the consumers in both countries, that under such circumstances, the wine and the cloth should both be made in Portugal, and therefore that the capital and labour of England employed in making cloth, should be removed to Portugal for that purpose. . . .

Experience, however, shows, that the fancied or real insecurity of capital, when not under the immediate control of its owner, together with the natural disinclination which every man has to quit the country of his birth and connexions, and intrust himself, with all his habits fixed, to a strange government and new laws, check the emigration of capital. These feelings, which I should be sorry to see weakened, induce most men of property to be satisfied with a low rate of profits in their own country, rather than seek a more advantageous employment for their wealth in foreign nations.[33]

Were he alive today, David Ricardo would be very sorry indeed to see the evisceration of ties between place and capital. He might remind economists that comparative advantage, as he conceived it, is now virtually impossible. The country with the lowest wages achieves a condition of *absolute advantage,* drawing capital and labor from other countries and redounding to the advantage of Portuguese property owners. Ricardo was wrong on one count: The English capitalists might join their Portuguese counterparts in cheering this condition, but not the English consumers who, also being workers, would have to migrate to find new work in Portugal.

This is not an inaccurate portrait of the global economy today, in which unanchored corporations move to low-wage countries throughout the world to take advantage of unemployed labor forces and to achieve absolute advantage. The richest countries in the world now are experiencing declining wages (the United States) or rising unemployment (much of Western Europe).[32]

The opening of free trade is certainly not the only cause of these problems. MIT's Paul Krugman and Harvard's Robert Lawrence point out, for example, that manufactured goods once produced by high-wage industries have become cheaper because of technological advances.[35] The result is that American consumers are spending less to acquire the same goods, which has freed them to spend relatively more on services delivered by lower-wage workers. Doug Henwood, editor of the *Left Business Observer,* argues that in the airline and trucking industries, both of which have virtually no foreign competitors, deregulation is the culprit ("it's hard to think of sectors where so many formerly high-wage jobs have been so massively transformed into low-wage ones").[36]

Yet even these causes are linked at least indirectly to free trade. Opening the nation to cheaper foreign goods put the heat on U.S. manufacturers to reduce production costs. By threatening to leave their workforce behind, U.S. firms have been able to extract wage- and job-reduction concessions from labor, rather than put cost-cutting burdens on management. And both the reality and rhetoric of maintaining global competitiveness have been used to induce U.S. politicians to deregulate numerous industries.

Whatever the exact contribution of free trade to falling wages up to now, there's no doubt that it will intensify if exports and imports become a larger fraction of the U.S. economy. The price of many goods may fall, but fewer Americans will be able to afford them. The global economy, as my colleagues Richard Barnet and John Cavanagh recently argued in their book *Global Dreams,* has increasingly become bifurcated between haves and have-nots in both rich and poor countries: "Of the 5.4 billion people on earth, almost 3.6 billion have neither cash nor credit to buy much of anything. A majority of people on the planet are at most window-shoppers."[37]

Freer trade not only affects communities unequally, but also those living within them. Communities in the United States that claim to be winning gains from trade, like Cleveland, still have growing pockets of losers whose ranks are disproportionately made up of the poor, African-Americans, Latinos, women, and children. As divisions in the United States widen between rich and poor and between black and white, the destruction of community accelerates. Privileged neighborhoods wall themselves off from the expanding ghettos and set up their own schools, shopping malls, and community centers. The rage felt by the poor over this mounting inequality explodes into occasional riots, as Los Angeles discovered in 1992.

Free trade also weakens communities by freeing corporations to exhaust the local natural-resource base. In an economy *free* of environmental standards, communities win if they exploit their forests, mines, and fisheries for short-term profits rather than long-term sustainability. "Competitiveness," as the term is widely used today, is achieved by communities that allow pollution to continue unabated, since the costs of cleanup need not be incorporated into the products. The "winners" are cities like Santiago, São Paulo, Manila, and Mexico City, where the air is practically unbreathable.

None of this is an indictment of trade per se, only of trade without rules that protect communities. There are many ways in which trade can be harmonized with communities, as Chapter 6 details, but this requires thoughtful government intervention to level the playing field for responsible businesses. It requires, for example, that global rules apply to the one-third of trade which, in fact, is only transferred among different branches of the same multinational firm, and therefore carried out in anything but a free marketplace. Unfortunately, current free-trade regimes like GATT do exactly the opposite: They systematically strip national, state, and local governments of the powers needed to regulate mobile corporations and to ensure payment for the environmental and social damage they cause.

Ironically, free trade purports to enhance people's choices, yet winds up actually limiting them. Workers have only a few opportunities for work in the specializing industries. Consumers have less money to spend on the global cornucopia of goods and services. Subsistence farmers, once able to eke out a decent living off their own land and to barter for extras, are suddenly drawn into a global economy where they have to sell crops to buy food, water, clothing, and shelter. And communities, once able to choose their own paths of development, now find themselves following marching orders from distant corporate managers. Free trade has become the biggest oxymoron of our time.

A NEW ECONOMICS OF PLACE

A handful of critics have raised these points for many years. In *The Great Transformation,* written in 1944, economic historian Karl Polanyi decried the "economistic fallacy," which unwisely subordinated society and social relations to market analysis.[38] *Every* market, he argued, is embedded in a social context:

> *While monetary interests are necessarily voiced solely by the persons to whom they pertain, other interests have a wide constituency. They affect individuals in innumerable ways as neighbors, professional persons, consumers, pedestrians, commuters, sportsmen, hikers, gardeners, patients, mothers, or lovers—and are accordingly capable of representation by almost any type of territorial or functional associations such as churches, townships, fraternal lodges, clubs, trade unions, or most commonly, political parties based on broad principles of adherence. . . . [N]o*

purely monetary definition of interests can leave room for that vital need for social protection, the representation of which commonly falls to the persons in charge of the general interests of the community. . . .[39]

After World War II, urban studies and environmental studies departments were established in hundreds of universities that tried to make economics useful for communities. E. F. Schumacher, who helped lay the foundation for the British welfare state and whom John Maynard Keynes regarded as his intellectual successor, sought to create a "Buddhist" economics centered around people and nature in his 1973 classic *Small Is Beautiful*. Other important works on community economics also have appeared over the past generation: *The Economy of Cities* (1969) and *Cities and the Wealth of Nations* (1984), by Jane Jacobs; *Soft Energy Paths* (1976), by Amory B. Lovins; *Steady State Economics* (1977), by Herman Daly; *Neighborhood Power: The New Localism* (1974) and *Self-Reliant Cities* (1982), by David Morris; *Human Scale* (1980), by Kirkpatrick Sale; *The Politics of the Solar Age* (1981), by Hazel Henderson; *The Living Economy* (1986), edited by Paul Ekins; *Environmental Protection and Economic Well-Being* (1988), by Thomas Michael Power; *For the Common Good* (1989), by Daly and John Cobb, Jr.; and most recently *Short Circuit* (1996), by Richard Douthwaite. These thinkers have diverse perspectives and employ very different analytical tools, but their recommendations converge around one central concept—*community self-reliance.*

The term "self-reliance" is admittedly an awkward one. The word *self* suggests an individualistic, atomized, antisocial framework. The goal of self-reliance has been seized upon by libertarian conservatives who seek to dismantle the welfare state and much of government altogether. It is invoked by leaders pushing for dangerous visions of separatism, from the survivalists and militias of Montana to the Reverend Louis Farrakhan, who wants a new, self-reliant black nationalist community. But self-reliance, appearing initially in the Bible and given a distinctly American spin by Henry David Thoreau, also has many positive connotations. It suggests personal responsibility, respect for others, and harmony with nature. And the addition of the word "community" to self-reliance underscores that the ultimate objective is a social and caring one. As Neil Seldman of the Institute for Local Self-Reliance emphasizes, *all* people within a community should be enabled and empowered.

Johan Galtung, a leading peace theorist from Norway, elaborates the rationale for communities to become self-reliant:

> [P]roduce what you need using your own resources, internalising the challenges this involves, growing with the challenges, neither giving the most challenging tasks (positive externalities) to somebody else on whom you become dependent, nor exporting negative externalities to somebody else to whom you do damage and who may become dependent on you.
>
> . . . The justification for so doing is clear: we will enjoy the positive externalities, rather than giving them away, and at the same time will be responsible ourselves for the negative externalities. . . . We can fight the negative consequences ourselves, the distance between cause and effect being a short one.[40]

Galtung's definition of self-reliance weaves together several important strands. One is the importance of minimizing dependence on others. If a community can achieve full employment and provide for the basic needs of its citizens without relying on other communities, it will be less vulnerable to decisions and disasters outside its control. Having satisfied its needs, a community will have less need to meddle in the affairs of its neighbors. As ecologist Kirkpatrick Sale writes:

> [A] self-sufficient town cannot be the victim of corporate-directed plant closings, or a truckers' strike, or an Arab oil boycott or California droughts; it does not have to maintain lengthy and tenuous supply lines of any kind, nor pay the shippers and jobbers and the middlemen who are clustered along them; it does not have to be the accidental victim of toxic fumes or industrial poisons or nuclear wastes produced by or passing through the town; it does not have to bow to always rising prices set by distant A&Ps and GMs and GTEs in disregard of what the local farmer is in fact growing or the local shop producing; and ultimately it does [not] have to sway in the winds of the hurricanes of boom and bust as regularly generated, as it were offshore, by distant and uncontrollable economic forces.[41]

Minimizing dependence on others also means maximizing on all kinds of challenges, whether intellectual, technological, or social. Observes Sale,

"It makes a place expand instead of contract, create instead of borrow, use instead of discard: just as a man left on his own, thrust on his own devices, develops strengths and uncovers inner resources and becomes the fuller for it, so too a community."[42] This points out a fundamental flaw in neo-classical economics. Efficiency, economists argue, requires specialization. The narrower the range of tasks an individual performs, the better he or she becomes at it. But, as any person who has sweated on an assembly line knows, a job reduced to the turning of a screw does little to satisfy the soul or self-esteem. Real people are not satisfied with the role of Chaplinesque automatons that economists have assigned them, and they look for more from a job than just a paycheck.[43] They seek a challenge, pride, and respect. And, if given the choice, many people will gladly choose a more exciting job with less take-home pay.

The same emotions are at play in a community. Why should a nation's choice about specialization dictate everyone's career choices? To invoke Ricardo's hypothetical, must the Portuguese become vintners and the English textile workers? Most of us believe that an indication of the health of a community is the breadth of jobs available. Many of us had parents or grandparents who experienced some version of a community in which neighbors included their doctor, baker, butcher, banker, stationer, accountant, and lawyer. Like a well-balanced ecosystem, this kind of diversified economy was not easily vulnerable to outside events. Those who worked in small businesses, even those who didn't own property, had more of a stake in them. Even within sprawling cities there were well-defined neighborhoods in which people had lifelong attachments. Evenings might be spent sitting on the porch or wandering around the town square, as is still done in small towns in southern Europe.

Today's typical communities center around a large factory or office complex. If you're lucky, you have a specialized job that pays well, and spend your money at the mall on the outskirts of town. As production at the plant expands or contracts, so does the influx of newcomers or the outflow of oldtimers. The revolving door means that you know fewer of your neighbors, and that more of your relationships are based on impersonal economic exchanges. The breakdown of personal ties makes it easier not to care about the have-nots, to commit crimes against anonymous victims, to retreat into walled subdivisions.

A third feature of self-reliance, noted by Galtung, is the absence of *externalities*. An external cost, according to economists, is one that is not reflected in the price of a good. If a chemical manufacturer dumps sulfur dioxide into the air, the deaths, illness, and property damage caused by acid rain downwind are considered external costs. A self-reliant community makes sure that external costs are imposed only on itself. A guaranteed way to ensure that a car does not pollute is to stick the exhaust pipe into the passenger section. Similarly, a community committed to self-reliance will be mindful not to foul its own nest. Self-reliance therefore is a tool for ecological protection and restoration. As many Native American tribes demonstrated for thousands of years, a community that relies exclusively on its own forests, rivers, and farms—and doesn't see the use of outside resources as either necessary or desirable—will take special care to safeguard its natural resources for future generations. A community that refuses on principle to export pollution and waste will take greater care to minimize or eliminate them.

It's easy to dismiss the principle of self-reliance by pointing to many complex products that communities cannot manufacture on their own. The goal of a self-reliant community, however, is not to create a Robinson Crusoe economy in which no resources, people, or goods enter or leave. *A self-reliant community simply should seek to increase control over its own economy as far as is practicable.* It should try to encourage local investment in community corporations, and local consumption of goods made or service delivered by them. These community corporations, in turn, should be encouraged to hire local workers and use local inputs for production. This strategy maximizes the number of dollars that circulate within the community, which in turn pumps up its levels of employment, business, income, and wealth.

The qualifier "as far as is practicable" underscores that community self-reliance is a guidepost, not a diktat. Not every industry can be built in a given community, especially in a small one, and not every producer can rely exclusively on local inputs for production. Nor should self-reliance be used as an excuse to waste public funds on money-losing businesses. But if a company only needs to achieve a positive rate of return (whereby revenues exceed costs) rather than a maximum rate of return, many more goods and services can be made and sold locally than are today. Moreover, wise policy decisions by local, state, and national governments can greatly expand every community's universe of business possibilities.

A community can—indeed, must—maintain economic relationships with the rest of the world, provided it retains *control* of these relationships. Three strategies can help accomplish this. The first, discussed in Chapter 2, is to nurture businesses that reduce imports for basic needs. A sound local economy is one that provides everyone with the necessities of life, and trades surplus production for less-essential goods and services. The second, covered in Chapter 3, is to keep ownership of business local, so that the sudden departure of a firm on which a community depends is virtually impossible. The third strategy, the subject of Chapter 4, is to channel local savings and investment capital into the building of the local economy.

All three strategies strengthen what economists call the *economic multiplier*. The expenditure of a dollar generates more than just a dollar's worth of activity. A worker who receives a paycheck of say $500 might spend half on food and half on rent. The market that sold the food might use its $250 in revenue to buy more produce from local farmers, and the landlord might spend his or her $250 on electricity from the local utility. Every expenditure cascades into a larger number of transactions that enrich the community. Once the multiplier leaves the community, the benefits of subsequent transactions are lost. A community in which money flows out quickly and never returns slowly bleeds to death. The primary virtue of import substitution, community corporations, and local investment is that these strategies increase the likelihood of the economic multiplier's staying at home.

Community self-reliance may or may not be consistent with the goal of traditional economists, efficiency, or the goal of their critics, equity. A community that chooses to become self-reliant may well decide to accept more expensive goods and services in the name of a better quality of life. Likewise, principled adherence to community self-reliance may mean saying "no" to certain federal grants and loans which could stymie income redistribution. But a community can—and *should*—be responsive to *all* these goals. The key is to start with self-reliance and frame local business, labor, and environmental laws and policies around it. Exactly how economics can serve the basic needs of a community is the focus of the next chapter.

Needs-Driven Industries 2

Community self-reliance may be difficult to imagine, but it has been the norm for most of human history. Somewhere around 10,000 B.C., *homo sapiens sapiens* pioneered agriculture and used crude tools to plow fields for millet and rice in Southeast Asia.[1] At roughly the same time, counterparts in France were building structures capable of sheltering 400 to 600 people. Three thousand people lived within the walls of the city of Jericho as early as 8,000 B.C. Fragmentary records suggest that these early communities were capable of producing enough grains, vegetables, fruits, and livestock to feed their residents. Wood, grasses, stones, and mud provided the essentials for housing and furniture. Animal hides, furs, and fibers were fashioned into clothing. Locally harvested plants and minerals became sources of the first medications. The burning of wood and manure generated warmth and light, and even facilitated basic metallurgy. Mechanical energy from running water and from draft animals helped process raw ingredients like wheat into more usable products like flour. These "simple" communities, the first outposts of human civilization, left an impressive legacy of folklore, music, art, and science.

Few communities in the United States today are this self-reliant. They require oil brought in by truck, coal by rail, natural gas by pipeline, and electricity through expansive power grids. The typical food item travels 1,300 miles before it winds up on the dinner table, and is distributed through supermarkets and chain stores.[2] Wander through your house and you'll probably find more evidence of resources from places thousands of miles away than from your own bioregion: tuna caught in the Gulf of Mexico; beer brewed from water and hops in Germany and bottled in New Jersey; Evian water extracted from southern France. Your closets are filled with shirts and blouses that traveled from silk producers in China to production plants in Malaysia, on to packaging facilities in Guatemala, and finally to the racks at Macy's.

The variety of these well-traveled goods certainly enhances the quality of our lives, but our growing dependence on them carries profound risks. The more essential an item is for our survival, the more dangerous it is to depend on someone outside the community selling it to us. Basic necessities, of course, are difficult to define. But if you were to write down a list of what you need to survive, chances are good you would include what most nations assented to in Article 25 of the Universal Declaration of Human Rights: "Everyone has the right to a standard of living adequate for the health and well-being of himself and his family, including food, clothing, housing, and medical care and necessary social services. . . ." To provide these basics, a community needs farmers, water suppliers, loggers, materials processors, and social-service providers. But is it really possible to structure a viable community around just these economic sectors? Can community-scale businesses meet local citizens' needs cost-effectively?

IMPORT REPLACEMENT

Nowhere are the dangers of depending on imports of basics more clear than with oil. Over the next decade the United States is expected to import 60 percent of its oil from foreign suppliers (up from 52 percent in 1994).[3] Just as OPEC's sudden boycott and price hikes in 1973 and 1979 triggered long queues at gas stations, shortages, inflation, and recessions, our continued dependence threatens economic instability in the years ahead. A 60-percent import rate means a trade deficit in oil of $100 billion per year.[4] Leaving aside the costs of spills from offshore oil-drilling and air pollution from oil-burning, the transportation of oil across oceans poses huge environmental risks to harbor and coastal ecosystems, as well as to the entire oceanic food chain. Another decade of imports will provide $1 trillion of revenue to Persian Gulf states, much of which will be spent on weapons, wars, and saber-rattling that are hardly in the interests of U.S. foreign policy. America is once again in a position where a handful of governments, most of them undemocratic, can bring the nation's economy to its knees by turning off the spigots.

Dependency on necessities from outside the community means that a remote crisis can reverberate into a local one. A study for the Pentagon concluded that in a single night, without ever leaving Louisiana, a few saboteurs could cut off three-quarters of the natural gas supplies to the eastern United States for more than a year.[5] It also found that low-technology sabotage of any one of the nation's more than 100 power stations could trigger a catastrophic core meltdown, inflicting a Chernobyl-like accident, or worse, on the country. In November 1965, a faulty relay in Canada cascaded into a series of equipment failures that blacked out 30 million electricity customers in the Northeast for up to 13 hours.[6] On July 13, 1977, the chair of the Consolidated Edison Company in New York assured his customers that he could "guarantee" that a recurrence was extremely unlikely. Three days later, a combination of lightning and equipment failures blacked out nearly nine million Con Ed customers for up to 25 hours, and set the stage for $121 million worth of looting. Two decades of reflection and planning did not prevent another major collapse of the electric grid on August 10, 1996. A tree falling into a transmission line near the Columbia River in Oregon toppled a series of mechanical dominoes and left millions of consumers in 14 states and two Canadian provinces without power for several hours. Dependence holds a community hostage to mistakes, misdeeds, and misfortunes totally outside its control.

A dependent community also loses the economic benefits of producing necessities for itself. A community that chooses not to generate its own electricity, not to grow its own food, not to process its own lumber, and so on, winds up losing the jobs and income that might have come from these commercial ventures. The more these activities are performed outside the community, the weaker the economic multiplier inside.

Economists are skeptical about the principles of self-reliance and import-substitution, because they deprive a community of the benefits of trade. A community focusing inward narrows the range of goods and services available to its citizens, and deprives its businesses of the new machines, new production methods, and competitive forces necessary for progress. Moreover, if local goods and services cost more than those produced outside, going local means losing money, which condemns a com-

munity to less consumption and lower investment. Economies that have
sought to seal themselves hermetically from the world—like the former
Soviet Union, Albania, and Burma—soon crumble from obsolescence.

A better way to think of the goal of import substitution, however, is that
it motivates a community to move the most important and valuable types
of production back home, not to unplug completely from the national or
international economy. And the means to accomplish this need not be tariffs or heavy-handed regulation, but simply smart choices by residents and
local officials to buy, invest, and hire locally. Viewed this way, "the theoretical case for emphasizing import substitution is strong," according to
Joseph Persky, David Ranney, and Wim Wiewel, three economists at the
University of Illinois at Chicago.[7]

Import-substituting growth facilitates the diversification of the local
economy and the accumulation of its own capital, skills, and experience.
Jane Jacobs, in her 1969 book *The Economy of Cities,* provides two examples of cities that were able to pump up their economies through import
substitution:[8] The Los Angeles export industries that nourished the U.S.
military during World War II, like aircraft manufacturing, shipbuilding,
and petroleum refining, all declined after the war ended in 1945. Yet the
number of jobs in the city expanded because of the growth of new import-
replacing businesses. Automobile companies in Detroit, for example,
opened branch plants to serve customers in southern California.

In Chicago, between 1845 and 1855, the city's population grew by nearly a factor of seven, as did the overall economy. The reason again, writes
Jacobs, was import substitution:

*[A]t the beginning of the decade Chicago, like any other little
Midwestern depot settlement, was importing most kinds of things that
every town supplied. But by the end of that decade it was producing a
very large range of the common city-made goods of the time and some
of the luxuries too—clocks, watches, medicines, many kinds of furniture, stoves, kitchen utensils, many kinds of tools, most building components.*[9]

Import substitution actually incorporates some of the export-oriented
thinking of mainstream economists. As a community replacing imports
grows in size, it naturally attracts more businesses that target national and

global markets. Persky, Ranney, and Wiewel summarize the export-led theory of development in the following terms:

> [A]n area that is able to increase significantly its sales of a major export will experience population growth related to the new employment in the basic export sector. This population growth in turn implies that an area may pass thresholds for new products. Now the metropolis will provide some commodities for itself that formerly it imported. Export growth leads to import substitution.[10]

A community committed to import substitution, however, aims to *minimize* population growth. The goal is to expand the quantity and quality of jobs without drawing new people. University of Montana economist Thomas Michael Power has shown that the states in which jobs grew fastest during the 1970s, such as Alaska, Arizona, Nevada, and Utah, also saw family income grow more slowly than the national average.[11] In states like New York and Rhode Island, where employment growth was slowest, income growth was above the national average. The reason for these seemingly paradoxical results is the inflow and outflow of people. Power concludes that "there is no reliable connection between mere quantitative expansion of the local economy and local economic well-being."[12] Expansion of economic activity should be targeted carefully at those people, institutions, and businesses that have a long-term commitment to the community. He winds up recommending a concerted local effort at import substitution:

> The import substitution can be direct, as in the case of energy or of a local bakery replacing imported bread, or it can be indirect. As the variety of goods and services produced locally expands, the richer commercial economy attracts and holds more of the residents' dollars. Local dollars that would have otherwise flowed out of the community, to purchase things that would add variety and quality to residents' lives, stay in the community to purchase local services. Live theater and music, instruction in personal skills, recreational facilities, and so on attract and hold dollars that otherwise would have flowed out to finance imports.[13]

If import-replacement leads to greater exports, is the distinction from export-led development simply a matter of semantics? Hardly. A typical export-led development strategy targets just one or two industries. The World Bank pushed dozens of poor countries in the 1980s to specialize in the production of a few primary commodities like coffee, sugar, cocoa, copper, aluminum, and lumber. The fatal flaw of this approach was that each country's economy became so specialized that it was vulnerable to the collapse of the price of a targeted commodity. And this is exactly what happened. The nosedive of coffee prices in the late 1980s and early 1990s, for example, destabilized coffee-exporting countries worldwide, from Guatemala to Indonesia. In Rwanda, another country dependent on coffee exports, the consequent economic turmoil set off a chain of events that culminated in the Hutus massacring an estimated million Tutsis.

Development led by import-replacement rather than export promotion diversifies, stabilizes, and strengthens the local economy. As Jane Jacobs writes:

In the case of an export-multiplier effect, some of the new imports earned by the export growth go directly back into the export work, the way ore imported into Pittsburgh goes directly into exported steel, or a high proportion of the textiles imported into New York go into exported clothing. The other imports earned by exports go into a city's local economy; but even so, many of them go indirectly into the export work that earns them. In the case of an import-replacing multiplier effect, however, none of the different (seemingly additional) imports go either directly or indirectly into exports from the city. All are added to the growing local economy. The greater volume of the locally produced jelly, lamps or tombstones—relative to the imports they replaced—is one result. The rounding out of the local economy is another.[14]

Can a small community embark upon an import-replacement development strategy? Don't certain industries need a large enough local market to be set up in the first place? No, respond Persky, Ranney, and Wiewel: "[W]e do not observe a well-defined threshold population at which a given industry enters a community. For most industries, we only observe that the share of local demand supplied locally tends to rise with size."[15]

A small community like Eugene, Oregon, couldn't operate a factory to produce cars solely for its own needs, but it *could* build a plant that met the transport demand of the Pacific Northwest region. The key issue is what economists call the optimal *economy of scale*. Whenever the economy of scale of production is large and a plant needs a very high output to operate competitively, it must export to consumers outside the community. And any good or service for which this is true, by definition, can facilitate import substitution in only a limited number of communities. Because the economy of scale of automobile construction is large, it's neither possible nor desirable for every one of America's 36,000 municipalities to manufacture cars.[16]

The prevailing wisdom among economists and businesspeople is that large economies of scale are the rules of thumb for industrial production. Huge factories with global distribution networks are assumed to deliver cheaper and better products than are small factories serving just local markets. This is because certain fixed costs, such as management, machinery, warehouses, marketing, and lawyers, can be spread over more and more units of production. Business consultants like the Boston Company and Wall Street investment houses like Drexel Burnham Lambert have accumulated vast fortunes acquiring, merging, and reorganizing firms to achieve larger economies of scale.

Yet, as the dinosaurs learned, bigger is not always better. Bigger businesses also tend to develop certain *dis*economies of scale. The larger the distance between producers and consumers, the harder it is to fine-tune products to the particular tastes of local markets. Local businesses set up to serve the exacting demands of local consumers can be started more quickly, with smaller investments and smaller risks. Once a conscientious process of import replacement begins, a company may be surprised to discover other savings inherent in local production and distribution. Transportation costs go down. So do the costs of marketing.

So do the costs of excessive preservatives and packaging. A study in Europe found that a jar of strawberry yogurt traveled 2,166 miles before reaching the typical German consumer.[17] Most of the mileage wasn't logged by the food; the main ingredients—milk and sugar—came from the surrounding countryside, and the strawberries were grown in Poland. It was attributable to the packaging. Glass for the jar, paper for the label, paste for the paper, aluminum for the top all were produced from sites across Europe.

The bottom line depends on how these economies and diseconomies add up. For basic necessities, economies of scale appear to be shrinking to the point where hundreds or even thousands of U.S. communities could move toward self-reliance. Recent breakthroughs in technology, workforce organization, and resource management are enabling local entrepreneurs to provide food, water, wood, energy, and materials in cost-effective ways. While few communities have deliberately tried to replace all their imports of basic necessities, a number of examples in each of these economic sectors testify to the possibility and promise of doing so.

FOOD INDUSTRIES

One of the saddest stories of the past century in the United States is the destruction of community-based family farming. The number of Americans on a farm today is less than one-fifth what it was in 1920.[18] Those involved in farming have substantially expanded their land holdings. In 1994, 2 percent of all the farms in the United States were so big that they were responsible for half of all food sales, while three-quarters of the farms were so small that they accounted for only 9 percent.[19] A closer look at recent developments in agriculture, however, suggests that small-scale systems to grow, process, and market food are becoming not only cost-effective—in both rural and urban areas—but also essential to preserve the genetic integrity of the world's edible plants.

Leaving aside inflation, the value added to the economy by food-growing farms has remained constant throughout this century. What has changed is the explosive growth of the food-marketing business and of corporations providing inputs into farming (seeds, fertilizers, herbicides, pesticides, etc.). In 1910, for every dollar Americans spent for food, 41 cents went to farmers and 59 cents to marketers and input providers; now 9 cents go to farmers, 24 cents to input providers, and 67 cents to marketers.[20]

Economists celebrate these statistics, because fewer farmers can grow more food for American consumers at a lower price. But the costs have been the decimation of once-vibrant rural communities, and increased dependency of urban and suburban communities on far-off sources of nutrition. Another look at the numbers suggests that community-scale production might actually *lower* the cost of food for local consumers. Community-scale agriculture, even if it means higher-cost farming, might be able to bring down the cost of inputs through organic growing methods and the cost of marketing through local distribution.[21] When farmers are involved in distribution, they also have an opportunity to retain more of the "value added."

The economics of small-scale farming actually is improving, though it varies across the country. The valleys of the Mississippi, Missouri, and Ohio Rivers offer richer farming opportunities than do the Mohave desert or Fairbanks, Alaska. But the presence of *some* commercially viable agriculture in every one of America's 50 states (as well as in the less hospitable provinces of Canada) is a reminder that wherever there is land and water, growing one's own food is possible. One out of four fruits and vegetables distributed in today's commercial systems never makes it to the consumer's table, because it spoils during shipment or on the grocery-store shelf.[22] Less locally grown produce, in contrast, needs to be thrown away, and because it's closer to the customer (a typical item travels 200 miles instead of 1,300), transportation costs are lower. Finally, direct relationships between farmers and consumers can greatly reduce or eliminate the costs of packaging, marketing, middlemen, and supermarkets.

A recent study by the United Nations Development Programme suggests that even dense urban areas hold enormous potential for cultivation.[23] Some 800 million people in the world who live in cities are engaged in urban agriculture, mainly for their own consumption.[24] In Hong Kong, which has an extraordinary population density, nearly half of all vegetables consumed are grown within the city limits, on 5 percent to 6 percent of the city's land. Squatters in Lusaka, Zambia, grow one-third of their food in the city. Residents of Kampala, Uganda, meet 70 percent of their poultry and egg consumption with local production. Data from the 1980s suggest that the 18 largest cities in China met over 90 percent of their vegetable needs, and half their meat needs, through urban farming. And Singapore raises 80 percent of its poultry, and a quarter of its vegetables, within city limits.

A nation's food system is rooted deeply in its history, culture, diet, and land-use policies, and therefore these experiences abroad may not be entirely transferable to the United States. But enough farming is occurring in or near U.S. cities that the opportunities for expanded urban agriculture are certainly worth exploring. More than 30 percent of the dollar value of U.S. agricultural production originates from farms within major metropolitan areas.[25] Over the past 20 years, New York City has opened a thousand community gardens on public land, and 18 public markets to sell produce grown in them.[26] Boston and Philadelphia have even more gardens per capita. Recognizing the potential of urban farming, several cities such as Chattanooga and Hartford, and states such as Massachusetts and Oregon, have developed comprehensive urban food policies.

Several trends in American cities make the economics of urban agriculture increasingly attractive. First, more land is becoming available for farming. Most U.S. cities are spreading out over larger geographic areas, while their populations are remaining stable or declining. Some 40 percent of all the land in Detroit is now vacant. The exodus of industry and people from Pittsburgh has left more than 37,000 empty lots. These lots, once cleared of garbage, toxics, and abandoned buildings, have potential for cultivation, along with parkland, greenhouses, and even rooftops. Second, cities have a growing supply of idle labor. The highest unemployment rates in the country are in urban areas. In principle, much of the work required for municipal farming could be done by unskilled inner-city residents, though some training would be required and psychological barriers to manual labor would need to be overcome. Third, with recent cuts in Aid to Families with Dependent Children, cities will continue to have serious unmet demands for more food. The Food Research and Action Center estimates that nearly half the children under the age of 12 who live in urban households below the poverty line are "either hungry or at-risk of hunger." Developing new, cheap sources of nutrition for these young people is imperative—for their future and for the future of America's cities.

A handful of nonprofits have seized this opportunity in intriguing ways. In South Central Los Angeles, Reverend George Singleton's Hope LAS Horticulture Corps trains young and at-risk gang members to plant flowers, herbs, vegetables, and trees in vacant lots. Sales of the produce grown pay for the project, which combines agricultural coursework with hands-on training. Singleton is now working with organizations to spread the program to five other sites in the Los Angeles area, and to the Bronx.

Farms need not be within a city's limits to contribute to its economic well-being. Linking farmers just outside a city with consumers inside it can boost the regional economy. One indication that this is happening is the revival of farmers' markets across the country, in which local growers set up stands (or use the backs of their station wagons) to sell fruits, vegetables, and nuts. This produce often is not as pretty as what's available at the local supermarket; it may well be discolored and irregular. But consumers are attracted to it because it tastes better, holds more nutrition, and often is free of pesticides.

Some clever farmers have organized groups of consumers (and vice versa) into subscribers' clubs. One model of what has become known as community-supported agriculture, or CSA, is that each member family agrees to pay a fee for the growing season, and in exchange the farmer promises to deliver a box of vegetables each week, enough to feed a family. The contents of the box vary throughout the season; one week it might be mostly asparagus and melon, another it might be potatoes and pumpkins. Some CSAs add farm products like eggs, milk, honey, spices, flowers, and firewood. Subscribers can pick up their box of produce at a nearby distribution point or have it delivered to their doorstep.

Some 600 such community-supported agricultural or horticultural operations now exist in 42 of the United States, with 100,000 members.[27] A typical participating farm has about 3 acres (plus grazing land) and serves the needs of 60 to 70 families who each pay about $400.[28] With the subscription fee paid up front, consumers share the risks of failure with the farmer. If consumers were to become co-owners of the land and equipment, effectively shareholders, this model could be seen as a community corporation.

If you can't imagine taking a box of produce chosen and packed by someone else, but still want to support local farmers, you might just try to shop only at community-friendly markets. Retailing food, of course, is another viable business for community corporations, which can set up outdoor farmers' markets or indoor stores, or take over and revitalize failing stores. The Village Retail Services Association (ViRSA) in England has a simple mission: to save small shops endangered by shopping malls and gigantic outlets. It organizes customers to invest in local shops, with the goal of strengthening their buying loyalty and the incentive of advertising by word by mouth. It also works with management to improve the efficiency and quality of operations. Sometimes ViRSA purchases the entire operation and hires new management; and occasionally, where there is very broad local commitment, it will organize the shop to be run entirely by volunteers. In ViRSA's first year it assisted 12 British communities.[29]

How far urban agriculture, CSAs, farmers' markets, and village stores can go in feeding a community is unclear. Even if these innovations can deliver fruits and vegetables cost-effectively, can they also provide grains, meat, and other kinds of food? The answer may only be positive if more and more value-added activity is undertaken by farmers themselves. One recent study found intriguing evidence that small-scale farmers could do well supplementing their incomes with homestead chicken production, small dairy herds, and on-farm food processing.[30] Certainly if growing numbers of consumers continue to prefer food grown, raised, processed, packaged, and sold by local farmers, the economics of community food production will steadily improve.

Besides the economic bottom line, there is another reason why communities should vigorously promote local agriculture: to insure the long-term integrity of the world's food supply.[31] Richard Douthwaite, a community-economics specialist currently living in Ireland, details this argument in his recent book, *Short Circuit: Strengthening Local Economics for Security in an Unstable World*. He begins with a story his countrymen know all too well—the Irish potato famine. In the late 1500s, explorers of the New World brought back two types of potatoes to Ireland, and left the plants' natural enemies behind. For three centuries, potato growing in the country flourished, even given relatively little genetic variation. But this eventually left them easy prey for various New World molds, viruses, and bacteria that ultimately found their way across the ocean. Between 1825 and 1849, two-thirds of the nation's potato crops went bad. Famines during eight of those years took the lives of a million people, and convinced another million to pack their bags for more fertile fields elsewhere.[32]

Agriculture around the world today is set on the identical course toward disaster. Eager to find a superspecies that can resist pests and microbial enemies, growers around the world are relying on dwindling numbers of carefully designed seed species. These monocultures are genetically "stable," which means that each seed grows into fruits and vegetables similar in size, color, and taste. Like their predecessors in Ireland, today's farmers are being blinded by short-term success. Yes, monoculture crops enable them to achieve ever-larger yields of marketable produce or grains at lower costs. But while these crops remain the same, year after year, their enemies are mutating, evolving, catching up, and spreading. Sooner or later, every superspecies meets its superpredator.

Mindful of these dangers, scientists set up the International Board for Plant Genetic Resources in 1972, to create "seed banks" in which diverse crop species could be collected, catalogued, stored, and protected. Seed banks provide a sort of an insurance policy: if disaster strikes one species, others with different genetic strengths and weaknesses stand ready for reintroduction. Most banks, however, are poorly funded and inadequately maintained. The repository of the world's rice seeds sits between two active volcanoes in the Philippines. And the U.S. National Seed Storage Laboratory in Fort Collins, Colorado, has fought a losing battle with power shortages and outdated refrigeration technology while trying to keep seeds stored at an appropriate temperature.

It turns out that even well-maintained seed banks cannot protect genetic variation. In the real world, seeds continue to evolve from generation to generation in response to changing local conditions of temperature, soil, air, water, and pests. If thousands of communities introduce one type of seed, thousands of subtle genetic variations inevitably emerge with thousands of unique defenses. A seed bank cannot possibly mimic these variations. Moreover, seeds cannot survive in cold storage forever. They must be periodically replanted, and offspring seeds are then put back in storage. But these specially grown seeds inevitably reflect the artificial conditions of the bank, not of the real world.

The inescapable conclusion is that there is only one way to ensure that global agriculture maintains its genetic diversity: As many communities as possible must develop their own species of seeds that are adapted to local conditions and immune to local enemies. Cary Fowler and Pat Mooney, two experts on sustainable agriculture who won the Right Livelihood Award (often called the alternative Nobel Prize) for their work in 1985, have written: "Saving farmers is a prerequisite of saving diversity. Conversely, communities must save their agricultural diversity in order to retain their own options for development and self-reliance. Someone else's seeds imply someone else's needs."[33]

The dangers of monoculture agriculture, like those of global warming, will never be reflected in free-market prices before it's too late to act. It may not be until one or two monocultures fail on a massive scale, causing millions to die from famine, that markets will sharpen the resolve of governments and entrepreneurs to revive community farming. Localities mindful of their own survival, and smart entrepreneurs living within them must act sooner. The goal of every community needs to be to collect, plant, and develop, through new community businesses, seeds uniquely suited to its bioregion.

ENERGY INDUSTRIES

Energy industries, like modern agribusiness, have long been thought to be an exemplar of the benefits of large-scale production. The states awarded gigantic monopolies to electric utilities and natural-gas companies because they were convinced that the economies of scale of these businesses were large. Oil companies also have been among the most powerful U.S. corporations throughout the twentieth century, so much so that they have provided much of the impetus for antitrust legislation. The economies of scale for producing electricity and liquid fuels, however, are fast shrinking.

Over the past decade, electric utilities have had to face a radical change in their business: Saving a unit of energy is now cheaper than producing a unit. And exploitation of cost-effective savings can proceed very far before the construction of a single new power plant can be justified. Installation of the best lighting technologies can save up to three-quarters of the lighting energy we now use, displacing dozens of large power plants.[34] An analysis of 35 types of improvements to electric motors and their components found a potential to save about half of all electrical motor input, which uses over half of all electricity in the world, at a fraction of the cost per kilowatt–hour of just operating either a coal or nuclear plant.[35] If the United States were as energy efficient as its Western European competitors, it could save about $200 billion annually—much more than the size of the federal deficit.[36]

These changes in the electricity business, reinforced by long-overdue reforms in state regulatory and price-setting policies, have prompted utilities across the country to launch programs to conserve energy. Many now have divisions that help residential users replace inefficient air conditioners and refrigerators, caulk leaky doors and floorboards, replace windows with double-paned glass, insulate walls and roofs, and so on. They work with industrial customers to upgrade the efficiency of lighting, motors, and production processes. In California, utility investment in energy efficiency yielded $2.4 billion in net benefits (from avoided production costs) to customers between 1990 and 1994.[37] It's true that some utility "demand-side management" programs are beginning to be scaled back, but those moves aren't because conservation has become less cost-effective. Two other important factors are responsible.

One factor is deregulation. Economists have long viewed the electrical industry as a classic instance of a natural monopoly. It doesn't make sense to have a half-dozen electric companies competing with one another, each hooking up wires to a new residential block. A crazy quilt of wiring systems crisscrossing subdivisions would be enormously wasteful, resulting in companies continually ripping away or digging out one set of wires and installing a new set. Consequently, the federal and state governments gave utilities a monopoly over both the generation and the distribution of electricity. However, in recent years economists have made the case that even if a distribution system should be a monopoly, electrical generation systems need not be. Just as the phone system has been broken up between local-service monopolies which own the wires, and competitive long-distance carriers, so too are electric utilities. The entire industry is undergoing radical reorganization. Competitive pressures among generators of electricity are inducing some to abandon conservation programs that assisted all their customers, rich and poor, and instead to "cherry pick" the biggest customers, and abandon the rest.

A second factor is growing competition from small business. Nothing about conservation inherently requires a large economy of scale and certainly not a protected monopoly. Hands-on inspection, conducted from house to house and from business to business, is probably the best way to evaluate which walls and ceilings need to be insulated, which appliances need to be replaced, which energy-use patterns need to be altered. Some energy-saving devices, such as compact fluorescent lightbulbs, superefficient windows, and reflective materials for rooftops, may be best manufactured in large, centralized plants. But the installation of these devices can be done best by a local workforce intimately familiar with its local terrain, architecture, and business culture.

Because of these changing economies of scale, a whole new industry of "energy-service companies" (ESCOs) has taken root. The National Association of Energy Service Companies has estimated that, to the time of this writing, ESCOs had provided nationwide $2 billion of energy-efficiency hardware, software, and services.[38] The typical ESCO is a small or medium-sized company that oversees energy conservation projects for a period of seven to 10 years. It enters a contract with a business, school, or public agency, and promises to save a certain amount of both energy and energy expenditures. It conceptualizes, implements, and finances the project. And it receives payment based on achieving or surpassing the promised efficiency targets.

In the late 1980s the Desert Sands Unified School District (DSUSD) in Indio, California, announced that it was taking bids to retrofit its 21 buildings. After three ESCOs submitted plans, the contract was awarded to Onsite Energy, based in Carlsbad, California. Onsite carefully measured the District's consumption patterns of electricity and natural gas, then arranged for a third party to provide a $1.4 million loan, and offered additional financing itself. In the first phase of the project, completed in 1991, Onsite replaced inefficient lights and installed electronic systems to control heating and cooling levels. Carol Miller, the business manager for the District, says:

> *Our system's efficiency has improved dramatically simply by our ability to now have all [heating and air-conditioning] units automatically shut off at night and brought back up in the morning. At the same time, individualized needs, like the need to maintain temperatures over a weekend for a classroom pet, can be met through the computerized system.*[39]

Onsite guaranteed the District energy savings of $326,410 per year for 10 years, and thus far has exceeded this goal. The District also has enjoyed other benefits from the deal, such as training for its maintenance personnel and ongoing technical support.

ESCOs are gradually moving beyond conservation and into small-scale energy production. NORESCO, a company based in Framingham, Massachusetts, recently helped the University of Rhode Island save more than $1 million by supplementing conventional conservation measures with the installation of three natural gas-fired engines that cogenerate electricity and steam for dorms. Under the Public Utility Regulatory Policy Act of 1978, utilities must buy electricity from small producers at a price they otherwise would have to pay to buy electricity from other utilities or to generate the electricity themselves.

Whether ESCOs ultimately replace or supplement the electricity-generating capacity of utilities or just supplement them will depend in part on how utility deregulation proceeds at the national, state, and local levels. But, since both types of business can be owned and operated locally, it doesn't much matter. Either structure will enable communities to harness special natural endowments for local needs for electricity.

Communities on open plains, mountainsides, or coastlines have wind resources that can be used either for pumping purposes or for making electricity. Southern communities are bathed in solar energy usable for heating, cooling, and electrical generation using both photovoltaics and solar-thermal-electric power technology. Western communities can tap geothermal resources. Landlocked communities can harness the power of rivers through small-scale hydroelectric dams. Rural communities have a surplus of agricultural, forestry, and animal wastes that can be used as or converted into combustible fuels. Urban areas may have a high enough population density to construct an economical district heating system in which a central heating unit pumps hot water and steam to nearby houses and factories. Technological innovations of recent years are steadily improving the ability of communities endowed with renewable energy resources to tap them economically.

ESCOs or utilities in areas with decent wind resources can take advantage of increasingly sophisticated wind turbine designs. Compared to former generations', today's machines operate over a greater range of wind-speeds, in a wider variety of sites, and without the earlier problems of television interference, noise, and broken blades. Global wind capacity has grown from 10 megawatts in 1980 to nearly 5,000 today, which is the output equivalent of five to eight large nuclear-power plants.[40] About 40 percent of this capacity is in the United States. Major wind-power projects are under way in Maine, Minnesota, Montana, and Texas, and the Electric Power Research Institute (a research arm of the utilities) estimates that an additional 2,600 megawatts of capacity are now on the drawing boards of U.S. utilities.[41] Royal Dutch/Shell projects that annual sales of wind turbines by the year 2020 could reach $50 billion.[42]

Basic economics have driven the spectacular growth of wind-generated electricity. In 1994, the average retail price of electricity in the United States was eight cents a kilowatt–hour—and rising.[43] Some areas, like New York State, face prices as high as 15 cents. Wind "farms" are now delivering highly competitive electricity for five to seven cents per kilowatt–hour, with facilities in the windiest areas pushing the cost below four cents a kilowatt–hour.[44] The cost of wind-generated electricity has fallen by 10 percent a year for the past 15 years, and as the technology matures and enters mass production, it should fall still further.[45]

Shell is even more bullish about the prospects for photovoltaic (PV) cells, which convert sunlight directly into electricity, predicting annual global sales growing to $100 billion by 2030. Currently, PVs are most cost-effective in specialized uses, such as electrifying homes (100,000 U.S. residences use PV power), pumping, signaling, and communicating in remote areas. To avoid spending an estimated $40,000 to $60,000 per mile to extend an overhead power line (or $130,000 for an underground line), utilities already find the installation of PVs at the point of use cost-effective.[46] PVs also may be cheaper than upgrading or rebuilding old distribution systems.

However, even in places where conventional electrical hookups are available, the economics of PVs are rapidly improving. Their cost has steadily dropped from $75 a peak watt in 1975 to about $4 today.[47] The Sacramento Municipal Utilities District (SMUD) is pioneering the use of photovoltaics on residential rooftops at a cost of 17 cents per kilowatt–hour, which is less than the cost of peak power in 35 U.S. cities.[48] (The comparison with peak power is relevant because the output of PVs varies with the intensity of the sun and peaks at mid-day, which coincides nicely with the peak of demand in certain locations for electrical needs like air conditioning.) Solec International, the only U.S. manufacturer of PVs to make a profit up to 1994, projects that the commercialization of several recent breakthroughs will soon bring PV-electricity costs down to 12 cents a kilowatt–hour.[49] In 1994, Enron Corporation entered a contract with the U.S. government to build a 100-megawatt solar-cell power plant using a thin-film PV technology, and agreed to sell electricity for 5.5 cents per kilowatt–hour.[50]

Global annual sales of PVs have skyrocketed from under seven megawatts in 1980 to 96 megawatts in 1996, nearly half produced by U.S. businesses.[51] Major companies around the world are racing to bring a wide range of PV technologies to the marketplace. One of the most promising ideas is to integrate PVs with the "skins" of buildings—roofs, walls, and skylights—and thereby obviate the costs of PV installation. A Swiss company, Atlantis Energy, is already selling PV roof shingles that simultaneously generate electricity and capture emitted heat for space heating.[52]

ESCOs in communities near farms can make use of a wide range of agricultural wastes to provide low-grade heat. Facilities that can burn special crops and crop waste are generating as much electricity in the United States today as eight large nuclear-power plants.[53] The Department of Energy predicts that biomass fuels will be competitive with gasoline and diesel by the year 2005.[54] Other analysts anticipate that the U.S. biomass industry, currently employing 66,000 people, could more than double by the year 2020.[55] The actual rate of expansion, of course, will depend on the prices of oil, natural gas, and other conventional fuels.

But the potential for community corporations to expand biomass as an energy source is best suggested by recent developments *outside* the United States. The harvesting of four tons of grain leaves two tons of straw, which can produce as much heat as a ton of coal—with less pollution.[56] Two hospitals in Birmingham, England, are taking advantage of this and burning straw pellets to heat their main buildings.[57] In Denmark, 12,000 farms are using straw-fired boilers for heat, and 60 communities burn straw to pump hot water and steam through district-heating systems.[58] The Danish Energy Agency estimates that straw-burning soon will be providing 7 percent of the nation's total energy needs.

Biomass is more environmentally attractive to use than fossil fuels, for several reasons. Because plants and trees are photosynthesized from air and water, a steady pace of harvesting and regrowth year after year does not increase the net accumulation of carbon dioxide in the atmosphere. For each unit of heat generated, a given amount of fossil fuel creates four times as many nitrogen oxides and 50 times as much sulfur dioxide as the burning of biomass.[59] Ash from some types of biomass combustion actually can enrich farmlands. And special plants like elephant grass, energy cane, and switchgrass can remove pollutants from contaminated soil and water.[60]

Still, there are environmental problems that accompany the use of some biomass wastes for fuel. The best nutrients in trees are in the branches and leaves, and harvesting forestry wastes can mean gradually depleting the soil. Fortunately, another biomass option is available with no such problems. The most plentiful plant in the world, and the easiest to grow, is algae. A collaboration between the University of the West Indies and the University of the West of England in Bristol has developed an ingenious system in which algae is grown, mixed with small amounts of diesel oil, and then burned for electricity.[61] The process uses the waste heat to dry the algae, and carbon-dioxide emissions to stimulate algae growth in the tanks. A new company—Photosynthesis, Ltd.—plans to market, to diesel-importing islands like the Seychelles, 300-kilowatt power stations using this technique.

The economies of scale for these technologies are naturally small. Ultimately, the devices for tapping renewable resources (windmills, PVs, boilers for burning straw or algae) might be mass-produced economically by a small number of global producers. But the installation, operation, and maintenance of these devices is best done by local firms in each community. Some renewable resources, like agricultural waste and algae, weigh too much to haul around cost-effectively. Others, like electricity from wind-power and PVs, are most economic if they are used locally and can avoid expensive and inefficient long-distance transmission.

If the price of oil rises over the coming decades, as most government and industry experts expect, the economics of local energy production will improve. Economically recoverable reserves of oil are physically limited, and new discoveries are occurring far slower than increases in consumption. With expected rises in global population and per capita consumption, the U.S. Energy Information Administration projects that, by the year 2010, demand for oil worldwide will grow by 20 million barrels a day (total consumption today is about 60 million barrels a day).[62] The speed with which an oil price rise ushers in what some predict will be a "renewables revolution" also depends on what happens to the price of natural gas. In recent years, cheap gas has slowed the spread of renewables and efficiency in the United States, and accelerated Japanese efforts to develop competitive "fuel cells"—devices that convert natural gas and other fuels into hydrogen, which can then be burned cleanly to power automobile engines or to produce heat and electricity for residential, commercial, or industrial use.[63]

Governments will be increasingly inclined to put a tax on oil, as well as on other fossil fuels, to account for the environmental effects of burning them. There is a virtual consensus among scientists today—except for a few cranks published by the *Wall Street Journal* and supported by interested industries and the Reverend Sun Myung Moon—that human progress is warming the planet. A recent report of the United Nations–sponsored Intergovernmental Panel on Climate Change, which represents 2,500 scientists from around the world, suggests that, over the next century, current trends in fossil-fuel use will release enough carbon dioxide and other waste gases into the atmosphere to raise global temperatures anywhere from 1.5 to 6 degrees Fahrenheit.[64] This will melt enough polar ice to raise ocean levels an additional 10 to 32 inches, and displace tens of millions of people living in coastal settlements from the Maldives to Bangladesh. Global warming also is predicted to unleash many violent hurricanes, diminish the productivity of certain agricultural regions, accelerate the extinction of plants and animals, and spread tropical diseases like dengue fever and malaria to new regions. By the time the multi-trillion-dollar costs of global warming are clear enough to affect the market price of fossil fuels, it will be too late to prevent it. But political pressures will surely mount on governments to place taxes on these fuels, per unit of pollution (a carbon tax) or per unit of energy (a BTU tax), that will raise their prices and reduce releases of carbon into the atmosphere. International negotiations are also under way to set ceilings on each nation's carbon emissions, and (more controversially) to allow nations to bid for emissions permits from one another.

Whether caused by dwindling supplies or higher taxes, a rise in fossil fuel prices will improve the economics of both efficiency and renewable-energy production. And that, in turn, will spur on the proliferation of ESCOs and local utilities.

NATURAL-RESOURCES INDUSTRIES

Judicious uses of land to produce food and of solar energy to produce electricity demonstrate how a community business can transform natural assets into a profitable product that serves local needs. But most communities are richly endowed with other natural resources that are inadequately tapped for their economic potential. Two prime examples are water and wood.

Few communities pay attention to the complicated networks of rivers, lakes, canals, reservoirs, wells, and aqueducts on which their survival depends. In the coming decades, however, many parts of the country are heading toward serious water shortages. In the West and Southwest, where the politics of water has always loomed large, periodic droughts and rationings have become a way of life, and are likely to become worse. Cities built in deserts, like Los Angeles and Las Vegas, whose explosive growth depended upon cheap water, are in for an especially rude awakening. Many of the most important agricultural regions in the country now rely on unsustainable mining of groundwater. Present rates of extraction will within three or four decades exhaust the Ogalala Aquifer lying under the Great Plains.[65] As the water tables of these regions drop, concentrations of minerals and pollutants will increase to the point where the remainder of the precious resource will be unusable.

Whatever the uncertainty about the timing and severity of water shortages, the price of water is almost certain to rise. Water is one of the most subsidized resources in the United States, with federal water projects selling each gallon at about one-fifth the cost to Uncle Sam.[66] And these costs do not include the environmental costs of excessive water use, such as the destruction of farmland, marshes, forests, and rivers, as well as the loss of animal and fish species that depend on these natural resources. Either public authorities will become more diligent about adding the environmental costs of depleting water supplies, or clean water supplies will simply run out.

The impact of an increase in water prices is clear: Transportation of water over long distances by pipelines, canals, and aqueducts, as we've gotten used to, will become increasingly uneconomical. The commercial advantage will move to communities that develop their own water supplies and use water more efficiently.

Just as ESCOs have profitably helped households and businesses to tighten energy efficiency, water-efficiency service companies (WASCOs) are beginning to do likewise. The efficiencies of energy and water use are of course linked. An air-assisted, low-flow showerhead cuts by nearly three-quarters the water needed for a shower, and three-quarters of the energy needed to heat the water. WASCOs can help households replace water–hungry appliances—toilets, washing machines, and dishwashers consume more than half of residences' water—with new, more efficient models. A typical U.S. toilet, for example, uses five gallons per flush, while common new models in Germany use half as much, and those in Scandinavia one-third.[67] Front-loading clothes washers can cut water use by 43 percent over conventional top-load models.[68] WASCOs also can help wean U.S. consumers away from one of the most ecologically destructive features of American life—the lawn. The city of Tucson introduced its citizens to the fine art of desert landscaping as part of its "Beat the Peak" program, which was able to cut peak water use by 26 percent in a decade.[69]

WASCOs can introduce local businesses to industrial processes that require less water. In Sweden, 80 percent of the country's industrial water use is for pulp and paper processors.[70] In the 1960s and 1970s, these processors cut water use in half while doubling production—by recycling used water. Farmers addicted to cheap water might prove to be especially important clients. Drip-irrigation saves a quarter of the evaporation and waste that occurs with sprinkler systems, and half that from conventional, gravity-fed irrigation.[71]

While newer and fewer than ESCOs, WASCOs are already demonstrating their business potential. Since 1988, American Water and Energy Savers, a company based in Miami, Florida, has plugged water leaks and replaced inefficient appliances in hundreds of thousands of buildings. VIEWtech, with offices in various cities across the country, has replaced 775,000 toilets in New York City, saving residents 20 to 35 percent of their water bills and relieving city officials of the need to construct billions of dollars' worth of new water-delivery facilities.

Some WASCOs like Consumers' Water Company of Portland, Maine, offer municipalities the opportunity to hand over their entire infrastructure for collecting, purifying, and reusing water. They then rethink its design, top to bottom. Why should clean rainwater be mixed together with human wastes, garbage, and various pollutants, and *then* be treated extensively (and expensively) before being reused? And why must crops, trees, and industry be fed water fit for human consumption? Systems are then rebuilt to collect different qualities of water for different purposes.

The same history of careless extraction and export of precious natural resources describes how Americans have treated their forests. When the Pilgrims arrived at Plymouth Rock, 954 million acres of forest covered what's now the lower 48 states.[72] More than one-third of this forest resource has been lost since, primarily on the East Coast. By 1982, forest cover fell to an all-time low of 577 million acres, 10 percent less than the area in 1963.[73]

As in the case of water, producers have had an economic incentive not to exploit forest resources sustainably, because of subsidies and unpaid external costs. In 1992, the U.S. government gave away half a billion dollars' worth of timber in the national forests to logging firms.[74] Meanwhile, legal mandates on firms to maintain forest ecologies have ranged from minimal, in national- or state-designated wilderness areas, to none whatsoever on private land. These kinds of policies make it economically rational for logging companies in the Pacific Northwest to clearcut the last 3 percent of ancient redwoods, ship them to Japan for processing, and then sell the finished lumber back in the United States.

Were the prices of forest products to reflect real costs, including the environmental ones, business would have a greater incentive to manage forests sustainably. Businessman Paul Hawken has noted that the Menominee Indians, motivated not by law but by a devout respect for nature, have selectively harvested trees on their land, and sold them profitably, for 150 years.[75] Today, after sales of 2 billion board-feet of wood, their forest remains as healthy an ecosystem as it was in the 1850s, with 25 percent *more* harvestable trees.

Communities need to recognize that permitting the destruction of forests for short-term profit is tantamount to burning down local banks. Annual sales by U.S. producers of wood, pulp, and paper products top $200 billion.[76] Placing this industry on a sustainable footing would ensure that these economic benefits would be available in perpetuity.

Forests also have innumerable benefits besides wood, pulp, and paper. The countries of Southeast Asia sell $3 billion a year of rattan, which are the stems from palm trees, to producers of wicker furniture.[77] The harvesting of forest products is not only viable in the Third World. An engineering firm in Corvallis, Oregon, found that the global market for bear grass, huckleberries, salal, and sword fern, all of which grew in abundance in nearby national forests, was $72 million a year.[78] In 1992, the direct-sales value of all nontimber forest products was about $1 billion.[79] Furthermore, annual sales of drugs derived from wild plants, animals, and microorganisms that are primarily found in forests probably top $100 billion.[80] These economic opportunities should all be seized by new community corporations.

MATERIALS INDUSTRIES

A traditional assessment of natural resources also would include mining. A community committed to local self-reliance, however, would seek to minimize its use of aluminum, copper, iron, and the like because these resources, like petroleum, are finite and their extraction carries enormous environmental costs. This does not imply that a local economy needs to abandon their use, for as David Morris, cofounder of the Institute for Local Self-Reliance, argues, every American community has aboveground mines that are carelessly ignored, and ripe for exploitation by community corporations. Just check the garbage.

The United States is the world's premier throwaway culture. Every week, every American consumes an average of 36 pounds of resources, and creates (directly or indirectly) more than 2,000 pounds of waste.[81] Much of this waste lies in landfills, where contaminants leach into the soil and the groundwater. Some is incinerated, sending toxic substances like mercury and lead downwind or leaving them in ashes that are placed in leaky landfills. Over the past generation the United States has spent more than a trillion dollars to curb pollution and manage wastes, but the problem seems only to be worsening.[82]

A self-reliant community would seek ultimately to eliminate waste altogether.[83] All industrial outputs would be rendered harmless or, better still, valuable. When, for example, industrial waste heat cogenerates electricity, additional money can be made. Each of these strategies opens up new opportunities for community corporations.

A growing number of U.S. communities have discovered that recycling not only is ecologically better than incineration or landfill, but also saves money. Recycling creates more jobs per dollar invested, and lays a foundation for setting up local scrap-based manufacturing enterprises. West Palm Beach, Florida, saved $43 per ton of material ($700,000 per year) by replacing expensive landfill practices with recycling.[84] New Jersey was able to use its recycling programs to provide materials to five glass-manufacturing plants, 13 paper mills, and eight steel mills, which together employ 9,000 people and generate over $1 billion in sales each year.[85]

Recycling of nonrenewable resources may be less desirable than substituting materials made from renewable resources, but the process of gathering, separating, purifying, and refabricating materials never can be perfectly efficient. And, even with recycling, a growing economy may seek to introduce a small amount of new nonrenewable materials. The challenge is especially acute as society begins to search for natural alternatives to materials derived from dwindling supplies of petroleum. Few appreciate that petroleum is now the basis for most plastics, fertilizers, paints, inks, medicines, and synthetic fibers. How can these materials be replaced? The answer is to look to the fields and the forests.[86]

In 1935, Henry Ford joined 300 other scientists, industrialists, and agronomists in forming the Farm Chemurgic Council, which aimed to enable "a variety of surplus products of the soil to be transformed through organic chemistry into raw materials usable in industry."[87] During World War II, Ford converted soy beans into plastic and envisioned manufacturing a new vegetable-car, with its wheels made out of goldenrod and its fuel derived from corn. Cheap oil after the war doomed the idea for two generations.

Now the dream of creating a "carbohydrate economy" is emerging again, thanks largely to the work of the Institute for Local Self-Reliance. The analysts at ILSR point out that Americans use 109 million tons of petrochemicals each year, compared to only 7 million tons of biochemicals.[88] But the potential supply of an organic feedstock is huge. U.S. farms generate 350 million tons of agricultural and forestry waste a year in the form of corn cobs, husks, straw, saw dust, pulp-mill wastes, vegetable oils, cheese whey, and many other substances. Conversion of just half these wastes could replace virtually all petrochemicals.

Most products derived from oil are now cheaper than their plant-based substitutes. Inks made from renewable resources cost 25 percent more than their petroleum-based counterparts, detergents 60 percent more, dyes 75 percent, paints 120 to 140 percent, and plastics 400 percent.[89] But some industrial products, such as acetic acid, adhesives, fatty acids, surfactants, and carbon black, can be produced from organic materials at the same cost—or cheaper. And the economics of biochemicals are improving. Improvements in technology and economies from greater production levels have cut the costs of many biochemical products, such as inks and dyes, by one-quarter or more since 1985. And, as the price of oil rises and governments impose green taxes on oil and oil-based products, the cost advantages of petrochemicals may disappear altogether.

Already, regional differences in input costs, as well as an emerging market of environmentally minded consumers and businesses, are enabling green products to displace petroleum-based competitors. Half of the 9,100 newspapers in the country print with soy ink, and 10 percent of detergents on the market are plant-based.[90] Minnesota Corn Processors runs a cooperatively owned biorefinery that is the largest corn-to-ethanol converter in the state.[91] Since 1990, processing plants have been built to convert sawdust to oil in Missouri, wood waste to chemicals in Wisconsin, whey to ethanol in California, and yard and paper waste to ethanol in Texas and Florida.[92]

The carbohydrate economy promises vast commercial opportunities for community corporations. Because agricultural and forestry waste is harder to collect and to ship than oil is, the most efficient location for processing plants will be close to the farms or forests providing the feedstock. David Morris of ILSR estimates that conversion of half the country's agricultural waste could provide the inputs for as many as 2,000 new biorefineries, meaning at least one plant for every rural county in America. One interesting implication is that while urban agriculture moves farms into the cities, the carbohydrate economy will move industry back to the countryside. This is welcome news for many rural areas where poverty rates often rival or exceed those in the inner city. The blurring of the once-rigid line between urban and rural communities will make *both* kinds more economically viable.

BEYOND NECESSITIES

Suppose a community were to start a network of locally owned and operated corporations which took care of most of its needs for energy, food, water, housing, and clothing. Would this really add up to local self-reliance? There are thousands of other sectors in the economy, from steel smelting to skiing. What good does it do to achieve self-reliance in just the necessities?

The benefits turn out to be impressive: In the short term, the community expands the local economic multiplier. As jobs and income grow, so do the local tax base and the public services. The provision of basics for local needs means that the community, through either the market economy or public assistance, can provide a baseline of decency for *all* its citizens. The long-term benefit of weaning the community away from depending on outsiders is that the community reduces its vulnerability to events outside its control.

It's astonishing how removed the priorities of today's local elected officials and urban planners are from this goal. They focus on luring nonlocally owned corporate giants to construct factories that produce nonbasics for nonlocal consumption. Or they build glitzy casinos, freeways, stadiums, shopping malls, and convention centers, and pray for the right multipliers. These strategies can't come close to meeting the basic needs of the middle class or the poor. They don't create a diversified economic base with secure jobs. Nor do they make the economy less vulnerable to oil embargoes, electrical brownouts, beef contaminated by "mad cow" disease, global grain shortages and price hikes, regional droughts, or skyrocketing interstate trash-disposal fees.

Achieving community self-reliance in basic necessities hardly precludes further opportunities for economic growth. Consumers secure in the basics have the ability to spend additional money on other professionals who provide valuable services like accountants, artists, dentists, doctors, mechanics, pharmacists, plumbers, and shopkeepers. Workers secure in the basics are happier, stronger, and more motivated. Decent conditions for consumers and workers ensure a stable economy with a reliable tax base. A community self-reliant on the basics usually has some ability to deliver public goods and social services to everyone (like roads, parks, firehouses, police cars, schools, and elections), including those who are not in a position to support themselves, such as the elderly, mentally ill, and disabled.

A self-reliant community can still import and export, provided the items involved are less essential for daily survival. Many of us want coffee from Guatemala, tea from Sri Lanka, software from Seattle, shoes from Milan, cars from Tokyo, watches from Zurich. A *smart* community will educate its citizens to appreciate the difference between needs and wants, and between basic necessities and luxuries that only seem essential because of advertising. But a needs-driven economy need not eliminate all imports, and otherwise purge residents of global tastes; the aim is only to minimize imports of the basics and create a local economy where much more can be done in the backyard.

A needs-driven economy is just the starting point for community development, not the end point. Once a community achieves self-reliance in basic necessities, it can promote other homegrown businesses to serve less essential needs. Local entrepreneurs interested not only in the bottom line but also in the welfare of the community might continue to focus on import replacement beyond the basics. By studying import patterns, entrepreneurs can identify key dependencies, and work aggressively to reduce them. These community corporations may well export and import, but overall they would facilitate the shift of control back to community decisionmakers.

Place was once a serious constraint on a community's universe of business possibilities. Corporations situated themselves in big cities because of the proximity of ports, railyards, airports, universities, skilled workforces, and complementary businesses. But the plummeting costs of communication and transportation are now making location less and less critical. A growing array of such services as data entry, accounting, strategic planning, and even legal analysis can now be performed anywhere in the world. Businesses that were once unimaginable—stockbrokering on a Montana ranch, software development in Key West, desktop publishing in rural North Carolina—are commonplace.

Recall economist Paul Krugman's point that Americans now spend proportionately more of their income on services, and less on manufactured goods. Scholars at Princeton's Center for Energy and Environmental Studies have documented that historically Americans and Western Europeans have been consuming fewer raw materials as the Gross Domestic Product (GDP) rises.[93] U.S. steel use per dollar of GDP has dropped to the 1880 level.[94] Similar declines can be observed in our consumption, per dollar of GDP, of most basic materials, including cement, ammonia, chlorine, and aluminum.

There are several reasons for this uncoupling of consumption from wealth. Advances in technology have liberated products from the need to incorporate bulky materials. Cars are increasingly made with composite materials that are stronger, lighter, and cheaper than steel. Once an industrial society builds an infrastructure and saturates the consumer market with basic appliances like TV sets and air conditioners, the demands for materials like concrete and steel go down. Repairs to infrastructure and replacements of appliances require fewer materials. Finally, people with rising incomes tend to buy goods featuring higher levels of technology, such as VCRs, personal computers, software, and medical instruments. The delinking of production from bulk materials diminishes the importance of locating a factory near natural resources. And this opens up more opportunities for community corporations almost anywhere to produce a greater variety of goods.

These changes, Krugman argues, are moving the U.S. economy inexorably toward what he calls *localization:*

> *A steadily rising share of the work force produces services that are sold only within that same metropolitan area. In 1894 Chicago's base employment was probably more than half the total—that is, more than half the workers were hogbutchers, steelworkers, etc., making the distinctive wares Chicago sold to the world. In Los Angeles today that fraction is probably no more than a quarter.*[95]

Krugman believes that services requiring a high degree of human skill—which are becoming a larger and larger fraction of the nation's economy—will necessarily remain local. "And that's why most people in Los Angeles produce services for local consumption, and therefore do pretty much the same things as most people in metropolitan New York—or for that matter in London, Paris and modern Chicago."[96]

If services, knowledge, and technology are substituting for materials, it follows that the most competitive communities will be those that are smartest, not largest. A small community is not limited by its size in the skill it can develop, knowledge it can retain, or technology it can acquire. Nor, as many small college towns demonstrate, does size determine the quality of local research or public education.

Even for industries whose economy of scale is large, regional alliances of community corporations might be able to compete effectively with today's privately owned globetrotters. In northern Italy small, locally owned firms involved in flexible manufacturing networks have been exporters of high-tech products like robotic arms. Of the 90,000 manufacturing companies in the Emilia–Romagna region, 97 percent employ fewer than 50 employees.[97] A network typically forms temporarily to create a specific product for a well-defined "niche" market. Participating firms pool their resources and share the risk. Once the project is complete, the network disbands. Following successful models in Europe, more than 50 flexible manufacturing networks have been set up in the United States.[98]

Political economist Bennett Harrison argues that the era of the "large, vertically integrated, multidivisional, often multinational corporation" is now giving way to "lean and mean core firms, connected by contract and by handshake to networks of other large and small organizations, including firms, governments, and communities."[99] The Fortune 500 may continue to dominate some segments of the economy like oil, autos, and cigarettes, but there are many new opportunities for decentralized production:

[T]he increasing capability to span boundaries and borders that networking affords to business would seem to have tilted the playing field decisively against locally elected and appointed economic development planners, vis-à-vis the plant location managers of the multilocational companies at the hubs or apexes of the network. Yet at the same time, precisely because the networking principle allows concentrated business organizations to coordinate operations across an ever more dispersed field of play, more decentralized production becomes increasingly feasible.[100]

Harrison does not suggest that location is irrelevant. He, along with many economists and urban planners, makes much of the concept of "clustering." The proximate siting of related and interrelating firms is believed to create certain economies of scale. The clustering of computer software and hardware manufacturers in Silicon Valley, for example, creates a pool of skilled individuals who share their knowledge with one another and carry that knowledge when they move between firms; intense competition among firms like Apple and Intel spurs innovation; linkages with world-class universities like Stanford and U.C. Berkeley turn out Ph.D.'s hired by these firms and integrate their discoveries quickly into new products; connections with support services like computer-part suppliers and patent attorneys motivate them to develop specialized expertise of optimal use to these firms; and personal relationships among all these players at the local bars and health clubs simplify every business transaction. This explains why Harvard business professor Rosabeth Moss Kanter urges communities to decide whether they are Thinkers, Makers, or Traders, and to develop clusters of business accordingly.

Michael Porter, a colleague of Kanter's at the Harvard Business School, argues that the proximity inherent in clusters helps make possible the achievement of a global competitive advantage.[101] Local government can help create the necessary "factor conditions," such as specialized education for employees within a cluster or specialized infrastructure. Local markets can ensure closer communication between producers and customers that improve the quality of the product. Local suppliers of inputs to production have a closer relationship with the producers which ensures that the engineering is exactly to specification. And together these factors can generate the local rivalry and competition needed to improve product quality.

A community should understand the clusters which already exist within its boundaries, or could exist, and then seed corporations that strengthen them. There are more than 500 examples of U.S. communities which have set up low-cost space and services intended to incubate small businesses.[102] These incubators, along with Kanter's and Porter's recommendations, would be stronger if they specified that the beneficiary corporations should be locally owned. Anchoring a cluster with one or more privately owned corporations can be dangerous, because if the private owners skip town, the community corporations that depend on the cluster could go under. A better approach might be for an alliance of community entrepreneurs, bankers, and officials to create a new cluster from scratch.

Harrison fears that even strong industrial clusters, once integrated into global commercial networks, may be vulnerable to "large organizations possessing concentrated economic, financial, and political power."[103] He warns that "with each passing year, even home-grown companies nurtured by local development agencies will face the growing likelihood of being drawn into the orbits of distant corporations whose managers have the power to decide the long-term fortunes of the no longer quite so 'local' firm."[104] Perhaps. But Harrison also assumes that ownership of these firms is unconnected to the community. And one of the virtues of local ownership is that it helps inoculate a firm from being bought out, merged, or manipulated.

Therefore, a critical feature of a needs-driven economy is local ownership. The relatively small size of CSAs, ESCOs, WASCOs, and recycling makes local ownership not only possible but probable. And for complex goods and services that can be produced only on a larger economy of scale, networks of locally owned businesses—whether clustered in one community or spread out globally—can do the job. The next question is: Exactly which model of local ownership is most likely to serve *all* the interests of a community economy?

Community Corporations 3

American activists tend to see business as the enemy. Richard Grossman and Frank T. Adams, long-time organizers, begin a thoughtful essay on corporations with the following observation: "Corporations cause harm every day. Why do their harms go unchecked? How can they dictate what we produce, how we work, what we eat, drink and breathe? How did a self-governing people come to let this pass?"[1] David Korten, one of the most articulate advocates of "people-centered development," entitled his most recent book *When Corporations Rule the World*.[2] And Jerry Mander, acting director of the International Forum on Globalization, writes:

> *Corporations are inherently bold, aggressive, and competitive. Though they exist in a society that claims to operate by moral principles, they are structurally amoral. It is inevitable that they will dehumanize the larger society as well. They are disloyal to workers, including their own managers. . . . They must attempt to dominate alternative cultures. . . . They are intrinsically committed to destroying nature. And they have an inexorable, unabatable, voracious need to grow and expand.*[3]

It's fair to add that these writers have quite practical ideas about how corporations ought to be restructured. Unfortunately, their activist audiences tend to pay less attention to the constructive alternatives than to the anticorporate rhetoric. Most of the left in America scoffs at the potential of business as an ally of social change.

Elsewhere in the world, advocates of social change have developed a far more nuanced relationship with business. For more than a generation the Democratic Party of the Left (formerly the Communist Party) has governed the city of Bologna in Italy. Party leaders unambiguously rejected state socialism of the Soviet and Chinese varieties, and instead pursued a decentralized vision of development rooted in worker-owned cooperatives. The key to transforming the local economy, they felt, was not to combat business but to remake it. Today, more than 1,800 cooperatives in the Emilia–Romagna region, where Bologna is located, employ 60,000 workers.[4] Many of these small businesses export high-tech products that compete internationally. The Left's probusiness strategy, creatively blending public–private partnerships with worker ownership, transformed a once impoverished agricultural area into the fastest-growing part of Italy, with the tenth highest per capita income among the 122 official regions in the European Community.

In the 1950s in Mondragon, Spain, a one-eyed priest named Don José Mariá Armendiarrieta organized local steelworkers to form a technical school. Armendiarrieta and five of his top students decided to open their own factory to manufacture paraffin stoves. With $362,000 raised from 100 friends, they bought used equipment from a bankrupt company and overhauled it. They opened a bank to manage fellow workers' savings and pension funds, and then reinvested them into new business ventures owned by the workforce. Today, Mondragon is the home of a network of 160 affiliated cooperatives, 90 of which are industrial producers. Among these businesses are Spain's biggest refrigerator and machine-tool manufacturers, and its only producer of computer chips.[5] The profitability of each cooperative is twice the average of that of a typical Spanish corporation.[6] The Mondragon cooperatives created 800 new jobs a year between 1960 and 1976, and continued to grow through the late 1970s and early 1980s, a period when most of Europe had fallen into a deep recession.[7]

Bologna, Mondragon, and hundreds of other such "experiments" around the world demonstrate that an enterprise started, owned, and run by members of a community can be a stunning success. And none of this would have come about if business had been seen as the enemy of social progress. Being either for or against business is antithetical to creating self-reliant communities. It's better to sort out which kinds of businesses are the best partners for community self-reliance, and which kinds are the worst. For environmentalists, labor organizers, and other progressive activists in the United States, this means moving beyond crude tirades against corporations. For those Americans who are uncritically probusiness, this means carefully asking which kinds of businesses can best serve the interests of their community.

A TAXONOMY OF AMERICAN BUSINESS

If you wanted to set up a business that would strengthen your community, what kind of corporate structure would you choose? To answer this question, you would first need to understand your basic options.

One possibility is to create a firm with stock owners, which can be either privately or publicly held. A small number of individuals, perhaps members of the same family, typically set up what's called a *privately held* firm. They personally have shares of stock, but these are not traded on public stock exchanges, as are shares of publicly held corporations. Under the 1934 Securities Act, the U.S. Securities and Exchange Commission (SEC) oversees all businesses with shares traded on a national securities exchange, as well as those with 500 or more shareholders and at least $5 million in assets. A publicly held firm issues shares of stock at a "par" value which anyone can buy or sell. The market value of each share is then determined by the perceived value of the company, divided by the number of shares issued. If the stock market is *bullish* about a company's future, more people buy the stock and the price rises; a *bearish* market depresses the price.

A publicly held corporation is arguably more responsive to the common good than a privately held one. SEC regulations mandate that publicly held corporations regularly disclose certain pieces of financial information and hold an annual meeting at which shareholders elect the board of directors. The practical impact of shareholder participation, however, is limited. Either a small number of investors control a majority of the public shares (in which case oversight resembles that of a privately held corporation), or a large number of individuals own the shares but are unorganized, leaving control in the hands of management. In any event, the managers of modern corporations have become adept at making most decisions autonomously of their boards, thus making board elections rather inconsequential. Other kinds of shareholder votes are usually advisory.

Worker-owned companies are privately or publicly held corporations in which employees own a majority of the shares. Some corporations, like Home Depot and Microsoft, supplement employee salaries with stock bonuses, though a small number of investors still are the principal owners (three of the top 10 billionaires in the United States effectively control Microsoft). In 1993, the National Center for Employee Ownership estimated that nearly 11 million workers in the United States were participating in from 9,000 to 10,000 Employee Stock Ownership Plans (ESOPs), and holding $60 billion in corporate assets.[8] Firms in which employees are majority shareholders include Publix Supermarkets, EPIC Healthcare, Avis, Weirton Steel Company, Morgan Stanley, Graybar Electric, Arthur D. Little, American Cast Iron Pipe, North American Rayon, and Spartan Printing.[9] In 1994, the employees of United Airlines (except the flight attendants) agreed to take 55 percent of the company's stock in exchange for $5 billion worth of pay and benefit cuts.

One type of for-profit that deserves special mention is the cooperative. Following the Rochdale principles developed in England in the mid-nineteenth century, cooperatives give every member one vote in the governance structure—regardless of the number of shares held. Consumer co-ops, like Recreational Equipment Inc. (REI) based in Seattle, encourage regular customers to become voting members. Worker co-ops, such as Cooperative Home Care Associates of the Bronx, are owned by their employees. Various producers also can join forces through a cooperative structure. A good example is Mondragon, which has a central community congress of representatives from constituent cooperatives that elects and oversees a governing board. The National Center for Economic and Security Alternatives estimates that there are more than 47,000 cooperatives in the United States, including 4,000 consumer co-ops, 6,500 housing co-ops, 12,600 credit unions, 1,200 rural cooperative utilities, 115 telecommunications and cable co-ops, and more than 100 cooperative insurance companies.[10]

Another type of corporation, the nonprofit, accounts for nearly 5 percent of the U.S. economy.[11] One out of three nonprofits is a tax-exempt foundation or charity that falls under Section 501(c)(3) of the Internal Revenue Code. The rest are primarily made up of universities, hospitals, fraternal organizations, and day-care centers. Nonprofits have no shareholders and are not owned by anyone except, in some abstract sense, the board and the public. The board has control over expenditure of revenues to further its public purpose. But, upon dissolution, a nonprofit cannot distribute its assets to any individuals; instead, the proceeds must go to other nonprofits. A few states allow some nonprofits to issue stock, which means that shareholders hold some equity but receive neither dividends nor capital gains upon sale (which explains the peculiar corporate structure of the Green Bay Packers).

No profit does not mean no surplus. In recent years, nonprofits have supplemented charitable gifts from individuals and grants from foundations and government agencies with earnings from the sales of everything from Girl Scout cookies to pharmaceutical patents, fuzzing the traditional dividing line between nonprofits and for-profits. Community-development corporations (CDCs), for example, were set up by the federal Office of Economic Opportunity and the Ford Foundation in the late 1960s to spearhead President Lyndon Johnson's "War Against Poverty." The National Congress for Community Economic Development estimates that by 1988, between 1,500 and 2,000 CDCs had built almost 125,000 low- or moderate-income housing units, developed over 16 million square feet of commercial or industrial space, made loans to or investments in 2,200 community businesses, launched and owned another 427 businesses, and, over the most recent five-year period, created or retained 90,000 jobs.[12]

A final type of corporate structure available to a community is public ownership. U.S. state and local governments have established more than 6,300 public authorities to build highways and bridges, run electric and water utilities, dispose of hazardous wastes, operate ports, and perform public services.[13] A few public enterprises have moved into other areas of activities. For example, the state of North Dakota runs its own bank and features both checking and savings accounts. David Osborne and Ted Gaebler, in their book *Reinventing Government,* show how local governments are making money by turning sludge into fertilizer (Milwaukee), extracting and selling methane gas from a wastewater treatment plant (Mesa, Arizona), licensing software developed by the police department (St. Louis County), and purchasing an amusement park (Santa Clara, California).[14]

An entrepreneur committed to community self-reliance soon discovers that each of these corporate options has notable strengths and weaknesses, and that choosing among them is not easy. Yet some are clearly more community-friendly than others.

ENGINES OF SELF-RELIANCE

How does a corporation's structure help or hurt a community? Some corporate structures, it turns out, are more likely than others to produce goods and services that serve the needs of local residents. Certain structures are more inclined to create good workplaces or to be exemplary environmental citizens. Some types of corporations have strong incentives to operate efficiently, while others don't. And only a small number are likely to have a reliable, long-term commitment to stay in the community. The following overview suggests that certain specific nonprofits, cooperatives, and public enterprises usually perform reasonably well, but the most promising model may well be a for-profit with a residential restriction on stock ownership.

COMMUNITY USEFULNESS

No corporation should be considered community-friendly unless it provides something useful for the people living within its boundaries—that is, more than just decent jobs. Is the business selling grains and vegetables to put on residents' tables, or tobacco leaves that will addict and slowly poison smokers? Is it generating electricity needed to run local industry, or churning out machine guns, sold to repressive governments abroad, that wind up in the hands of gangs back home? Is it providing medical services to improve the health of community members, or manufacturing dangerous dune buggies for export?

Most businesspeople don't really care about these questions (or their answers). They're interested in any market in which they can sell products, not just in the community market; and they're eager to produce any good or service that a group of customers will buy, not necessarily those basic to people's lives. Even firms claiming to be "socially responsible" often target national or international markets with products that are anything but essential. Visit any major city in America or Europe these days and you'll find a Body Shop, Gap, and United Colors of Benetton—each of which claims to be doing lots of social good, yet has no linkage to a particular place, and produces vanity and fashion items well beyond the budget of the vast majority of the world's people.

Worker ownership does surprisingly little to change the basic corporate imperative to maximize profits without reference to what's being produced. The worker-run Mondragon cooperatives in Spain rooted their businesses in manufacturing products for export, not in meeting basic local needs. Among the first products they produced were butane cookers, lawnmower parts, and food-handling equipment.[15] By 1990, Mondragon cooperatives shipped 40 percent of these capital goods outside Spain.[16] The cooperatives in Bologna also saw themselves as producing machine tools, pasta- and espresso-makers, and trendy clothing for export. When the workforce of United Airlines became the owners, the company certainly did not suddenly refocus transportation services on a few key communities.

The only two corporate structures that are naturally linked with community needs are nonprofits and publicly owned corporations. CDCs, for example, are formed to tackle specific local problems, such as housing rehabilitation and credit shortages. Publicly owned corporations primarily serve local infrastructure needs like maintaining roads, repairing bridges, running harbors, purifying drinking water, and distributing electricity. Even these bodies, however, lack the kind of governance that might make them truly responsive to community needs.

Almost every community has experienced pitched battles between neighborhood associations and publicly owned transportation authorities eager to bulldoze hundreds of blocks to make way for a highway or an airport. Public enterprises often wind up being run by political cronies who award contracts to local contractors, who in turn line the pockets of the appointing politicians. The patronage systems of Chicago under Mayor Richard Daley, Sr., the District of Columbia under Mayor Marion Barry, and Louisiana under Governor Huey Long are only the most blatant examples of the vulnerability of public business to corruption.

As Jane Jacobs argues in *Systems of Survival,* the conflation of "guardian" and "commercial" roles creates dangerous conflicts for decisionmakers.[17] A politician whose fortunes depend on how well public enterprises perform will be inclined to use subsidies to cover for embarrassing mismanagement, look the other way if the firm has horrendous labor and environmental practices, and cook the books to bury a problem from public scrutiny. The larger the commercial activity a government undertakes, the more vulnerable its civil servants become to bribes and manipulation.

Politicians who mastered the ideology and slogans of socialism were hardly immune to such favoritism. Indeed, bribery was an essential part of getting anything done in the old Soviet Union. In Italy today, more than 3,000 leading corporate heads and politicians—among them, the former Socialist Prime Minister, Bettino Craxi—have been indicted on numerous charges of corruption, including routinely accepting kickbacks for public-works contracts. (The Italian communists, by contrast, who favored privately owned cooperatives like those in Bologna, emerged from these scandals relatively unscathed.) In countries as diverse as Brazil and South Africa, the managers of the "parastatal" corporations have regularly been implicated in scandals of kickbacks and embezzlement.[18]

Nonprofits also are capable of shockingly self-serving behavior. A nonprofit's vision of the public interest, after all, is defined by its own leaders and board members, not by members of the community. For years, the National Rifle Association had its national headquarters in Washington, D.C., and fought gun control across the country with remarkable success, utterly indifferent to the devastating effects its "public-interest work" was having in its violence-ridden home town. (The NRA has since moved to the cushy and relatively disarmed suburbs of northern Virginia.)

Many CDCs stray from developing poor neighborhoods to ensure a steady stream of contracts for well-heeled developers who are predominantly black or Latino.[19] As Christopher and Hazel Gunn conclude after reviewing the performance of several prominent CDCs, "Yes, CDCs provide development potential, but it is safely mainstream. CDCs may end up providing apprenticeships for members of chambers of commerce."[20] Nonprofits are not inherently representative of community interests for one simple reason: They are run by board members who reelect themselves, their buddies, and their contributors. If broad community participation occurs, it's by chance—not by design.

RESPONSIBLE PRODUCTION METHODS

A community-friendly corporation is one that treats its work force and local ecosystems well. By this criterion, the production methods chosen by conventional corporations, whether privately or publicly held by shareholders, are unimpressive. In the absence of legally enforceable minimum standards, profit-driven firms are motivated to keep wages low and to minimize investments in environmental protection. Every wage hike, every worker benefit, every new smokestack scrubber threatens to weaken profitability.

The exceptions only prove the rule. Aaron Feuerstein, owner of a textile mill in Lawrence, Massachusetts, made headlines in late 1995 when, after a fire destroyed the plant, he decided to rebuild the factory and rehire the workforce.[21] Television and radio reporters made much of his compassion to his employees, and especially his gesture to pay their wages during the Christmas season. Peter Jennings knighted him "Person of the Week." President Bill Clinton strategically sat him next to Hillary during his State of the Union Address. What made this story newsworthy was its departure from the cruel logic of the bottom line. Every day, managers in similar predicaments collect the insurance, fire the employees, and carefully evaluate where a new factory with cheaper workers might be more profitable.

Businesses that call themselves socially responsible try to attract politically correct consumers by advertising their investments either in the workforce or in environmental protection. That a company like Dow Chemical, infamous for disastrous products ranging from Agent Orange to breast implants, can advertise itself as "socially responsible" suggests how vapid the term has become. (Hannah Arendt might have called this kind of deceit "the evil of banality.") But even firms with more-sincere intentions wind up capitulating to the almighty bottom line.

Consider the following examples. For years, Ben & Jerry's made much of its decision to keep the spread between the highest- and lowest-paid employees in the corporation to 7 to 1. As the firm grew, and tried to hire more-experienced managers, however, business reality forced it to abandon the cap on high salaries. IBM tried to live up to its image of being one of the best places to work in America by providing employees with generous salaries, benefits, stock options, country club memberships, and travel discounts. As profits began to melt in the mid-1980s, the benefits were peeled back, and more than half of the company's workforce—an estimated 200,000 employees—were laid off.[22] A professor and a graduate student at Carnegie Mellon recently surveyed 54 large U.S. corporations claiming great commitment to environmental protection.[23] Only one-third were willing to substitute more environmentally safe inputs for production when they raised costs by a measly 1 percent. With a 5 percent price hike, the number of companies willing to make the switch dropped to two.

Socially responsible companies invite public inspection, but all too often when it comes, stunning hypocrisies are uncovered. Ben & Jerry's promised its sweet-toothed customers that money from sales of Rainforest

Crunch ice cream would be used to "help Brazilian forest peoples start a nut-shelling cooperative that they'll own and operate."[24] The campaign was so successful that the cooperative couldn't keep up with the demand, and 95 percent of the nut purchases ultimately had to be made from the very agribusiness concerns that were systematically destroying the supposed beneficiaries. Moreover (as Hanna Rosin pointed out in *The New Republic*), calling the Xapuri, descendants of Portuguese rubber tappers who ran the cooperative, "forest peoples" was "a stretch" which infuriated the indigenous peoples living there.[25]

The Body Shop also has come under sharp attack for misrepresenting its do-good behavior. Consumer writer Debra Dad-Redalia has pointed out that a hair gel claiming to be based on a natural Ethiopian recipe using ochre, butter, and acacia in fact contains *none* of these ingredients.[26] A German environmental group testing a number of skin creams flunked the Body Shop's Carrot Moisture Cream because it contained formaldehyde.[27] The firm's public position against animal testing of cosmetics turns out to be a legalistic commitment to eschew ingredients tested on animals within the past five years. A New Jersey sewage authority fined one of the Body Shop's factories three times for illegal dumping.[28]

Of course, those looking for dirt on socially responsible businesses have their own axes to grind. Hanna Rosin's brief against Ben & Jerry's turns out to be a conservative plug for multinational corporations: "Caring capitalism is perhaps best left to larger enterprises."[29] True, big oil and chemical companies have the research and development budgets to make products more ecologically friendly, to redesign factories top to bottom, and to clean up past messes. "In fact," writes Rosin, "some of the most innovative environmental solutions have come from the worst polluters, responding purely to fear of punishment. . . ."[30] But larger enterprises also have more lawyers on retainer who would rather fight than switch, plus global linkages that make relocating to pollution-friendly countries the preferred alternative.

The obvious point is that the behavior of *any* corporation must be judged by what it does, not what it says. As David Moberg, a writer in the progressive newsweekly *In These Times,* argues: "[I]t still takes the pressures of vigorous, independent forces—unions, consumer groups, government, the press—to watch and challenge any business, even one that parades as a paragon of leftist virtue. . . ."[31] And the structure of conventional stock-held corporations dictates that even enlightened managers will be held accountable to shareholders who prefer to maximize profit rather than to serve a community.

Does worker ownership change a business's production methods? Certainly, where the workers actually control the enterprise (and are not just passive owners of stock), treatment of the workforce improves. Even if wages and benefits aren't higher, the shared sense that business decisions will help or hurt all employee-owners, that "We're all in this together," boosts morale. Still, not all workers have equal say in management, and conflicts can erupt. Shortly after becoming owners of United, for example, one group of its workers legally challenged the new management's decision to plow recent profits back into the company rather than to distribute them to the employees.

Whether worker ownership promotes environmental protection is unclear. The Vermont Asbestos Group made a major investment in pollution-control equipment after it was bought by its employees.[32] But workers and management also can unite around sharing the spoils from a good bottom line, and too often environmental protection is perceived to reduce both investor and employee profit shares. This explains why relations between labor and environmental groups remain uneasy (though they're improving). Unemployed loggers in the Northwest have practically declared war on forest preservationists who threaten their jobs. Friends of the United Auto Workers, like Democratic Congressman John Dingell of Michigan, have served as reliable henchmen of the auto industry to kill legislation to clean up auto emissions and to improve fleet gas-efficiency requirements. (The UAW, to its credit, has remained officially neutral in these fights.)

Publicly owned enterprises may treat their workforces well, but have an unremarkable environmental record. The American Federation of State, County, and Municipal Employees, an exceptionally powerful union, has pushed for strong laws protecting civil-service employees and ensured relatively high wages and job security for public employees. But environmental regulation of public utilities or port authorities creates the difficult dilemma for politicians which was noted earlier, between protecting the public and keeping the enterprises profitable. (When private corporations grease the palms of politicians with campaign contributions, of course, similar moral hazards occur.)

Some of the least environmentally sensitive utilities that plunged ahead with ambitious plans to build nuclear power plants in the 1970s were publicly owned. The Washington Public Power Supply System (WPPSS) earned the nickname "whoops" for leading the region to embark upon an environmentally and economically crazy scheme to build five gigantic nuclear power plants. Projected originally at a few billion dollars, the price tag ultimately escalated to over $12 billion, triggering a major default on bonds and a spate of expensive lawsuits. In the end, four out of five WPPSS reactors never produced a single kilowatt–hour of electricity.

Most nonprofits are service providers, and therefore place few burdens on the environment. Those that do have environmental impacts—such as agencies like CARE that work abroad to assist refugees—have developed guidelines to ensure a high level of ecological sensitivity. Nonprofits are, however, notoriously unpleasant places to work. Few are unionized, and most pay low wages with limited health-care, retirement, and leave benefits. Each year's budget depends on very unpredictable flows of membership donations and foundation grants, and job security is practically nil.

EFFICIENCY

A community inevitably depends on the economic performance of its businesses. When a corporation suddenly skips town, the high public costs discussed in the Introduction suggest that what's efficient for the community may differ from what's efficient for the firm. A business with a 3 percent rate of return that stays is more valuable to a community than a business with a 30 percent rate of return that leaves. But even from a community perspective, the minimum expectation of business should be that it have a positive rate of return. No uncompetitive industry can last indefinitely. The costs to the public of propping up even one major money-losing venture, as the Pacific Northwest discovered with the WPPSS debacle, can be enormous. There is no escape from basic principles of good management. Efficiency is an important goal for community economics—not the only goal, but a necessary one. Once a business is serving local needs and using responsible production methods, it should take advantage of any opportunities to do more at a lower cost.

Efficiency is the singular strength of shareholder-owned corporations. For-profit corporations are structured to induce their managers to strive for the highest rate of return and to be attentive to every cost. The managers of for-profits are driven by both punishments and rewards. If they fail to achieve a decent profit, they are sacked by the board of directors. If a corporation's budget bleeds red ink, and the board and shareholders fail to act, then sooner or later bankruptcy court and the creditors will step in and do the job. To the successful manager, of course, comes raises, bonuses, good press, and bargaining power for the next job. Whether a for-profit firm is worker-owned or socially responsible, efficiency is the overriding goal.

Nonprofits must operate with a positive cash flow, but any rate of return above zero will do. For-profits have increasingly complained that permitting nonprofits to deliver the same goods and services that for-profits produce puts them at a competitive disadvantage, since nonprofits have unique access to "soft money," tax-deductible contributions from individuals or foundations. The office of the Small Business Administration issued a report in 1984 entitled *Unfair Competition by Non-Profit Organizations with Small Business: An Issue for the 1980s,* which sent tremors through the nonprofit community.

A recent study by the Roberts Foundation, however, suggests that nonprofits actually have a competitive *dis*advantage:[33] "In many cases, the nonprofit business manager is under pressure as a result of his social mission to offer wages substantially above the market rate, something a for-profit would only do to secure an exceptionally productive employee."[34] The best performers in nonprofits often move into the private sector, which means that turnover in nonprofits tends to be higher, as are the resulting costs of training, transition, and severance.

The prerogatives of business may be at odds with the mission of a nonprofit. Many nonprofits view as suspect the bonuses, major salary hikes, and other perquisites that the private sector uses to induce and reward exceptional performance. The boards of nonprofits are often more hands-on than those of for-profits, which forces nonprofit managers to spend more time preparing reports, answering questions, and involving their trustees—and less time running the business. Meanwhile, the Internal Revenue Service and myriad state and local agencies impose all kinds of special reporting requirements.

Another problem facing nonprofit businesses is finance. While a for-profit can navigate cash-flow difficulties through debt or equity, a nonprofit *must* turn to debt. Without much in the way of assets to serve as collateral, a nonprofit cannot easily qualify for a loan. These factors mean that even well-run nonprofits tend to grow very slowly, if at all. With a social mandate to spend accumulated earnings, most perpetually operate on the brink of bankruptcy.

The Roberts Foundation concludes that "were there a significant competitive advantage to being a nonprofit engaged in revenue-generating activities, we would have witnessed a marked increase in the number of businesses seeking strictly to take advantage of the added financial benefits of nonprofit status in the marketplace. In fact, we see just the opposite."[35] Recently, for example, for-profits have been gobbling up nonprofit hospitals and health maintenance organizations. Nonprofits have many valuable attributes serving the public welfare, but economic efficiency is not one of them.

The efficiency of public enterprises is more complicated. The prevailing wisdom today is that the private sector operates more economically than the public sector, except in special circumstances. Laissez-faire economists begrudgingly admit that the state has a role to play in overseeing natural monopolies and public goods.

The delivery of electricity, natural gas, water, and telephone services is a good example of the former. But, as we saw in the previous chapter, technology is eliminating the natural monopoly once held by electrical utilities. Americans also are choosing among competing phone services. A century from now most energy may come from rooftop solar cells, and most communication via microwaves. Moreover, even where a natural monopoly exists, a smart local government will open up the business to competitive bids every few years.

Since they include products and services that benefit the community as a whole, public goods are best delivered by public agencies. The classic example is policing. Everyone in a community knows police are needed, and that if individuals each had to buy security, armed bands would roam the countryside (as in the film *Mad Max*) and anarchy would reign supreme. How broadly a community defines public goods varies enormously. Most U.S. communities believe that every child is entitled to a decent education, and every citizen should be able to enjoy public parks. Local governments in Western Europe fairly pump money into not just political participation, but also nonprofit activities.

A lively debate has ensued in recent years over whether private firms working under government control can deliver public goods more efficiently than public agencies.[36] The jury is still out. Certainly there are government functions that cannot be measured strictly by private-market efficiency considerations. Efficient health care may mean skimpier services for those who cannot afford to pay for fuller ones. Efficient schooling may produce students who perform well on standardized tests but poorly as community-minded citizens. Efficient policing may result in the triaging of certain neighborhoods with a high density of crack houses and gangs. Yet, even in these cases, one can imagine instances in which a local government is bad enough, and the private contractors good enough, to support privatization.

One strong argument in favor of minimizing government involvement in commercial activities, and of privatizing government services, is the moral hazard (discussed earlier) of mixing the functions of commercial regulation and commercial promotion. Once again, the history of nuclear power illustrates the dangers. *No* U.S. utility has ordered a new commercial reactor since the late 1970s. Nuclear-power expansion continues primarily in countries where public ownership of utilities has enabled state accountants to "excuse" gigantic debts. French politicians, for example, kept up appearances of a healthy reactor program by forgiving a debt of 5 billion francs in 1980.[37] Whenever politics can trump markets, business managers will be tempted to stroke the "good ole boy network" rather than run an enterprise efficiently—to the public's detriment.

COMMUNITY LOYALTY

The last criterion of a community-friendly corporation is that it have strong ties to its base. Most publicly and privately held corporations, as we've seen, have no such loyalty. Focused on the bottom line, the managers of these firms have few reservations about moving an operation elsewhere to increase labor productivity.

To be sure, certain kinds of privately owned firms may be *relatively* loyal to a community. A small, family-owned business is unlikely to pick up and move its operations to Singapore. Businesses that specialize in delivering local goods and services, such as a tractor repair shop in rural Kansas or a small law firm with a local clientele in San Diego, probably harbor few global ambitions. Worker ownership of for-profits, cooperatives, or nonprofits also can inhibit mobility if the workforce is small and lives nearby. When the workforce is large and dispersed, however, as is true for United Airlines, worker ownership has no real advantage for a community.

The conventional wisdom is that mobility is a bigger temptation for manufacturers and banks than for service providers. This distinction, however, is rapidly disappearing. Service industries like insurance and accounting now have data entered halfway around the world. As more of the trillion-dollar-per-year health-care industry in the United States involves claims processing (something like one dollar in four now goes to administration), sizable chunks of America's largest service industry can be farmed out overseas.[38] The infiltration of low-price chain stores in almost every product line—including clothing (K-Mart), groceries (Safeway), stationery (Office Depot), coffee (Starbucks), books (Borders), music recordings (Tower), and banking (First Interstate)—means that less and less economic control resides on Main Street.

A few socially responsible firms deviate from this logic. The South Shore Bank, which is a publicly held corporation, targets loans to poor and middle-class neighborhoods in Chicago. Ben & Jerry's restricted its first stock issue to residents of Vermont, and continues to prioritize the use of local ingredients like milk in its ice cream. But most firms claiming to be socially minded have no real home base. Indeed, for companies like the Body Shop and United Colors of Benetton, which market themselves as responsible *global* citizens, it's hard to know where their home is.

The only firms that almost never skip town are cooperatives, nonprofits, and publicly owned enterprises—since they are set up to serve specific community needs and governed by people connected with the community. But, as we've seen, even these models can go off track. The cooperatives in Mondragon and Bologna recently entered joint ventures with multinational corporations that effectively dilute community control. And the National Rifle Association's departure to Virginia underscores how a larger nonprofit can move to an adjacent community, just like their for-profit brethren, to find cheaper land, rent, or labor.

NEW MODELS

What kind of corporation, then, should communities seeking self-reliance turn to? If publicly and privately held corporations care little about producing for community needs or show little loyalty to the community, if cooperatives and worker-owned enterprises are still prone to environmental neglect, if nonprofits have serious impediments to being competitive, and if public ownership carries inefficiencies and moral hazards, which forms of business are in fact community-friendly?

One approach, of course, is to enact laws at the local level that mandate strong performance for all types of corporations in each area. If a for-profit firm is *required,* for example, to produce only certain kinds of needed goods, to pay high wages, to meet stringent environmental standards, and to give at least a year or two of notice before moving, then it will become community friendly—by law. But as long as companies are capable of moving, high standards only provide an incentive for existing businesses to move and for potential businesses to stay away. This underscores why community loyalty is so critical. Without anchoring firms to place, all other efforts to improve community friendliness wind up being irrelevant.

Since the only companies linked strongly to place are cooperatives, nonprofits, and public enterprises, it's worth asking whether the other problems associated with each can be overcome. The answer, generally speaking, is "Perhaps." Nonprofits with imaginative leadership, as many universities and hospitals demonstrate, can become quite successful in the marketplace. And public enterprises can be structured in ways that minimize their inherent defects. Empowering residents to elect boards directly, rather than leaving appointments to local politicians, can insulate them from politicking and corruption, especially if tough campaign-finance and lobbying laws are in place. Consumer groups, such as Ralph Nader's Public Citizen, are pushing public utilities to allocate a small percentage of every electricity bill to fund a special consumer advocate's office within the enterprise that could serve as a watchdog of corporate behavior. These intriguing ideas deserve to be tested and refined. Let a thousand experiments unfold.

But two final concerns raise doubts about how big a role nonprofits, cooperatives, and public enterprises can play. First, Americans are unlikely to hitch their future to these unconventional corporate forms. The nation's ideological commitment to private property and the profit motive, reinforced by the mythology of the rugged individual, are too deeply etched into our collective psyche. Even if the political pendulum swings back in favor of government initiative, municipalities are unlikely to do much more than modestly "reinvent government."

Second, there is a fundamental problem with public enterprises that *cannot* be overcome: A healthy democracy will experience wide ideological swings over time, and even the most progressive electorate will occasionally swing conservative. The swiftness and ease with which neoliberal governments in Russia and Mexico are selling off at bargain prices assets built up over generations should give pause to even the most committed advocate of public ownership. These patterns of privatization are now being replicated in communities throughout the United States, as local governments ponder selling off schools, parks, community centers, ports, and other enterprises to the highest bidders. This is hardly an accident. Politicians looking no further than the next election have a natural incentive to auction community assets. Just as President Reagan saw the virtues of pumping up the U.S. economy by amassing a huge deficit, so do local politicians see the virtues of cashing in on public assets to make their budgets look artificially healthy. It's usually years before the public fully understands the costs, and by then the politicians have happily retired.

Is there a type of business that is community-friendly, profit-oriented, and resistant to government sellouts? One interesting option might be to create for-profit enterprises that are not owned by a local government (or an adjunct agency), but by the citizens in the area. As with other for-profit enterprises, the shareholders would elect a board of directors to oversee management. *The key distinction from conventional corporations is that only members of a community would be allowed to own voting shares of stock.* Shareholders could exchange or sell the stock freely, but only with other community members. Whenever a shareholder decided to move out of the community, he or she would be obligated to sell off the shares, either to other community members or back to the company.

This kind of community corporation could create, if it wanted, two classes of shareholders: residential shareholders with voting rights, and nonresidential shareholders without them. Conventional corporations often issue different classes of stock, each with a unique set of rights. "Common" stock usually carries the right to vote, whereas "preferred" stock doesn't. The classes also may have different rights to dividends or liquidation proceeds, and to different redemption privileges.

This structure is only a slight modification of the conventional privately held corporation, yet radically improves community friendliness. Shareholders probably would set up such an enterprise to meet a particular community need; if they cared only about the private bottom line, they would set up a conventional corporation. If the corporation veered from its original purpose, other members of the community would be able to buy its stock, take over the firm, and reorient it. The shareholders may or may not be workers, but in either case the two groups, normally separated by hundreds or thousands of miles, would now be neighbors. If the owners of an enterprise live close to the work force, go to the same church, synagogue, or mosque, send their children to the same school, have picnics in the same parks, and drink the same water, they have a greater incentive to make decisions responsive to their neighbors' needs. Because the enterprise is for-profit, there remains a strong incentive for competitive, efficient management. And, with all voting shareholders residing in the community, it's unlikely that the firm would move operations elsewhere (unless relocation were clearly in the interest of the community).

Local ownership of a for-profit does not automatically ensure that the firm's products are in the community's interest or that production methods are responsible. But it enables regulation to proceed without today's fear that the firm automatically will skip town. No longer would higher labor and ecological standards have to mean a less attractive business environment.

Another helpful feature of a locally owned for-profit would be a limitation on the percentage of the company that one citizen in the community can own, effected through either a provision in the bylaws or a local antitrust ordinance. Obviously if one person can own 51 percent of the corporation, then it ceases to have a community character. Even smaller ownership shares that permit two or three people to dominate a board do this. A community might want to limit citizens to owning no more than, say, 1 percent of the corporation, which would mean that at least 51 people would have to achieve some kind of consensus, before the company could depart or dissolve.[39]

While the 50 states each define corporate law in the United States today and thus make generalization difficult, it's fair to say that *some* kind of community corporation could be set up in every state under current law. Normally, a shareholder has the right to sell or transfer his or her shares freely. But a corporation can restrict these rights through its articles of incorporation, bylaws, or an agreement with or between the shareholders. Some states, like Delaware, expressly permit limitations on transfer rights.[40] In other states without such statutes, courts hold as a matter of common law that limits on transfer rights are permissible as long as they are reasonable and lawful.[41]

Fearing concentrations of power, the states passed corporate laws early in their history that actually placed numerous restrictions on stock ownership.[42] William Penn's Free Society of Traders, chartered by the King of England in 1682, limited voting rights to shareholders living in Pennsylvania. Between the Revolution in 1776 and 1801, the U.S. government chartered more than 300 companies, and most of these charters limited voting rights. One common restriction gave a shareholder with many shares proportionally fewer votes per share than a smaller shareholder. A statute in Pennsylvania, in effect between 1849 and 1874, stipulated that "each stockholder shall be entitled to as many votes as he owns shares of stock in said company, but no person shall in any case be entitled to more than one-third of the whole number of votes to which the holders of all the shares would . . . be entitled. . . ."

The cases in which the courts have found residential limitations on ownership unreasonable are rare.[43] As a Wisconsin appellate court said in 1989, "Restrictions on the transfer of corporate stock are very common. . . . One authority estimates that the shares of stock of at least half the corporations in the country are subject to such restrictions."[44] One of the key factors courts review in making these decisions is the interest of the corporation. If a community corporation states at its inception that a transfer restriction is central to achieving its mission, judges will respect the firm's vision.

Today, residential restrictions on shareholders of for-profits are rare. The reason is simple: In closely held companies, the founders usually want to limit share ownership to family members, partners, or friends. The goal is to run the company with only those people you personally know and trust, a universe of people much smaller than a community. In publicly held companies, the goal is to maximize stock value and facilitate the greatest possible demand for shares. A residence requirement necessarily limits demand and dampens stock value. It will probably take some special initiatives by community-minded grassroots groups to seed and expand this kind of corporation.

Henceforth, the term *community corporation* shall refer to for-profits with a residential restriction, as well as to cooperatives, nonprofits, and public enterprises. The promoters of all of these kinds of business are effectively saying: "Yes, we aim to be commercially viable, like conventional for-profits. But we affirm in no uncertain terms that the mission of our corporation is to advance the well-being of our community."

One very successful type of enterprise in which residency restrictions can be found is the consumer credit union (CCU). A CCU is a nonprofit bank owned and run by shareholding members for their own benefit. Some CCUs are established through fraternal organizations or workplaces, but roughly 300 are linked to a well-defined neighborhood or community.[45] The first credit union was organized in the United States in 1909. By 1935, three-quarters of the states passed laws permitting them and more than 3,000 were in operation. Congress passed the Federal Credit Union Act in 1934, allowing CCUs to be chartered and insured by the federal government. Today, the National Federation of Community Development Credit Unions estimates that place-defined CCUs oversee half a billion dollars in deposits.[46]

Another structure suggesting the benefits of community ownership is the land trust, pioneered in the United States by Robert Swann and the Institute for Community Economics. A typical community land trust is owned by a nonprofit entity like a church or a grassroots group. A resident or business that wishes to use part of the trust's land acquires a long-term lease, which it can sell back at any time—but only to the trust. The trust agrees in advance to repurchase at the price paid plus an allotment for inflation. This arrangement ensures that all improvements of the land and increases in property values are shared equally by every member of the trust. It discourages the buying and selling of land for speculation.

The Community Land Trust in Burlington, Vermont, a college town with 39,000 people, has become one of the biggest landlords in the city. Started with a grant of $200,000 from the municipal government, the trust purchases and refurbishes old properties, and then selects low-income tenants based on their long-term commitment to Burlington. It currently has 150 homes with long-term leases and 135 rental units.[47] This land trust has inspired the founding of 25 other land trusts in New England. In all, there are 65 land trusts operating in 20 states.[48]

Community corporations can be viewed as essentially business trusts which, like land trusts, ensure that development proceeds with sensitivity to the needs of the community. Shareholders in community corporations, like land-trust leaseholders, buy stock for long-term investment, not for short-term speculation. The benefits from both are enjoyed by the entire community. And a community corporation, like a land trust, cannot sell, merge, or dissolve the enterprise without democratic approval by its members.

The community-corporation structure can be applied to all the new kinds of business discussed in the previous chapter, including energy- and water-efficiency service companies, urban farms, recyclers, and biorefineries. It represents an exciting hybrid between capitalism and socialism. It fosters competitive enterprises and private ownership without continued irresponsibility toward workers, ecosystems, and communities. It facilitates community decisionmaking without the bureaucracy and corruption of a large public sector. It provides communities with new opportunities for development, and simultaneously breaks down the unnecessary and inhibitive wall between advocates of social change and promoters of business.

EMPOWERMENT THROUGH OWNERSHIP

One early U.S. pioneer who understood the value of community corporations as a tool for social change was Reverend Leon Sullivan. The steps he took to transform his inner-city neighborhood in Philadelphia through business suggest opportunities available for virtually every city, town, and neighborhood in America. Sullivan, who later became well-known for spelling out ethical principles to guide U.S. corporate investment in apartheid South Africa, was angered over the dependency of the local black community:

> Ours was a tissue-paper middle class. Our best jobs were municipal, state, and Federal administrative and supervisory jobs, but there were white bosses for these. We were living on a different kind of plantation, except that we went to our own homes at night. Even the best jobs we had in business were highly terminable, dependent upon the whims and desires of the white management, which often gave us the jobs in order to protect a corporate image. I knew, though, that something could be done about the situation—and something had to be done.[49]

Sullivan decided to transform his parishioners from victims into owners. Starting in 1962, he asked 50 members of his church to contribute $10 a month for 36 months into what was effectively a community corporation. "This amounted to $360, or the price of a good television set."[50] Contributions over the first 16 months went into a charitable trust for scholarships. The remaining contributions were invested into a for-profit corporation, with each participant receiving one voting share of stock. Shares could be sold back to the corporation, but any participant who quit would not be permitted to return.

Demand for membership far exceeded Sullivan's original expectations. The number of shareholders expanded to 600 by 1965, and 3,000 by 1968. Zion Investment Associates, as the for-profit was called, built the first black-owned apartment building in an all-white neighborhood; a shopping center called Progress Plaza, with stores run by black entrepreneurs; a black-owned aerospace enterprise; and Progress Garment Manufacturing Enterprises. Profits from these businesses were split three ways, with 40 percent going to the nonprofit, 40 percent to shareholders, and 20 percent to workers. The nonprofit, with supplemental funding from foundations, then set up a technical school to train black entrepreneurs and managers.

Today, a generation later, Zion Investment Associates continues to operate with a somewhat more modest—and conventional—model of business. The number of shareholders has expanded slightly to 4,000, and they still reside primarily (though not exclusively) in Philadelphia. But the only for-profit enterprise that remains is the shopping mall, and its profits are distributed solely to the shareholders. Still, Sullivan's vision, simultaneously probusiness and procommunity, has inspired experiments in other inner-city neighborhoods. And it offers an important lesson to antibusiness community activists throughout the United States: "If others can build a house, we can build one too. If others can build a bridge, we can build one too. If others can build schools, factories, industries and banks, we can build them too. Whatever others can do we can do. Properly motivated, a man can do almost anything.[51]

Financing the Future 4

Being poor doesn't always mean being without resources. Anacostia is one of the poorest neighborhoods in Washington, D.C., yet the total income of all its households is $370 million per year.[1] Most of this money quickly departs in the hands of landlords, business owners, and bankers who live in more upscale parts of town. The thriving stores like Safeway, CVS Drugs, Popeye's, and Amoco all are part of regional or national chains. Some small local shops are doing well (hair salons, liquor stores, and bars seem ubiquitous), but the many boarded-up storefronts on the main thoroughfare stand as if tombstones to past economic development efforts gone bad. When President Bill Clinton spoke to a luncheon of the Rainbow Coalition in 1992, he said, "In the Washington, D.C., area there are 50 major banks, but only two have branches in Anacostia, and neither of them has a lending office."[2] New branches of several regional banks have opened since, but those Anacostians who maintain savings or checking accounts must accept that most of their money is being invested in a swankier part of town, or even hundreds of miles away. The lucky few with pensions place them in the hands of mutual-fund managers who probably haven't even heard of Anacostia. Residents speak longingly and bitterly of money that has come and gone.

To understand the essential problem facing the Anacostia economy, visit a landmark at 2529 Good Hope Road, the likes of which can be found in almost every community in the United States—McDonald's. Fast-food restaurants, to their credit, are among the few chain stores that venture into poor neighborhoods and provide a safe family environment, inexpensive meals, and local jobs. The McDonald's in Anacostia is situated in a commercial oasis of sorts, flanked by Burger King and Kentucky Fried Chicken. But every time the cash register rings in one of these stores, it's a signal that money is about to leave the community. In 1975, the Institute for Local Self-Reliance studied a McDonald's in another Washington neighborhood, Adams–Morgan, and found that of its $750,000 in gross monthly revenues, $500,000 was quickly respent outside the community.[3] Christopher and Hazel Dayton Gunn took another look at McDonald's 15 years later, and concluded that three-quarters of consumers' expenditures are exported.[4]

The principal affliction of poor communities in the United States is not the absence of money, but its systematic exit. Three out of four dollars the federal government spends within Indian reservations leaves within 48 hours.[5] In rural Britain and Ireland, only about one in four dollars deposited in banks gets reinvested locally, and in some areas the ratio is as bad as one in six.[6] The positive side to these dismal statistics is that even poor communities have money sloshing around—lots of it—in the form of checking and savings accounts, pension funds, stocks, bonds, and life insurance. Few individuals have much to their name, but the community as a whole may have discretion over how to invest resources totaling hundreds of millions of dollars. How then can the residents of such communities pool their wealth, and plant it into community corporations that will meet basic needs? And how can citizens recycle local finance, in order to bankroll community self-reliance?

BANKERS VS. COMMUNITIES

Historically, banks have been essential players in community development. When Florence became the first city-state in Renaissance Italy to replace papal power with a rudimentary democracy, the transition was led by the local bankers—the Medicis. Look at the skyline of any major city in America today and you'll see towering glass structures with brightly lit trademarks like Citicorp (New York), First USA (Wilmington), First Interstate (Los Angeles), and Bank of America (San Francisco). Banks are the titans of development, important to everyone in society—especially the poor.

"In modern American society," argue James Head and Kelly Mogle, "access to credit is one of the few routes to economic progress for those who are not born into privilege."[7] Credit is critical for fighting poverty for several reasons. Without a history of borrowing and repayment, a poor person cannot qualify for housing or business loans. A neighborhood made up of renters rather than owners remains transient, and if the renters cannot borrow for repairs and upgrade, the housing stock steadily deteriorates, and the riskiness—and interest rates—of all housing loans in the area increases. As long as business loans are unaffordable or unavailable, residents cannot become entrepreneurs, and remain either low-wage employees or unemployed.

Although poor people need banks, too many banks act as if they don't need poor people. Economist John Caskey studied five cities and found that, in four of them, black neighborhoods were significantly less likely to have a local bank than were nonblack areas.[8] In two of the cities (Atlanta and New York), poor communities generally had less access to a local bank than affluent ones. There's much more than a grain of truth in the saying that the rich get richer while the poor get poorer.

Banks once were the servants of communities, rich *and* poor. The McFadden Act of 1927 gave states the power to regulate banking, largely to encourage local reinvestment and to prevent interstate competition.[9] Julia Ann Parzen and Michael Hall Kieschnick, two of the pioneers in community banking, write: "Twenty years ago, a business lender—typically a commercial bank—raised most of its funds through local deposits and made most of its loans to local borrowers. The money was local, it was loaned locally, and the commercial bank evaluated its loan opportunities relative to other local borrowers."[10] Savings and loans, or *thrifts* as they became called, opened up to help Americans in every community become home owners. Populist farmers set up their own community banks in the late nineteenth century called credit unions, which were owned and operated by their members. In 1929, after the stock market crashed and many private banks collapsed, few credit unions defaulted.[11] Today, some 66 million Americans have deposits in credit unions linked to workplaces, fraternal associations, or communities.[12]

The trend in recent years, however, has been for U.S. households to remove their money from banks. On average, Americans place fewer than one in five dollars of assets in depository institutions.[13] Most of their assets go into pension plans (26%), stocks (20%), bonds and other securities (10%), mutual funds (8%), trusts (4%), or noncorporate business investments (13%). Intense competition from these new financial sectors has pushed traditional banks (with the permission and encouragement of federal and state deregulators) to loosen their ties with communities, consolidate, merge, and set up branches across state boundaries. In 1982, more than 10,000 banks in the United States had less than $50 million in assets; today these smaller banks number fewer than 5,000.[14] Banks with over $1 billion control 75 percent of all banking assets, up from 63 percent in 1982. Free of loyalties to any place, or any place-based economy, the managers of these ever-larger interstate banks seek out profitable loan opportunities wherever they might be found, even if thousands of miles away.

For the modern globally-minded bank, community corporations are hardly ideal borrowers. The kinds of needs-based businesses described in Chapter 2 tend to be small and are looking for start-up loans on the order of thousands of dollars rather than millions. Commercial banks do not regard the high administrative costs associated with processing these loans as worth the interest payments. (Since any loan requires similar paperwork, the bigger the loan, the smaller the administrative cost per dollar lent.) Most community corporations asking for loans also happen to be new businesses. Lacking a track record to prove their creditworthiness and business skill, they will be deemed too risky to merit loans.

Yet the prospects for community corporations' finding credit are not entirely bleak. In 1977, U.S. activists persuaded Congress to pass the Community Reinvestment Act (CRA).[15] The main purpose of the CRA was to outlaw lending discrimination, and particularly the practice, by banks and thrifts, of "redlining" poor neighborhoods as bad credit risks. It also placed obligations on all depository institutions receiving federal insurance to reinvest some of their capital in the community, particularly in low- and moderate-income areas, and to make information about their lending patterns public.[16] Whenever a bank or thrift decides to merge with another or to open or close a branch, it must apply to federal regulators for approval. Public hearings are then held, and residents in the affected community can comment. If the institution is shown not to be meeting its CRA obligations, regulators might decline an application.

The Association of Community Organizations for Reform Now (ACORN) and other grassroots groups have seized upon the CRA to pressure banks to behave more responsibly. Along with presenting challenges before federal regulators, they've mounted full-fledged campaigns against certain banks. The results have been impressive. Fear of losing business opportunities because of a veto by federal regulators, or customers because of adverse publicity and boycotts, has motivated banks to extend $30 billion in new credit to poor communities.[17]

Even $30 billion, however, constitutes less than 1 percent of all the assets of commercial banks. The CRA is hardly a panacea. The criteria for community-friendly performance are loose and enforcement lax. Strong grades can go to a bank that makes loans to local developers for pet projects, like stadiums or conference centers, that contribute little to the well-being of the average resident. Between 1985 and 1988, federal regulators reviewed 26,000 banks and gave fewer than 3 percent of them grades of "less than satisfactory" or below.[18] During the first decade of the CRA's operation, regulators examined 40,000 applications for bank expansion and denied only eight.[19] By 1993, that number rose to only 15, with an additional 60 applications receiving conditional approval.

Some states have tried to enhance these duties on banks by passing their own community-reinvestment acts. New York State permits commercial banks to move into real estate only after they demonstrate diligent community reinvestment.[20] Minnesota's Commerce Commissioner would like to impose CRA standards on insurance companies and other securities firms.[21]

However, even *without* supplementary state laws, community activists might be able to use the CRA to push existing banks into financing community corporations. They might press a targeted bank, for example, to open up a special fund which depositors can elect to use to have their money reinvested exclusively in local business. A consortium of unions in the Netherlands did just this in 1960.[22] Forming a financial institution called ASN, they convinced Postbank (the nation's largest), to set up and administer a special fund run by ASN. ASN members made savings deposits at the Postbank by mail or telephone, and ASN officers based in the Hague then invested the deposited money in low-income housing, education, health care, and environmental protection. Both partners benefited: The Postbank received a small fee from ASN to cover expenses, and ASN circumvented the burden of building an entire banking infrastructure with vaults, tellers, offices, and the like. Because ASN follows national standards for low-risk investments, its depositors enjoy the same level of national insurance as do other Postbank savers. Today, about 135,000 ASN members have nearly $1 billion on deposit, and its officials feel ready to sever the umbilical cord to the Postbank and finally become an independent financial institution.

COMMUNITY-DEVELOPMENT FINANCIAL INSTITUTIONS

Another way to finance community corporations, of course, is to open a new bank with an unequivocal mission to invest locally. An estimated 350 community-development financial institutions (CDFIs) are operating in the United States, and their ranks include commercial banks, thrifts, place-based credit unions, and community-development loan funds. The best-known is the South Shore Bank of Chicago, a commercial bank which since 1983 has profitably provided hundreds of millions of dollars of loans to refurbish low-income housing.[23] The Community Capital Bank in Brooklyn (another commercial bank) specializes in loans for small businesses, nonprofits, and affordable multiunit housing in low- and moderate-income areas of New York City. An example of a community-oriented savings and loan is the labor-owned Union Savings Bank in Albuquerque, New Mexico. Among the credit unions that claim to be CDFIs are the Self-Help Credit Union in Durham, North Carolina, and the Quitman County Federal Credit Union in Marks, Mississippi.

President Bill Clinton was so taken with community banking during the 1992 campaign that he promised to spend a billion dollars to set up 100 banks like South Shore.[24] Once elected, Clinton pushed forward—but mainstream banks conditioned their support on a simultaneous loosening of federal oversight of banks. The final law on CDFIs, passed in 1994, offers limited matching support for both for-profit and nonprofit financial institutions.[25] The billion dollars initially proposed was pared down to $382 million. As one advocate of community lending noted, the bill is "just a beginning when you compare it to the need for affordable credit. It's just a small down payment."[26]

Most antipoverty loans from CDFIs finance housing, automobiles, and college tuition—but not business. However, as these banks standardize finance packages for the poor, they are also learning how to bring down the administrative costs of loans for small commercial borrowers. One approach is close personal contact between bank officers and borrowers before, during, and after the loan. Another is the focusing of loans on a small geographic area. South Shore renovated thousands of apartments near one another with a deliberate strategy to shift public perceptions of a single neighborhood. By making a major commitment to a neighborhood and pumping up local pride, the bank convinced others to invest in the community. Rising expectations can then translate into rising property values.

When it comes to loans for small business, no institution has done more to demonstrate the creditworthiness of the poor than the Grameen Bank in Bangladesh. For more than a decade, Grameen has given "microloans" of roughly $50 to an estimated 2 million poor women, to start their own businesses. Women are the targeted borrowers because they are seen as handling money more responsibly, and spending it more diligently on basic family needs, than men, who more often waste their paychecks on liquor and gambling. Grameen gives a series of loans to five-person collectives that support one another in the design and implementation of business plans. Once one woman in the collective successfully repays the first $50 loan, another loan is issued for the second woman in the collective, and so forth. The Grameen Bank not only provides loans but also trains recipients in the basics of running a business. It has achieved a repayment rate of 97 percent—remarkable even by Western standards.

A few microenterprise funds have opened up in America's inner cities, including one overseen by South Shore, but most do not yet incorporate all the features offered by Grameen. Unlike Grameen, they generally don't focus exclusively on the poor (some recipients are middle-class), target women, organize support groups, or provide much in the way of business training or ongoing technical assistance. Grameen's success also may have limited applicability to the United States. Bangladesh has a huge informal economy which provides special opportunities for single-person enterprises. And the women in Grameen's support groups have known each other all their lives, whereas U.S. lending circles often bring together strangers.

Despite these challenges, however, a few U.S. microenterprise funds have managed to achieve respectable results. The Women's Self-Employment Project (WSEP) in Chicago provides loans to single mothers committed to starting their own businesses and leaving the welfare rolls.[27] Like Grameen, WSEP creates support groups of five women from the same neighborhood who must help one another design and implement business plans. WSEP also gives between six and 10 weeks of business training; participants must pay tuition for more classes if they wish to receive larger loans. Initial loans, each under $1,500, go to two designated members of the group. If timely payments on these are made over the next six weeks, two more loans are made. Full repayment of the principal and of 15 percent interest on each loan is expected within a year.

Since 1986, WSEP has made 575 loans totaling over $1.2 million, and launched enterprises in apparel, arts and crafts, cosmetology, food preparation, and business services.[28] It estimates that it has provided business tools, information, training, and technical assistance to 5,000 women in the Chicago area. Its repayment rate is 93 percent.[29] A study in 1995 found that of 400 businesses started, 85 percent were still operating.[30]

Another example is Working Capital, a nonprofit program based in Cambridge.[31] Since 1991, it has provided more than 1,300 loans worth more than $1 million to 770 small-business owners, mostly women. First-time loan recipients get $500, and once a repayment record is established, new loans are issued in successively larger sizes, up to $5,000. Working Capital obtains financing from regional and local banks, foundations, corporations, and federal agencies. Its repayment rate is 98 percent.

In all, more than a dozen "lending circles" are operating in the United States, in locations as diverse as South Central Los Angeles and the Pine Ridge Indian Reservation in South Dakota. While these funds do not require recipients to structure their firms as community corporations, most microbusinesses are in fact run by one person, one family, or a small partnership that's well rooted in the community. Some community corporations might require more capitalization than microloans provide, but it's easy to see how small loans could capitalize the launching of a neighborhood energy-service company or a community-supported agriculture initiative. Enterprises with growth potential could graduate from microloans to conventional loans and even to stock sales.

One interesting model is suggested by the Triodos Bank in Sussex, England, which stands the typical banking paradigm on its head.[32] Rather than attracting depositors and then finding businesses for loans, Triodos *begins* by assembling interesting community projects. It then asks potential depositors not only to pick projects for their loans, but also to choose an interest rate they would like to be paid—usually between zero and 2.5 percent. The bank adds a 4 percent service charge. Depositors are fully covered by national banking insurance.

The vast majority of U.S. communities that do not have a CDFI should consider setting one up. Probably the easiest structure available is a community-based consumer-credit union. Remember, however, that a credit union can give loans only to its members. If a community wants a larger pool of capital, it might set up a commercial bank or thrift with a community ownership structure. Creating a new bank from scratch is of course a formidable task. But two of the biggest obstacles—sufficient capitalization and good banking expertise—might be overcome with assistance from local government, labor unions, or public employee pension funds.

One of the most difficult requirements facing a new commercial bank that seeks to qualify for federal insurance of its deposits is to secure at least $2 million in capitalization.[33] Even if a typical customer put $1,000 in the bank (which is higher than many families can afford), the bank would need 2,000 such customers just to reach the insurance threshold. It seems doubtful that 2,000 customers would agree to switch to a new bank *before* federal insurance became available. But a local government could help the bank clear this threshold. It could provide the bank with a $2 million grant, in exchange for concrete commitments to provide loans to new community businesses. It could issue tax-exempt bonds to finance the venture. Or it could place $2 million of city or pension money into certificates of deposit in the institution.

As for expertise: Larger cities have numerous financial experts who work for banks or recently retired, who might be willing to help create a new local bank. The mayor might lobby members of the private banking community to help. A smart politician could view a community banking project as a newsworthy opportunity to bring together conservative businesspeople and progressive activists. Plus, there are plenty of outside groups with expertise in community banking that can be tapped for help, such as the National Federation of Community Development Credit Unions and the National Association of Community Development Loan Funds.

Once a community bank is up and running, clever advertising might attract customers away from other commercial banks: "Invest in Your Community's Future," "Don't Let Your Money Leave Town," "Only a Fool and His Money Stay Parted," "Switch Banks for Your Children's Future." Even in conservative communities, as the classic film *It's a Wonderful Life* suggests, the one corporate institution residents love to hate is the bank.

Even though CDFIs of all kinds are rapidly proliferating, their numbers are few and their assets limited. South Shore, the largest CDFI, has assets of $625 million. The next largest, the Self-Help Credit Union in Durham, has only $94 million, and other CDFIs down the list are much smaller. Compared to the elephantine assets controlled by FDIC-insured commercial banks—$4.3 trillion—the CDFIs look like mice. Still, they are likely to become important fixtures in more and more communities. Besides providing depositors with the satisfaction of knowing that their money is financing local business, community banks have one other advantage over the multistates: They're more efficient. The Southern Finance Project has found that, compared to banks with far-flung portfolios, those lending only to geographically restricted borrowers were typically twice as profitable, had lower overhead costs, and wound up with fewer bad loans.[34]

UNCONVENTIONAL LOANS

Even small microenterprise funds usually require seed capital from a government agency or a large foundation. How can a tiny, impoverished community with absolutely no capital resources finance new corporations? The answer is simple—talk with your neighbors.

The value of family and friends pooling resources and extending each other credit has been established again and again. One reason why Jewish and Korean communities, for example, often fared well after coming to America was their well-established traditions of helping each other financially. In Santa Ana, California, the Civic Center Barrio Corporation has been leading Latino families to follow this tradition by consolidating their resources to help Latino renters finance the purchase or upgrade of more than 1,200 apartments.[35]

A striking example of how neighbors unified to create credit—not by ethnicity or religion but by place—occurred in 1989 in Great Barrington, Massachusetts. One of the city's major landmarks, Frank Tortoriello's delicatessen, suddenly lost its lease, so a new site had to be found. Lacking the $4,500 needed to acquire a new lease, Tortoriello turned to the nearby Self-Help Association for a Regional Economy (SHARE), a project of the E.F. Schumacher Society, for advice. The staff economists, Robert Swann and Susan Witt, recommended that Tortoriello arrange a loan with his customers by issuing Deli Bonds for $9 apiece and promising to pay them back with $10 of sandwiches and deli food, over a one-year period beginning four months after the bond issue. With interest rates effectively between 11 and 33 percent, customers eagerly snatched up all 500 bonds, and Tortoriello was able to make the move and keep his business alive.

Inspired by the success of Deli Dollars, SHARE applied the concept to two nearby farms that needed credit. One wanted to expand a greenhouse in order to grow off-season houseplants; the other had to rebuild a road-side-sales stand damaged by fire. Following SHARE's advice, both issued Berkshire Farm Preserve Notes, promising houseplants and vegetables several months later, in exchange for immediate cash. They were able to raise $7,000. SHARE has since used similar schemes to help the nearby Monterey General Store get through the slow winter months and to finance a new Japanese restaurant.

Another novel source of credit SHARE has pioneered is the largesse and goodwill of vacationers. Many affluent New Yorkers have second homes in the Berkshires of western Massachusetts, an economically depressed area where SHARE is based. Whenever one of these out-of-towners asks a member of SHARE what can be done to help boost the local economy, he or she is invited to open a savings account jointly with SHARE. Up to three-fourths of the account is then used as collateral to support local business loans brought to the bank by SHARE. Depositors who wish to withdraw their funds must give four months' notice, which usually is enough time to find new depositors. Going into its fourteenth year, this scheme was operating without a single default either on the records or in sight.

Debt relationships need not be structured exclusively between two people. Imagine a barter transaction in which a filling-station owner gives $100 of gasoline to a dentist, the dentist provides a $100 tooth-cleaning to a taxi driver, and the taxi driver delivers $100 worth of airport rides to the filling-station owner. Arrangements like this are based on enforceable promises to pay between debtor and creditor. If the IOUs are transferable, they effectively become a kind of currency. And Deli Dollars were used exactly this way in Great Barrington. Anyone inside a barter system can trade an IOU for a good or service of equal value from anyone else in the system.

An example of this interplay between local banking and local currency is the Economic Circle in Switzerland, an association of 60,000 business and individual members set up in 1934.[36] If a Swiss business proprietor wishes to obtain a low-interest loan from the Economic Circle, he or she must join the network, demonstrate creditworthiness, and present collateral (usually a second mortgage on a house or business facility). Once the loan is approved, the proprietor receives a special checkbook and credit card, as well as a fat catalog listing all the businesses that are part of the circle. The loan must be used exclusively to purchase goods and services from businesses within the circle, and repaid exclusively with the proceeds from sales to member businesses. Real currency, Swiss francs, is required only to pay nominal service charges. Once the initial loan is repaid, a business is permitted to use a combination of real and internal currencies for transactions within the circle.

It would certainly be possible to set up similar circles among community corporations in a given city or area in the United States. Stronger and more established corporations could extend credit, technical assistance, and preferential purchasing to weaker and newer ones. An association of community corporations could provide a mutual support group, just as circles of poor people do in microenterprise schemes. It's helpful if at least one of the corporations is a bank, though nonbank members could leverage their own assets in order to extend credit.

Support groups, whether in an extended family or in a producer cooperative, differ from banks in one significant way: They want the borrower's venture to succeed. Most banks are more or less indifferent. They know that they'll make a profit either by collecting interest payments, or by foreclosing on assets held as collateral if the enterprise goes belly-up. Support groups care about success (because the viability of the local economy depends on it), and therefore usually incorporate some form of technical assistance. Good business practice should not be left to fate; it should be taught.

If a community depends on the success of its homegrown businesses, then debt may not be the best way to finance community corporations. Perhaps it's better to have a financing mechanism that gives the community a stake in the enterprise, one that spreads the opportunities and the risks. That's why community corporations should consider obtaining finance through equity.

LOCALLY OWNED EQUITY

An investor, like a local support group of borrowers, cares more about the success of an enterprise than does a creditor. If a business fails, an equity investor can lose everything. This is why investors usually demand some kind of influence over businesses they own as shareholders, and why venture capitalists who assume huge risks demand majority shareholder control. The larger an investor's ownership stake, the greater his or her incentive to ensure that the business is run well.

By issuing stock, a corporation can distribute the opportunities and risks of ownership to members of the community. Financial institutions and individuals within the community can use their equity shares to cement their relationship with local business. In a community committed to self-reliance, every effort would be made to convince members who buy stock—individuals, churches, nonprofits, fraternal organizations—to invest exclusively in shares issued by community corporations.

Finding a local owner for every equity share of a community corporation is possible only if community residents have enough resources to buy the available stock. This is possible in such cities as New York, Houston, and Los Angeles, where there are huge concentrations of wealth among bankers, oil tycoons, and movie stars. (How to convince the wealthy that local investment is in their interest is another question.) But what can a *poor* community do to generate equity financing? Perhaps recruit a community bank for investment, rather than for loans.

An interesting example of equity banking comes from Mondragon in Spain. Early in the development of the Mondragon cooperatives, Don José María Armendiarrieta convinced his disciples to pool their savings and set up a bank run by its workers and member cooperatives. But the Lankide Aurrezkia Bank was no ordinary bank offering loans to strangers and watching passively whether they succeeded or failed. Instead, it became the hub of a local industrial policy, connecting and strengthening the spokes of more than 100 industrial cooperatives.

To obtain finance, each Mondragon cooperative had to follow the bank's guidelines on worker rights and ownership. Minimum wages had to be within 10 percent of minimum wages in the bank, and maximum wages had to be no more than three times the minimum. Cooperatives were required to use the bank for other financial services like processing of paychecks, deposit of sales receipts, and payment of expenses. Also, following the principle that workers had to own the enterprises and risk their own capital, all employees of Mondragon had to purchase ownership shares in the bank; those without resources had their wages garnisheed until the principal was paid (but no interest was charged). Every dollar of profit generated by each cooperative was split according to a set formula: 10 cents for charity, 20 cents for business expansion, and 70 cents for pensions.

One important feature of the Lankide Aurrezkia Bank was that it oversaw and assisted the management of cooperatives receiving loans. The bank had a team of experts who could offer advice on accounting, marketing, management, legal issues, technology, and so forth. During rough times, the bank would step in and fire managers, change product designs, cut wages, shift around positions—whatever might help the situation. By exercising control over the enterprises and moving workers among enterprises, the bank has been able to achieve a remarkable record: Only three enterprises in the history of Mondragon have failed.

The Mondragon bank's technical team also supported workers who wanted to start a new cooperative. If a business idea looked promising, Mondragon would underwrite the salary of the group leader for a few months, to allow that person to prepare a business plan. This procedure benefited not only the new enterprise but also the bank itself, which built up expertise for future business ventures. The Lankide Aurrezkia Bank acted, in effect, more like a venture capitalist than a commercial bank. In exchange for start-up capital and expert advice, it insisted upon control and equity from member cooperatives. If a cooperative failed to repay the "loan," the bank had sufficient ownership to reorganize it.

Much of this story must be written in the past tense. The opening up of the European Economic Community (EEC) in the early 1990s precipitated dramatic changes at Mondragon. As tariff walls came down and regional competition intensified, Mondragon decided to shed some of its unique characteristics. The maximum-wage ceiling was relaxed several times and lifted altogether in 1992. The vast majority of the bank's business, some 85 percent, is now done outside the cooperatives, in joint ventures with private corporations and conglomerates that sell products throughout the EEC. In 1995, it sold nearly $100 million of equity shares with no geographic restrictions on ownership.[37]

It's worth noting that Mondragon really never was a community corporation. Branches of the Lankide Aurrezkia Bank were originally established in two neighboring provinces, Mondragon and Vizcaya, as a hedge against one of the provincial governments' deciding to shut it down. Ownership was held by workers, not by community members, and workers' concern for the bottom line was not balanced in corporate decision-making with an equal concern for place. Nor was there an effort to link Mondragon's products with basic local needs. Mondragon's business strategy was always oriented toward exports, not import substitution.

Still, Mondragon was a remarkable pioneer. It demonstrated the commercial viability of worker ownership, producer cooperatives, and reinvestment banking. It also showed that among the most important sources of capital for investment, especially in a poor region, are pension funds.

PENSION REINVESTMENT

Recall that Mondragon placed 70 cents of every dollar of profit into worker retirement funds, which were used by the bank to finance new cooperative enterprises. Retirement money turns out to be one of the most important sources of investment capital. Americans today have roughly $5 trillion in pension assets, broken down as follows: $1 trillion in the pension reserves of life insurance companies; $2.6 trillion in private pension accounts (including Keoghs and IRAs); and $1.4 trillion in state and local government retiree funds.[38] The potential for community development, were even a small fraction of these funds reinvested locally, is enormous.

Each of us should boost our community's economic future by investing pension funds in community corporations. If you own an IRA or Keogh, shop around for local retirement-account managers who focus on investment in local enterprises. Those who do not directly control their retirement funds should push their fund managers to make a similar commitment.

Public consciousness about pension-fund investment has grown considerably in recent years, because of conscientious moves by the managers of what is often the single biggest pension fund within the community—that of public employees. In the 1980s, hundreds of municipalities worldwide decided to stop investing public-pension monies in or entering into contracts with firms doing business in South Africa. In the United States, a total of 27 states, 25 counties, and 101 cities enacted sanctions.[39] These U.S. jurisdictions decided to reinvest more than $20 billion in "clean" firms with no ties to apartheid.[40] Some U.S. communities also refused to do their banking with, or buy goods from, companies involved in South Africa. Once these sanctions were put into effect, two-thirds of all American companies with ties to South Africa sold off their equity shares, and the U.S. Congress passed the Comprehensive Anti-Apartheid Act in

1986, mustering the supermajority needed in both legislative houses to overcome President Ronald Reagan's veto.

The antiapartheid campaign signaled the first time that many localities realized the kind of power their investment and contracting decisions could give them over global corporations. Since then, cities have added other "screens." By 1987, there were 10 cities and counties in the United States that refused to invest in or buy goods from firms involved in the manufacture of nuclear weapons.[41] A dozen cities recently divested from firms doing business in Burma, to protest its repression of prodemocracy and human-rights activists. Cottage industries have sprung up to promote "socially responsible investment" and "Green purchasing." According to the Social Investment Forum, more than $700 billion of investment money is being managed in some kind of screened account.[42]

These efforts can be criticized for not emphasizing a positive vision about which investments are in the interests of a community. The next step in the evolution of socially responsible investing is to put retirement funds to work within every pensioner's community. And what better investment opportunities than new community corporations?

There is yet another long-term pension reinvestment opportunity that cities might explore. Monies given to Social Security are supposed to be held in trust and invested until the potential recipient either reaches retirement age or becomes blind or disabled. Currently, over 90 percent of the surplus funds in Social Security are being invested in nonmarketable Treasury notes, in order to reduce the federal deficit.[43] As the deficit gradually is repaid, more Social Security funds could be used for community reinvestment. At the end of 1996, the total size of the Social Security Trust Fund was over half a trillion dollars, and various experts project that it will grow to between three and four trillion dollars over the next generation.[44] One intriguing use of these funds could be the planting and nourishing of CDFIs in every community in America.

THE ROLE OF PUBLIC POLICY

U.S. banking laws provide a wide range of options for financing community corporations. You can push your current bank to make more loans to community corporations, or organize your friends to start a community credit union. If you're short on cash, you can issue IOUs like Deli Dollars or Berkshire Notes, and also borrow from neighbors, customers, and visitors.

You might pool your assets with those of other community corporations, as the Swiss Economic Circle does, or follow in the footsteps of Mondragon and set up an investment bank that oversees community corporations. You can use your pension portfolio to buy equity in community corporations, and persuade your neighbors to do likewise. Most of these initiatives require no special support by the government.

Still, government does have an important role to play. By strengthening the Community Reinvestment Act, screening public employees' pension funds, or seeding CDFIs with public funds (whether from congressional appropriations or from the Social Security Trust Fund), the U.S. government can expand enormously the finance capital available for community corporations. The next two chapters elaborate the full range of tools that local and national governments have at their disposal to help prosperity go local.

Pro-Community Local Governance 5

Government these days seems to be everyone's favorite whipping boy. For nearly two decades, Republicans have promised to get Washington off of voters' backs, and now even prominent Democrats distance themselves from Big Government. This bipartisan endorsement of markets over bureaucracies is certainly understandable. A society in which individuals can freely produce goods, enter into contracts, purchase property, hire workers, and take jobs is certainly more desirable and more in keeping with notions of freedom than one in which faceless ministers impose dubious economic choices on resentful subjects. A vision in which millions of citizens acting in their own self-interest can somehow set society on the proper course appeals to our beliefs in individual initiative and participatory democracy.

But the choice for communities is not between public policy *or* markets. As we have seen, many threats to the integrity of communities simply cannot be solved through free markets. Indeed, markets cannot function, even in theory, without *some* government intervention. For example:

• Markets perform properly only when government enforces rules of contract, property, and tort. (For a glimpse of what an economic system looks like in the absence of basic rules, look at the new Russia, where capitalism is now synonymous with anarchy and oversight has been unofficially assumed by mafioso.)

- Because markets work best when consumers are well informed, government can play a constructive role in disseminating information to consumers. A free market that limits information to those who can pay for it necessarily means that the poor, and others who can least afford to make bad economic decisions, are the ones most likely to do so.
- Markets are unable to solve many of the social problems they help cause, nor are they held responsible to pay the costs of policing, health care, and mediation necessary to prevent such problems.
- Markets do not internalize the external costs of pollution, labor disputes, and defective products, so it is necessary for government to set minimum standards to protect the environment, workers, and consumers.
- Because markets rarely provide full employment (as noted in Chapter 1, most economists assert that 5 percent unemployment is a "natural rate" for a healthy economy), the government needs to provide relief or public jobs to the unemployed. Failure to do so leaves the rest of society vulnerable to crime, health epidemics (tuberculosis being the most recent example), and revolution.
- Markets alone will not deliver such public goods as defense, foreign policy, roads, bridges, trains, and harbors.
- Markets rarely lead to the spontaneous construction of community spaces like parks, libraries, schools, and civic centers, where all people can go, regardless of social status or ability to pay.

It took government initiative to put the market rules in place that allow global corporations to run roughshod over communities, and it will take government initiative to replace them with a new set that favors self-reliance. And the biggest role should be played by *local* government, where the public sector is most accessible, accountable, flexible, and innovative.

THE VIRTUES OF LOCALISM

You've probably heard the litany of reasons why local government can't be trusted. Conservatives worry that if every community erects its own trade barriers, the national economy will descend into the kind of trade wars that nearly destroyed the country during the era of the Articles of Confederation. Progressives warn that a weakened national government will only help corporations play communities against one another, and view "states' rights" as giving license to policies of racism, sexism, and parochial abuse.

A little reflection, however, suggests that both sets of fears are exaggerated. Community self-reliance does not require the dismantling of nation-states; it simply means greater tolerance of local freedom of action. Self-reliance can be pursued without building feared tariff walls, if the driving force is community corporations supplying local demands for necessities. And there is nothing inconsistent about the national government's maintaining minimal standards concerning corporate responsibility, equal protection, and affirmative action, while still permitting localities to legislate creatively within these restrictions.

One of the remarkable political transformations in recent years has been the convergence of left and right thinking on the value of localization. The only provision of the Republicans' 1994 Contract with America that attracted strong support from the Democrats was the promise to relieve states and localities of the burdens of "unfunded mandates." Conservatives fighting for states' rights have astonishingly common ground with progressives dedicated to community empowerment and bioregionalism. Even such top-down institutions as the European Economic Community, the United Nations, and the World Bank are seeking to promote "devolution," "decentralization," and "subsidiarity."

The term *subsidiarity* is perhaps the most useful of these three, because it implies a pragmatic relationship among different levels of government. Subsidiarity posits that power should always be exercised at the level closest to the people affected by a decision. At the community level, decisions can be tailored to special local circumstances. If mistakes are made, they usually can be easily corrected. The closer those affected by decisions are to the decisionmakers, the more likely the decisions will be efficient, fair, democratic, sensitive, creative, and disaster-proof.

Lest the reader think what follows is romanticism about decentralization, a clarification is in order: A preference for local action is not a presumption that local action is perfect. In fact, local leaders are as susceptible to incompetence, corruption, sycophancy, and blandness as are their national counterparts. Checks and balances within every level of government (including municipalities and counties) as well as among them are needed to keep politicians honest. And inequalities among people, as far as wealth, social status, and education are concerned, pose as formidable a challenge to democratic governance at the local level as at the national level. Subsidiarity is simply a *preference* that political participation and policymaking proceed first and foremost at the local level; if local action proves inadequate for whatever reason, then—and only then—move to a higher level.

Local decisionmaking is preferable to national decisionmaking first, because it peels away unnecessary layers of bureaucracy. Common sense suggests that the only people sitting around a table should be those who either have important input for a decision or will be affected by a decision. To involve outsiders who have nothing unique to add, and no real stake, only bogs down and muddles the process. Decisions that concern only people living inside a community should rarely be made by those at a higher level. Every additional layer of official intervention wastes time, distorts information, and removes power from those who deserve it. The less distance between those governing and those governed, the better the opportunity for real stakeholders to be heard. Also, for most Americans, a clear virtue of local politicians is that they are rarely farther than a telephone call or a meeting away.

What some people find so disturbing about local politics—that a community might enact policies that are loony, backwards, or mean—is exactly what others find so exciting. If there's anything that the ossifying gridlock of national politics reveals, it's that a country of 270 million people cannot easily reach consensus around difficult value choices. The right to choose to have an abortion has practically ignited a civil war in the country, and equally profound moral questions are presented by capital punishment, euthanasia, sex education, and welfare. Reasonable Americans have never agreed over the dread "r" word—redistribution. Should society pursue equality of opportunity or equality of result? If the latter, how much equality is just?

To say that a national consensus on these issues is unlikely is not to imply that it's undesirable. Settlement of divisive issues would certainly unify and strengthen the country. Greater national uniformity on public education and welfare benefits might reduce migration among the states and give children more-equal starting places in life. But consensus in a strong democracy should never be assumed. In the absence of consensus, to impose a national law or policy beyond the minimal standards articulated in the Constitution (which itself is a consensus document) only erodes the legitimacy of the national government and of government in general.

There are huge differences on many issues by region, each of which reflects critical religious, ethnic, racial, and cultural traditions. Putting such policies primarily in the hands of state and local governments increases the chances that citizens in each community will have the laws and policies they really want. Why should we expect or want Berkeley, California, to approach welfare and tax policies in exactly the same way as Lubbock, Texas? A country in which every community can move closer to its own utopia—even if it means that there are fewer communities outside our own where we would like to live—ought to enhance most people's quality of life.

One of the brilliant features of U.S. federalism is that national policy-making is *supposed* to be difficult. The Founding Fathers wanted the country to overcome difficult and time-consuming procedures before new national laws or new constitutional amendments were passed that might restrict state and local freedoms. Those who seek the latter action would be wise to develop a national consensus built on a foundation of local consent and local action.

The diversity of policies being tried at the local level makes it easier to identify those that really work. As Supreme Court Justice Louis Brandeis once wrote: "It is one of the happy incidents of the federal system that a single courageous State may, if its citizens choose, serve as a laboratory; and try novel social and economic experiments without risk to the rest of the country."[1] There is a tremendous virtue in letting the 36,000 local governments in the country each find its own way. We will thereby learn much more rapidly about what works and what doesn't, than if we engage in one clumsy national experiment after another. Brandeis added, "Denial of the right to experiment may be fraught with serious consequences to the Nation."

Community initiative can better unleash American ingenuity. The participants in Richard Harwood's focus groups (mentioned in Chapter 1), who were so pessimistic about "politics as usual," spoke of numerous examples of people rebuilding their communities outside the traditional channels of politics. According to Harwood's final report:

> *Perhaps what is most interesting about all this is how citizens seem to view "community." At first blush, they think of it in traditional terms: neighbors, town centers, city council meetings. Yet, through their community involvement, it appears that citizens have been able to create*

alternative communities for themselves—some new, some not so
new—around such things as an ad hoc issue group's seeking to preserve
open space, a local school committee, a crime-watch group, or the tra-
ditional neighborhood association.[2]

A final virtue of subsidiarity is that local failures tend to be smaller, less
disastrous, and easier to fix than national failures. Because the victims are
nearby, it becomes harder for decisionmakers to hide from their mistakes.
Warnings that plans are running awry can be heard, digested, and responded to more quickly if decisionmakers are within earshot.

None of these observations means that decisions at the local level are
always efficient, fair, democratic, sensitive, creative, and disaster-proof.
But the more responsibility that we can place for politics at the local level,
the more likely people are to take their politics seriously and act responsibly. As Alexis de Tocqueville observed:

It is important to appreciate that, in general, men's affections are drawn
only in directions where power exists. Patriotism does not long prevail
in a conquered country. The New Englander is attached to his township
not so much because he was born there as because he sees the township
as a free, strong corporation of which he is part and which is worth the
trouble of trying to direct.[3]

The principle of subsidiarity suggests that a local government seeking to
achieve self-reliance should not rely on the state or federal government,
but should take initiative on its own. And it should mobilize *all* its legal
powers of investment, purchasing, contracting, hiring, and taxation.

LOCAL REINVESTMENT

An easy way for a local government to change the course of community
economy is to stop allowing disloyal corporations to feed at the public
trough. Most major new plants or plant expansions enjoy local-government support in the form of industrial-development bonds, loans, loan
guarantees, and tax abatements—with little or nothing asked in return.
Community corporations, at a minimum, should be able to plead their case
for municipal goodies alongside the out-of-towners. The next time your
community considers giving a package of $150,000 per job to BMW, insist

that the city council open up the process so that community corporations can show what they could deliver for around $149,000 per job.

But why stop there? Why not make the case that community agencies should support only community corporations? A municipality should no longer bestow hard-earned tax dollars on a business unless it is firmly anchored to the community. (The actual implementation of this policy might have to be introduced gradually, perhaps even over five to 10 years, to facilitate a smooth transition.)

General-obligation and industrial-development bonds might be restricted to projects built by and for community corporations. Investors are drawn to municipal bonds because the federal government exempts interest earned from income taxation. Limiting tax-exempt bonds to community corporations certainly would spur entrepreneurs to form them. If your community wants to build an airport, make sure the bonds financing the project stipulate that the proceeds will be used to give hiring preferences to locally owned architecture, engineering, and construction firms. Want to develop a new industrial park? Stipulate that local companies qualify for a 25 percent discount on their leases.

All the benefits that municipal governments now give to globe-trotting corporations should be reviewed. Public-employee pension funds and surplus municipal revenues should be invested in companies that have not only high rates of return but also high degrees of community loyalty. City offices of economic development, which now help multinational corporations with branch factories in innumerable ways—to acquire private finance, secure state and federal contracts, team up with local universities, obtain public R&D funding, and so on—should refocus their efforts on community corporations. And the mayor and city-council members, who now travel thousands of miles to attract new firms to the community, or to open new markets abroad for locally produced goods, should use their frequent-flier miles to lobby against the anticommunity trade agreements emerging in international institutions. Once a city government appreciates that community corporations serve the local economy best, it should systematically confer to them (and not to multinationals) such public benefits as roads, water supplies, sewage systems, electrical utility hookups, schools, and housing subdivisions.

Local preferences like these, it needs to be said, do carry risks. The more that civil servants award government contracts and purchase orders to their friends rather than to the lowest bidder, the greater the dangers of public corruption and theft. But instances of multinational firms using bribery and favoritism to win bids are hardly unknown, and global corporations certainly have more resources at their disposal with which to buy contractors than community firms do. The best means of preventing corruption are incentives that reward civil servants for keeping contract costs down, tough restrictions on lobbying that insulate decisionmakers from business interests, and rigorous enforcement of antikickback laws at all levels of government.

There are also big sticks that U.S. state and local governments can use to ensure that conventional corporations do not depart unexpectedly and thus inflict unnecessary pain on the community. In 1983, the city of Chicago tried to enjoin the parent company of Playskool from shutting down, on the grounds that the firm had promised not to sell off its assets for 20 years.[4] The case was ultimately settled out of court, when Playskool promised to keep the plant open one more year, to set up a job-placement center for unemployed workers, and to contribute $50,000 to support displaced workers.

After General Motors announced its plans to relocate a plant from Ypsilanti, Michigan, the city sued to stop it.[5] A lower court held that the corporation had an implied, common-law obligation to compensate the community, but an appeals court reversed the ruling.[6] The city would have been on stronger legal ground had it entered a carefully drafted contract with GM spelling out the firm's community obligations, or had it enacted an ordinance to regulate corporate closures putting all local firms on notice about what is expected of them before they skip town. A community might demand that companies with more than, say, 50 employees provide at least three months' notice and two-months' severance pay before closure.[7] Violations could be punishable by a fine large enough for the city to pay severance to displaced employees. In fact, between 1979 and 1982, at least 10 state legislatures considered bills that would have required corporations to give one to two *years* of notice to the community before closure.[8]

Another stick against disloyal corporations could be a law requiring any business considering a shutdown to offer the workers or other investors in the community the option to buy the factory. Pittsburgh, Pennsylvania, passed an ordinance mandating that firms about to close issue an economic-impact statement exploring alternatives, including the possibility of an employee buyout.[9] (A Pennsylvania court, however, invalidated the law on the grounds that the city exceeded its home rule power.[10]) In 1992 and 1993, Washington state considered a "social compact" bill which would have given communities and workers the "right of first refusal"—that is, the right to be the first purchaser (at market value) of a plant about to be sold.[11] Some states have even created special funds to assist with worker buyouts: Illinois and Michigan have revolving loan funds for such purposes; and California, Illinois, and Michigan authorize the use of industrial-development revenue bonds for buyouts.[12]

A few states allow their municipalities to use constitutional powers of "eminent domain" to take over plants about to be closed. The U.S. and state constitutions require both that such takeovers serve a public purpose and that the owners receive "just compensation," but *just* can mean *below* (often far below) market value. The states of Illinois, Ohio, and Pennsylvania permit government takeovers whenever plant closure or relocation will adversely affect the local economy.[13] New Bedford, Massachusetts, temporarily prevented the closure of the Morse Cutting Tools plant by threatening to take it over (which convinced the owner, Gulf and Western Corporation, to sell the plant to a third party).[14]

These sticks hardly exhaust the universe of possibilities. Illinois considered passing a law requiring that no firm receiving a state tax abatement could shut down during the abatement period, lest the state "clawback" the subsidy and force the firm to repay the abatement in full, plus 18 percent interest.[15] A proposed bill in New Jersey would create an Industrial Retention Commission empowered to deny state subsidies, contracts, and pension investments to any company found to have hurt local employment through plant transfer.[16] Maine requires banks engaged in major takeovers to reinvest in the state.[17] Thirteen state legislatures recently began discussing the creation of an interstate compact under which they would collectively withdraw their pension-fund investments from firms that depart irresponsibly.[18]

All together, these laws constitute a powerful arsenal with which state and local governments penalize corporations for costly departures. Yet their limitation is obvious: The more onerous the restrictions, the less likely will mobile corporations be to set up shop in the community in the first place. But a community with an expanding base of homegrown corporations will have the confidence and ability to regard such threats by outside firms as irrelevant.

LOCAL PURCHASING

A second tool available to local governments is to buy goods and services from community corporations. For struggling communities, purchasing is more important than investment, because the poor spend most of their income on the consumption of basics like food, housing, utilities, and health care. Whenever citizens buy a good that is made locally they expand jobs, enlarge the tax base, and strengthen the economy. Every dollar spent on local goods and services provides income to local owners, local workers, and local suppliers. If they, in turn, respend the dollars on locally produced goods, the local economic multiplier expands and the community economy grows.

A smart municipal government can mandate that its agencies purchase products from local producers, if reasonably priced local substitutes are available. A decade ago in Chicago, Mayor Harold Washington's policy of giving a small advantage to local contract bidders increased their share of city purchases from 40 percent to 60 percent in just two years.[19] For several years, city attorneys in Burlington, Rutland, St. Albans, and Williston managed to keep Wal-Mart out of Vermont because the chain sold primarily nonlocal goods (they ultimately lost the fight, however, in three of the four towns). A local government can mandate that special labels or seals be put on products that are manufactured primarily with its local capital, labor, and resources. It might also launch a public-education campaign to encourage residents to "buy local" through billboards, TV ads, pamphlets, and public forums.

In 1983, the city of Eugene teamed up with a private bank and the Lane County Private Industry Council to set up the Oregon Marketplace, to help in-state purchasers and contractors find competitive in-state bidders.[20] The operation paid for itself by assessing a small finder's fee for every new regional contract. The initiative was so successful that in 1985 the state legislature appropriated a grant to a neighborhood-development corporation to find and train people to run 12 more offices in the state and link them by computer network. During a two-year period ending in 1991, Oregon Marketplace brokered an estimated $68 million worth of in-state deals.[21]

Two dozen communities in the United States promote local trade through yet another (and an even more daring) tool—local money. Many years ago, the wise guys in Las Vegas realized it was profitable to allow gamblers to use playing chips from one casino in other casinos and in various stores. Old-timers recall that everyone would gladly accept chips, from churches on Sunday (when the collection bowl was passed around) to prostitutes during the other days of the week.[22] Casinos hired young runners to make the rounds and buy back the chips for cash. The practice gradually went underground in the 1970s and was formally outlawed in the 1980s.[23] In retrospect, it was a brilliant economic development strategy. The losers dropped their chips at the craps tables, while the winners were encouraged to spend theirs throughout the city. Either way, gamblers' pockets were vacuumed clean before departing. Make it easy for people to spend their money locally and—*voilà!*—purchasing goes local.

Local currencies actually have a long history in the United States. The earliest colonial settlers used corn as a medium of exchange in Massachusetts and wampum with Native Americans.[24] During the Great Depression, an estimated 300 communities across the country scraped by, using their own scrip. Philadelphia, Pennsylvania, and Wildwood, New Jersey, printed homegrown money to pay teachers and other municipal employees. The city of Tenino in Washington State put $6,500 worth of wooden tokens into circulation, and promised to buy the currency back. By the time the date for redemption arrived, tourists and collectors had pocketed most of the coins, which left Tenino with a profit.

Today, hundreds of communities worldwide print their own currencies to induce residents to pump up their local economies. A community currency, whether in the form of coins, paper bills, checks, or computer-tallied credits and debits, is essentially a system to promote local purchasing. The managers of the system decide which goods and services qualify for exchange, and exactly what residents need to do to join. With the time-consuming tasks of screening already performed, consumers and producers know that *any* purchase or sale within the money system helps the local economy.

Once a local money system is in place, participation becomes a sign of good citizenship. Consumers who go outside the system are stigmatized. Firms that refuse to take local money risk losing local business. The use of national currency is still permitted, but it's regarded as anticommunity behavior.

In 1983 a Scottish-born Canadian named Michael Linton introduced the Local Exchange Trading System (LETS) into the depressed Comox Valley in British Columbia, where one-fourth of the population was unemployed. Using a simple computer program, he invented a currency called "green money." He invited residents to barter goods and services with one another, and report all transactions back to him. Over the next four years, the LETS system in the Comox Valley recorded $350,000 in trade, and the system has since spread to hundreds of communities worldwide.

Here's how a typical LETS works: Sam agrees to buy Zoe's yardwork for 10 green dollars. The exact price for the work is negotiated exclusively by Sam and Zoe. Once the work is done and reported, the computer notes that Sam's account is now minus 10 and Zoe's account plus 10. Zoe then might buy groceries from Isaac for 5 green dollars, leaving her account at plus 5 and Isaac's at plus 5. And so forth. At any given time, all accounts add up to zero.

Richard Douthwaite reports that his community of Westport, Ireland, issued participants a LETS check book and LETS tokens named after a nearby mountain, the Reek. The system overseers encourage participants to peg the value of a Reek to the average wage for a minute of work. To give buyers and sellers the greatest incentive to use only Reeks, Westport's leaders do not officially recognize an exchange rate between the national and local currencies. Indeed, to participate in the system, a seller must set a Reek price for goods and services. A seller is permitted to accept partial payment in national currency, but the exchange rate is up to him or her— and therefore varies from transaction to transaction.

Linton designed LETS to be both self-propelling and self-regulating: self-propelling because individuals whose accounts were in surplus would have an incentive to go out and strike deals with others in the community; self-regulating because anyone could log onto the computer system, see anyone else's tally, and decide not to do business with a person whose account was too deep in the hole. Linton assumed that every participant's account would go negative from time to time, and since this was an essential feature of the system, no interest should be charged. If someone's account went too far in debt, Linton imagined, the community as a whole would put collective pressure on the debtor to cut expenses or take offers of employment. Most operating LETS systems, however, recognizing that allowing some community members to rack up debts and leave town with no consequences following is an invitation to abuse, place at least some limits on debts. The largest system in the world, which is centered in Katoomba, Australia (40 miles east of Sydney) has more than a thousand participants, yet sets a debt limit—though as of this writing no one had reached it.

The biggest problem facing LETS is not deficits, but unspent surpluses. Losers who can't sell are more susceptible to peer pressure or shunning than are winners who can't find anything worthwhile to buy. If a key business like a grocery or hardware store cannot use its surplus for production inputs or other valuable goods and services, it may well drop out. And once the most important economic players lose faith in the system, it can collapse.

One of the shortcomings of existing LETS systems is that they tend to involve individual craftsmen and service providers, not larger businesses. Michael Linton's original LETS system had 500 participants, but only five were shops, all small. When a dentist who was one of the key participants left town, the system fell apart. As Richard Douthwaite observes, "[T]he Comox experience underlines the importance of ensuring that people's real needs, as opposed to their peripheral pleasures, can be met through a LETS."[25]

One local money system which has incorporated the business community from the outset is in Ithaca, New York. Paul Glover, an urban planner and journalist, set up LETS in this small college town in the 1980s. But the system attracted only about 60 members, and ground to a halt when the nonprofit group operating the computer program closed down in 1988. Glover found it cumbersome to keep track of accounts by computer, so set out to create a paper money system that anyone could use like national currency. Ithaca HOURS was born in November 1991. Glover writes:

> *We printed our own money because we watched federal dollars come to town, shake a few hands, then leave to buy rainforest lumber and fight wars. Ithaca's HOURS, by contrast, stay in our region to help us hire each other. While dollars make us increasingly dependent on multinational corporations and bankers, HOURS reinforce community trading and expand commerce that is more accountable to our concerns for ecology and social justice.*[26]

The name HOURS comes from the ultimate reserve backing up the currency—the labor of participating Ithacans. Each HOUR is worth $10, the wage for an average hour of work in surrounding Tompkins County. Notes come in five denominations: two, one, one-half, one-quarter, and one-eighth HOURS. Bills have the caption "In Ithaca We Trust," and state in the corner that "this note entitles bearer to receive one hour labor or its negotiated value in goods and services. Please accept it, then spend it." The production of each note is a source of considerable pride for Glover: "Multicolored HOURS—some printed on locally made watermarked cat-tail (marsh reed) paper, some with locally invented thermal-sensitive ink that vanishes briefly when touched or photocopied, all with serial num-bers—are harder to counterfeit."

Since 1991, organizers have issued $55,000 worth of HOURS, and 1,500 people—including 250 business proprietors—have used them for an estimated $1.5 million of transactions. Glover writes that Ithacans use the notes to

> *buy plumbing, carpentry, electrical work, nursing, child care, car repair, food, eyeglasses, firewood, and thousands of other goods and services. Our credit union accepts them for mortgage and loan fees. People pay rent with them. The best restaurants in town take them, as do movie theaters, bowling alleys, two large locally owned grocery stores, and thirty-five farmer's market vendors.*

It's no exaggeration to say that a person living in Ithaca can live quite decently without ever once touching a U.S. dollar—except to pay taxes.

How did Glover convince local businesses to participate? Every other month he publishes a newspaper appropriately named *Ithaca Money*. Businesses that accept HOURS are listed gratis in the paper, which is dis-tributed as a directory to all participants. Participating businesses also are given two HOURS to start with, and two additional HOURS every eight months for continued participation. In short, businesses are paid to par-ticipate—a technique some credit-card companies use. Businesses then can use the currency to buy work from more than 1,000 others.

A glance at Glover's paper suggests this isn't difficult to do. Under P, for example, are listed painters, patent consultants, payroll specialists, pet-car-ers, photographers, physical therapists, pianists, picture framers, plant-sellers, plumbers, poets, poster distributors, pregnancy counselors, preschool teachers (at a certified Montessori school), printers, pruners, psychotherapists, public-speaking trainers, publishers, and puppeteers.

Ithaca HOURS is overseen by the Barter Potluck, the local equivalent of the Federal Reserve Board. Unlike the interest-setting committee of the Fed, however, community decisionmakers meet every 60 days at a public dinner, rather than behind closed doors, and chomp on chopsticks rather than on cigars. Among the hot agenda items: Which professions should receive more than one HOUR for an hour of work? How much new money can be introduced to keep the system from veering toward either inflation or deflation? Who could qualify for interest-free loans of HOURS? Which nonprofits should be given charitable contributions of HOURS? (Twenty-five grants totaling $5,000 have been given thus far to groups like the Ithaca Rape Center, the Stop Wal-Mart Campaign, the Senior Citizens Center, and the Committee on U.S./Latin-American Relations.)

Economists who assume that Americans are driven solely by self-interest might predict that high-wage producers would never participate. Why would a lawyer making $200 an hour join a system paying $10 an hour? Recognizing the problem, the Barter Potluck does allow some professionals to charge somewhat higher hourly fees. But a remarkable number of doctors, lawyers, accountants, and therapists have agreed to take substantially lower wages because they are committed to boosting the local economy. A similar phenomenon can be observed in LETS systems worldwide, where many professionals are attracted to the philosophy of making wages more equal on behalf of the community's welfare.

Local currencies are gaining support from an astonishing range of organizations. The first grant to the E. F. Schumacher Society's newsletter, *Local Currency News,* came from the conservative Bradley Foundation, which has gained public notoriety funding right-leaning think tanks like the Heritage Foundation and the American Enterprise Institute. At the opposite end of the political spectrum, Resources for Human Development, a social service agency based in Philadelphia, has committed $200,000 to start a currency system because it believes it will stimulate local employment and help move its clients from welfare to work.

LETS, Ithaca HOURS, and other local currency systems in the United States all are undertaken unofficially, with neither support nor opposition from the local government. But the involvement of local government, especially if it backs up the currency with the municipal treasury, can accelerate acceptance of and confidence in the system. This was demonstrated in a famous experiment with local currencies that took place in the Austrian town of Wörgl in the early 1930s. With nearly one-third of the population out of work and tax collections falling far behind, the mayor printed a scrip to pay half the wages of city-council staff, and invited residents to use it to pay taxes. The local government guaranteed the money, which convinced businesses that they were taking no risk in using the currency. The system put Wörgl residents back to work, and the influx of new tax revenues funded new roads and sewers. Other towns in the country took notice and began to print their own currencies, until the Austrian Central Bank, fearful of losing control of national monetary policy, went into court and scuttled the initiatives.

Will U.S. communities that experiment with local currencies risk a similar backlash from the U.S. Treasury? Right now, the legality of paper currencies is well-established. Federal law prohibits private citizens only from issuing coins or bills with denominations of less than a dollar.[27] In a recent treatise on the subject, Lewis D. Solomon, a law professor at George Washington University, concludes: "[W]ith the possible exception of Virginia and Arkansas, federal or state currency laws would not restrain a system of alternative paper scrip."[28]

Were the U.S. government ever to fear, as the Austrian Central Bank did, that it was losing control over monetary policy, Congress might act to prohibit local currencies. The federal government certainly has the authority to do so. But, as a practical matter, the proliferation of modern financial instruments makes this kind of clampdown virtually unthinkable. Millions of Americans are beginning to undertake financial transactions over the Internet with a few keystrokes. As *Newsweek* observes, "Right now, anyone can put up a shingle and peddle his own private form of currency."[29] The possibility of the government's preventing people from creating a community tally of transactions (like LETS), exchanging paper IOUs (like Ithaca HOURS), or making on-line money transactions as they wish becomes smaller every day.

SELECTIVE PRIVATIZATION

A third means by which local governments can promote community corporations is to give them priority in taking on privatized public functions. A mantra of local officials in recent years has been "privatize, privatize,

privatize." Many communities have become convinced that private contractors often can deliver public services more efficiently than can government agencies. What started as a few experiments to place garbage-collection services into private hands has now become a political movement to privatize data entry, schools, hospitals, and even police and prisons. This movement is driven by three kinds of arguments, which—like Sergio Leone's classic spaghetti Western—might be called the good, the bad, and the ugly.

The *good* arguments boil down to a recognition that market competition spurs innovation, efficiency, and quality. The periodic auction of, say, the right to run a restaurant in an airport encourages the best entrepreneurs to come forward. Most air travelers would attest that the Jerry's Subs, Dunkin' Donuts, Pizza Huts, and even the Burger Kings are great improvements over the old, airport-run food commissaries. One of my happiest arrivals at Chicago's O'Hare Airport occurred when I discovered that Starbucks coffee outlets had replaced the dreary Hostess stands that once served dark, muddy water. (From the standpoint of community self-reliance, of course, replacing one national chain with a dozen others is not much of a step forward. How much nicer O'Hare would be, for example, if these outlets were occupied by locally owned deep-dish pizzerias, Jewish delicatessens, German beerhalls, and Polish sausage outlets.)

Intertwined with these good arguments, however, are *bad* ones about the horribles of government. The ideological assertion that government can do nothing right is an insult to every American who has benefited from public education, interstate highways, clean tapwater, rural electrification, student loans, social security, small-business support, job training, community block grants—in short, everyone. The numerous areas of market failure noted earlier underscore that not every inefficiency of government can be solved by tossing the responsibility back to the private sector. And the "government stinks" argument loses most of its force if, in the end, privatization simply transforms the role of government from tax, spend, and implement, to tax, spend, and contract-administer.

The final kind of argument for privatization is an *ugly* one. A close look at the interests arrayed for and against privatization reveals a not-so-hidden agenda to destroy public-employee unions and to weaken the bargaining power of workers in general. The cost-savings that private contractors muster are often the result of lower wages, fewer benefits, and more hazardous working conditions. Privatization, like outsourcing in the private sector, enables the government to dump higher-wage employees, particularly people with seniority and fewer prospects for rehire.

One of the benefits of community corporations is that they provide an alternative to public inefficiency and private inequity, an opportunity to reap the good without the ugly. A local government seeking to improve the performance of its operations might allow only community corporations to bid on public contracts or franchises. By further requiring bids to show that the community corporation's wages and benefits are commensurate with those of public employees, workers throughout the community can be protected. Meanwhile, control of the business would remain within the community, maximizing incentives for responsible behavior.

Many environmental initiatives undertaken by cities might be creatively reframed as contracts for community corporations. Recent studies indicate that if Los Angeles planted trees and covered its rooftops and roads with reflective material, it could reduce the ground-level temperature by five degrees and cut annual air-conditioning costs by more than $150 million.[30] This simple measure would reduce temperature-sensitive pollution by 10 percent, and create an estimated $300 million worth of health benefits—as much as removing three out of every four cars from the road would accomplish. Los Angeles might open a bidding process to community corporations to perform various pieces of work, including planting trees, manufacturing reflective materials, and installing them on roads and roofs.

If national trends toward privatization continue, so will opportunities to create new community corporations. Community corporations are exactly the right institutions to be entrusted to run hospitals and schools, supervise street repairs, and operate bus systems. Whether the checks and balances of community oversight within these corporations are better or worse than those of government agencies will depend on the quality of a given community's government, and the corporate alternatives. Generalization is difficult. The point is that whenever government is deemed undependable, the next resort should be community-owned and -operated private enterprise.

LOCAL HIRING

A fourth tool available to municipalities promoting self-reliance is local hiring. The virtues of putting local residents to work are obvious: more private spending, greater tax revenues, fewer welfare checks, less crime. And one way to accomplish this is to strengthen community corporations. Locally owned business may not exclusively be able to hire locals, but since most such businesses are small, chances are good that they will draw their employees predominantly from the local labor force. Still, it may be helpful for municipalities to look beyond the private sector.

Too many people in our communities are unemployed, underemployed, or unhappily employed, and the welfare reforms passed by Congress in 1996, which will dump millions of women into the labor force without creating new jobs, will only make the problem worse. Idleness imposes not only economic costs but also psychological ones; and the benefits of decent work are not just better macroeconomic statistics but also dignity, pride, and self-esteem. Local governments might contract with community corporations to provide more jobs.

Mickey Kaus, a senior editor at the *New Republic,* argued that a federal jobs program modeled after President Franklin D. Roosevelt's Works Progress Administration (WPA) could provide employment to every American for under $60 billion per year.[31] He proposed that the jobs pay a wage just below minimum. For a somewhat higher price tag, every able-bodied American could have a minimum-wage job (or better). Certainly there is no shortage of useful work that publicly employed Americans could perform: picking up trash, repairing streets, providing basic social services, taking care of preschool children, restoring ravaged ecosystems, refurbishing abandoned housing, providing recreational activities for teenagers—the list is practically endless. But is the federal government really going to implement a modern public-jobs program?

Even though $60 billion for full employment seems like a real bargain (especially compared to, say, our willingness to spend twice as much money each year to deploy troops in Europe against an enemy that no longer exists), don't hold your breath for a national initiative. Federal politicians who have spent the past decade wrestling with deficits, budget cuts, and tax revolts can hardly be expected to muster the political willpower for a new WPA. It will fall to states and localities to find creative ways to boost employment. To the extent that communities can improve and regain control over their tax base (as discussed shortly), they may be able to muster the resources to inject carefully targeted doses of public spending, as John Maynard Keynes would have recommended, into the local economy. Municipalities might then enter into contracts with community corporations to provide enough public services to ensure decent work for everyone living in the community.

For communities without surplus funds, another way to boost local employment is through a program known as Time Dollars. Conceived by law professor Edgar Cahn and underwritten initially by the Robert Wood Johnson Foundation, Time Dollars mobilizes people with extra time to work for one another and contribute to the community well-being. "The Time Dollar currency," says Cahn, "enables human beings to redefine themselves as assets, each and every one with something special to contribute. . . ."[32] A retiree might earn Time Dollars by tutoring young people—one Time Dollar for every hour put in. He or she might redeem credited hours when sick and needing help buying groceries or walking the dog, for example.

The Time Dollars system makes it worth everyone's while to give more hours to community service. Critics might complain about transforming once-voluntary activities into yet another economic venture, but Time Dollars actually expand the level of socially valuable work. "We have found that Time Dollars do more than simply pay for labor," says Cahn. "They reinforce trust; they reward acts of decency. They drive an information system about whom one can trust, about what neighbors can do and when they can do it—in a way that rebuilds community."[33]

More than 200 Time Dollar systems are operating in the United States, many with paid staff. Eighteen public-housing complexes in Washington, D.C., use Time Dollars to encourage residents to help one another care for small children and operate a food bank (where Time Dollars also can buy food). A health maintenance organization in Brooklyn gives Time Dollars to patients who, once they're feeling better, help hospital staff to administer wellness programs, and spend time with just-discharged patients to help them with recovery at home. (Saving even one day of hospitalization virtually pays the administrative costs of the system for a year.) In Pittsburgh, welfare mothers receive Time Dollars for running a consignment store where other Time Dollar earners can buy donated toys, infant clothing, and diapers. A Time Dollar Peer Tutoring Program in the South Side of Chicago moves 12-year-olds from gang mischief to teaching reading to six- and seven-year-olds, an extracurricular activity which reinforces and improves their own reading skills and allows them to spend Time

Dollar credits on refurbished computers. The District of Columbia Superior Court gives young people Time Dollars for serving as jurors in a Youth Court, where they render judgment on their peers for first-time, nonviolent offenders.

The current experiments rarely allow participants to convert hours into cash. As long as Time Dollars cannot easily be used to buy groceries or pay rent, they tend to be most useful for people who already have access to money, like retirees or children. But Cahn hopes to expand their convertibility. He envisions creating community corporations for day care, security, transportation, and senior home care in which employees gradually gain ownership through nonwage work. He wants local governments to contribute to the "Individual Development Accounts" of these participants.

A municipality also could expand and improve a local Time Dollar system. Were a municipality to provide a bounty of, say, one real dollar for every Time Dollar hour logged, community corporations would have an incentive to find more participants and to assign them to an expanding array of activities, such as community policing or trash-collecting. In return for municipal support, the franchise holder would be expected to keep accurate count of participants' hours, match skills to community needs, make sure jobs are performed well, and prevent fraud and other abuses. This type of system effectively cuts the labor costs of minimum-wage community-service programs by 80 percent.

A larger city might create several franchises, each focusing on a different service, such as sanitation, child care, human services, and environmental protection. Or it might open a franchise for every neighborhood. Already some industrious block associations—with no government or foundation support—are preparing rosters of barterable skills available from neighbors.

Olaf Egeberg, a tall, soft-spoken man in his late fifties, went door-to-door to create such a directory in Washington, D.C. The first directory had 11 entries, but within two years more than 300 neighbors decided to join. Here's Egeberg's description of how he personally has benefited:

The other day I needed an accountant to solve a major problem for me; with the directory, I found one right around the corner. Earlier I needed a graphic artist to do a book cover, and there was a good one two streets away. Someone to teach me more about using the Internet?

Again, just a five-minute walk. These are neighbors. The accountant
even brought his son over. They all remain friends.[34]

Neighborhood directories and Time Dollar systems enable a community to provide a wide range of services that the market is failing to deliver.
They not only improve the quality of community life and citizens' sense of
mutual obligation, but also provide real economic benefits. A community
with less trash and better services will attract new residents and see property values rise. A community with less crime and more beauty will draw
more tourists and more outside customers, which enhances the economic
multiplier and strengthens the local tax base. Municipal-government
investment in community corporations to administer Time Dollar systems
can be seen as a Keynesian stimulus on the cheap.

There is one other way in which officials can boost local hiring. They
can induce the smartest, most economically productive members of the
community to stay put. Today, the world economy draws the best and the
brightest toward a small number of "global cities" like New York, London,
and Tokyo.[35] While it may be impossible to stop such hemorrhaging altogether, a community could put in place modest incentives to encourage at
least some of its talented young people to stay. For example, it might give
special low-interest loans to promising high-school graduates, conditioned
on their agreement to resettle in the community after college. Those who
returned would receive repayment deferrals and perhaps also subsidies,
while those who abandoned the community would have to repay immediately, at market rates.

LOCAL TAXES

A fifth tool which local governments can use to stimulate the spread of
community corporations is taxation. Giving tax breaks only to community
corporations, already mentioned, is one useful approach. A community
also might consider abolishing taxes on community corporations altogether. Conservatives have long questioned the fairness and usefulness of corporate taxation, and it's time for progressives to reconsider their own views
on this. Businesses are really institutions comprising people. If government
is careful to tax the stocks and dividends of business owners as personal
income, why must it also tax profits again through special corporate taxes?
Shouldn't a society committed to fair taxation be more interested in taxing

rich people once, than in taxing all kinds of business owners, successful and unsuccessful, twice? The fear that owners would snatch up the tax breaks and move elsewhere is alleviated if the exemption is available only to anchored community corporations.

What would be the fiscal impact on state and local governments were they to abolish taxation on community corporations? Not very great. In 1990, corporate taxes accounted for only about 3 percent of state and local government revenues.[36] Even in the wildly unrealistic scenario in which every existing corporation converts into a community corporation to get the tax break, the impact on state and local budgets would be slim. Of course, from the standpoint of a corporation, the removal of local tax burdens can make a huge difference to the bottom line. The abolition of taxes on community corporations would be an incentive not only for existing corporations to transform themselves into community corporations, but also for entrepreneurs to create them. It also might provide an incentive for outside businesspeople to relocate to the community and convert their firms into community corporations. It would essentially transform the community into an enterprise zone, but with protections ensuring that the beneficiary businesses serve local needs, hire local residents, bolster the local multiplier, and remain committed to staying.

State and local governments actually need to rethink their entire tax systems. The vast majority of their revenues come from three sources: sales taxes (25 percent), property taxes (20 percent), and federal grants (18 percent). Two of these sources, sales and property taxes, are regressive—which means they fall disproportionately on people who can least afford to pay. Sales taxes are regressive because poor people spend relatively more of their income on taxed daily purchases like food, clothing, and rent than wealthy people do. Property taxes are regressive because some large landholders, like family farmers and nature conservancies, have relatively little disposable income. As long as the local tax base remains regressive, government is limited in its ability to raise revenues to pay for basic public services, such as schools, trash removal, infrastructure repair, parks, and the like. Moreover, as long as there is no local tax on income and wealth, an exemption for community corporations makes it possible for the rich to escape local taxation altogether by hiding their wealth in corporate stock.

Reformers might consider restructuring property taxes along the lines suggested by economist Henry George in 1879.[37] George proposed restricting property taxes to unearned income derived from appreciation of all land in the community. Why, he asked, should individuals profit from *social* investments in wise land-use planning, decent schools, beautiful parks, and so on? Returns on such investments should be taxed away and shared by the entire community. Property taxes would rise and fall with the overall performance of the community, which would eliminate any incentive for speculation. Moreover, if someone makes his or her land more valuable, for example, by converting a dump into a successful farm or by replacing a mansion with a block of 100 affordable apartments, no property taxes should be assessed on such investments. A Georgian tax system therefore is often called a split-rate tax: high property taxes on unearned income, and low taxes on income from improvements.

A city adopting Georgian taxes would enjoy many practical benefits. Investors would no longer find it profitable to hold onto empty lots or abandoned buildings. Residents living near new subway or light-rail stations would no longer risk being bought out by developers and pushed to resettle in distant suburbs; instead, the escalating value of such land would be taxed back and perhaps reinvested in more mass transit *within* the city. After implementing a modest split-level tax over seven years (with an effective property tax rate on buildings three times that on the land itself), Pittsburgh experienced a spectacular increase in new construction and a civic renaissance.[38] Carefully taking note, 15 cities in Pennsylvania are now using some form of split-level property taxation.[39]

Another, more radical proposal would be for state and local government to scrap their property taxes and sales taxes, and to replace them with simple income taxes. Today, the total share of state and local revenues made up by progressive income taxes is 14 percent.[40] This actually understates the regressive bias of local taxation. Forty-four states tax personal income, but few local governments do. Almost no states even *permit* their local governments to implement progressive taxes, and those that do so grant only limited rights. New York City, for example, must come begging to Albany any time it wishes to tinker with its municipal income tax. So reform must proceed simultaneously at the state and local levels.

Environmental economists argue that income taxes should be replaced by "green taxes." Why place burdens on labor, they argue, which we should want to do everything possible to encourage? Why not place them instead on pollution and consumption of resources (both renewable and nonrenewable), which we should want to discourage? The argument for green taxes is stronger, however, than the argument against income taxes. In the absence of taxes on wealth, income taxes are the best means to accomplish a very valuable social function—redistributing money from rich to poor. There is no good reason why a local government shouldn't aim to conserve *and* redistribute.

The problem is that green taxes, like sales taxes, fall most heavily on people who spend relatively more of their income on goods and services. When President Clinton proposed to implement a modest green tax on gasoline in 1993, arguments that truckers and blue-collar commuters would disproportionately shoulder the burdens helped kill the bill in committee. If we care about ensuring that most tax burdens fall onto those people most capable of paying, then income taxes and green taxes should be viewed as complementary. A local government should consider a package of tax reforms that simultaneously *raises* green taxes on local resource use and *lowers* income taxes on the poor and middle class.

Local green taxes could accelerate the expansion of the basic-needs industries. Take water conservation. By placing a tax on water so that its price reflects not only the real costs of production but also the environmental costs, a municipal government can cut water use, conserve water tables, and make water-efficiency service companies more lucrative. Rebates might be available to the poor, to remove the regressivity of the tax. The municipality could then invest the taxes in restoring the integrity of local water resources by cleaning up pollution and refilling exhausted groundwater supplies. A community that distrusted public agencies might use the collected funds to put local businesses and environmental groups on contract instead. If the tax did not produce enough revenue to restore the water resource and ensure that annual demand did not exceed the annual supply, it could be increased. Once a sustainable level of extraction was reached, the tax could be lowered.

This kind of model is relevant to the commercial exploitation of every natural resource. A public policy which places taxes on resource use decreases the competitiveness of businesses that rely on that resource. But it also stimulates new businesses which use the resource more efficiently. The loss to some businesses from no longer having unlimited rights to exhaust limited resources or to dump pollutants without charge is more than compensated for by the viability of new businesses based on low-resource use and clean production. Paul Hawken suggests that government should assess taxes on every fish taken from a river system through a "salmon utility." Municipalities might set up similar utilities for forests, wildlife, endangered species, and farmland.

Just as local governments can provide important incentives for community corporations to exploit the conservation of natural resources, they also can provide important incentives for community corporations to get started in waste management. A community that places a small tax on, say, local sellers of aluminum products like cans, foil, and car parts, improves the economics for aluminum recycling. Money collected can then be rebated to consumers who bring back the aluminum for recycling. If too much aluminum is still in the trash, the tax can be ratcheted up.

The city of Curitaba, Brazil, has received international recognition for its creative garbage utility. To rid itself of serious public-health problems associated with trash piling up in the local *favelas* (slum areas where the exploding numbers of poor Brazilians live), the city essentially paid residents to recycle. Anyone who brought separated trash to recycling centers on the edge of the favelas received chits for free bus service. Organic waste, which local farmers used for fertilizer, earned the gatherers chits for food. The plan simultaneously eliminated a municipal waste problem, removed a major cause of disease, promoted mass transit, and reduced the city's dependence on outside resources.

Most of the green-tax proposals bandied about are national in scope. But the chilly reception given to President Clinton's very modest green-tax proposal suggests the prospects for federal action are practically nil. Leadership is proceeding, however, at the state level.[41] In 1989, Minnesota placed a 6.5 percent sales tax on garbage collection, and directed that the revenues be used to finance programs for recycling, reducing waste, and cleaning up toxic landfills. Iowa's Groundwater Protection Act imposes taxes on pesticide and fertilizer sales and mandates that revenues be reinvested in the promotion of sustainable agriculture. Proposition 99, approved by Californians in 1987, collects a 25-cent tax on every pack of cigarettes, to pay for public programs to discourage smoking, treat nicotine addiction, and pay for public-health problems associated with smoking.

Communities certainly have an incentive to go further. Green taxes simultaneously help clean up local ecosystems, stimulate the creation of community corporations, and put new revenues into the hands of the local government. If local governments wait for state or national bodies to craft such taxes, they may find themselves legally preempted from doing so, and unlikely ever to see the revenues. A local government that takes the initia-. tive, in contrast, knows that every green-tax dollar collected goes into the local treasury and can be reinvested for local environmental protection and local business creation.

A QUESTION OF POWER

Armel Richardson, a propane dealer, was mayor of Nowata, Oklahoma, when Wal-Mart came in and built a store in 1982.[42] "We welcomed them," he reminisced to a *New York Times* reporter in 1995. The choice was apocalyptic. Half the local shopkeepers soon went belly-up as residents flocked for the huge selection of cheap goods from all over the world. "In an apparent departure from Wal-Mart's old emphasis on American goods," the *Times* reported, "this is a United Nations of merchandise. There are men's Gitano sports shirts made in Bangladesh, Western Frontier cowboy shirts from Qatar, $7 Gitano suede skirts from China. . . ."[43]

In 1994, Wal-Mart pulled out of Nowata. Not because its store was losing money, but because Wal-Mart wanted to open a still larger "supercenter" 30 miles away in Bartlesville, and didn't want its stores competing against one another. The closure stunned residents of Nowata and punched a hole in the local economy. The loss of sales tax from what was once the city's largest business created a shortfall of $80,000 in the municipality's budget. But Ken Murnan, a local newspaper publisher, reflects that if the town is honest with itself, it cannot hold Wal-Mart exclusively at fault: "I could argue that Wal-Mart came in and raped the community. By the same token, I could argue that we did this to ourselves."[44]

Few local governments in the world enjoy the powers that American communities have to prevent this kind of economic debacle. U.S. mayors and city-council members have a policy toolchest that enables them to invest, contract, zone, tax, lobby, and police. They have the ability to spend public funds on almost anything. While these powers are not unlimited, it's fair to say that the problem facing U.S. local governments is not the absence of powers, but the absence of political will to exercise them.

Antigovernment rhetoric has gone so far in recent years that we've forgotten many of the ways in which municipal initiative can promote local business. To the examples of local reinvestment, purchasing, hiring, and taxes previously discussed should be added the probusiness impacts of certain kinds of regulation. Starting in the 1970s, California began setting efficiency standards for manufacturers of refrigerators, air conditioners, TV sets, computers, and so forth. The result? Companies mindful of efficiency have thrived. In 1990, California mandated that car manufacturers make 2 percent of all vehicles sold in 1998 "exhaust-free." This mandate has since been relaxed, but not before seven of the biggest car manufacturers committed themselves to putting 800,000 electric cars on the state's roads over the next decade.[45]

The possibilities for action laid out in this chapter suggest how communities can sort out sensible economic policies from nonsense. The next time your city council meets to discuss economic plans for the future, here are some hard questions to ask:

• Why should the city provide support to any corporation that is not locally owned and operated? Shouldn't community corporations be the exclusive recipients of municipal subsidies, tax breaks, and pension investments?

• Why should the city lift a finger to help shopping malls that discourage purchasing from local producers? Why not instead underwrite local labeling, import substitution, and currencies that enhance the economic health of local businesses?

• Why throw money at the best and the brightest, only to have them move away from the community when they reach maturity? Why not, instead, create financial incentives for young adults to stick with the community that nurtured them?

• Why continue to place taxes on sales and property that fall disproportionately on those least able to pay? Why not restructure the tax system around income and resource use, to promote business expansion, environmental cleanup, and equity?

These policies only begin to scratch the surface of what a committed local government can do to move toward self-reliance. A city might link its citizens with its civil servants by computer, as Santa Monica does with its Public Electronic Network, so that creative ideas can keep flowing toward decisionmakers. (Affordable housing activists, for example, used terminals in Santa Monica's libraries and community centers to help officials design new public facilities to provide the homeless with showers, washing machines, and lockers.) A mayor might hold an annual set of public hearings requesting suggestions for new ways to promote local investment, purchasing, hiring, and taxation. However, to incubate a self-reliant economy over the long haul, it also must be vigilant that the federal government doesn't stand in the way.

Bringing Home Power, Not Bacon 6

Politicians across the United States see bringing home goodies from Uncle Sam's superstore as a central part of their job. Success is securing $100 million from the Department of Transportation for a new light-rail system, or convincing the Department of Defense to keep open the local Marine base, or winning a contract from the Department of Energy to be the site for a particle accelerator. The public may suspect that only big-spending Democrats are devout believers in the federal pork barrel, but the truth is that elected officials from both parties play the game and, come election time, brag about their accomplishments.

And so a natural impulse of a municipality trying to create a thriving network of community corporations is to figure out ways in which the federal government can finance its efforts. Which federal grants or loans might be available for new industries? Can proposals be fashioned around local groups of women, minorities, elderly, youth, and small-business people that might qualify for some special program? The temptation to rely on federal money to jump-start the local economy, however appealing, should be resisted.

Federal aid almost always undermines community self-reliance. A municipality dependent on federal dollars loses control of its economic future. Look at the communities that once enjoyed hundreds of millions of defense dollars being pumped into their local weapons manufacturers or military bases. Now, with military spending dipping below its Cold War peak, hundreds of defense-dependent communities are struggling to keep their heads above water. Some argue that the federal government should come to the rescue with "economic conversion"—*another* federal bailout. Addiction, however, cannot be solved by feeding a bad habit. A community should never allow its economic heart and lungs to be hooked up to a blood supply thousands of miles away.

Federal aid not only undermines community self-reliance, but also raises questions of fairness which should be as troubling to liberals as they are to conservatives. Why should some communities prosper from federal benefits while others suffer from neglect, if taxpayers across the country are footing the bill? A process in which the federal government picks winners and losers cannot help but become highly politicized. Should the economic fortunes of a community depend on the clout of its two senators, the committee assignments of its representatives, or the college connections of its mayor to key federal agency heads?

There *is* a legitimate role for the federal government to play in redistributing resources between rich and poor communities. Regional inequalities cause migration and economic upheaval. They create wildly disparate opportunities for children to receive basic nutrition, health care, and schooling that effectively punish poor kids for being born into poverty. But the federal government needs only one program to address these inequalities, not the complex web of 500 separate grant systems spun in the 1960s and 1970s.[1] That program should have been General Revenue Sharing.

President Richard Nixon sold Congress on General Revenue Sharing in 1972 with a simple premise: The federal government knows how to collect taxes efficiently, while local governments know how to spend tax revenues effectively. The program gave every community, every year, a no-strings grant. The size was determined by population, local tax effort, and per capita income—and the formula left no discretion to national bureaucrats. At its peak, General Revenue Sharing recycled about $7 billion a year, and it operated for more than a decade without any notable scandals. But in the early 1980s it fell victim to the budget-cutting axe of President Ronald Reagan. Devolution-minded politicians in Washington should consider bringing the program back.

There certainly are other legitimate rationales for federal involvement in community economies beyond remedying regional inequities. The national government should set basic standards for civil rights as well as for the protection of consumers, workers, and ecosystems. But if we take the principle of subsidiarity seriously, national standards will be relatively few, and enforced first and foremost by state and local authorities. This was in essence the view of the Founding Fathers.

The Constitution represented a grand compromise between nation-builders and state-protectors. Federalists like Alexander Hamilton and James Madison sought to remedy the defects of a weak Articles of Confederation by creating a strong central government with effective judicial, legislative, and executive powers. The Antifederalists, who controlled many of the state legislatures in 1787, believed that the key to participatory democracy was to keep power fragmented, checked, and decentralized. The two factions, meeting in Philadelphia, hammered out a plan in which the states and the national government were given enumerated powers. The national government held such powers as regulating commerce, collecting taxes, and declaring war, whereas state governments retained such powers as electing senators and organizing militias. When it appeared that the colonies wouldn't ratify the Constitution, the Federalists agreed to a set of amendments to appease the Antifederalists. The last of these, the Tenth Amendment, resolved any uncertainty about the proper allocation of authority in the new nation: "The powers not delegated to the United States by the Constitution, nor prohibited by it to the States, are reserved to the States respectively, or to the people."

What started as a meticulous balance of central and local spheres of power tipped toward a stronger national government over the next two centuries. The Civil War established that the national government was to have final, preeminent power over disobedient states. The New Deal expanded the federal government's involvement in the economic and social spheres. The Cold War created a gigantic complex of military and intelligence institutions insulated from normal political accountability by rules of secrecy, black budgets unreviewable by elected politicians, and an official ethos of "plausible deniability."

The gradual accretion of national power and diminution of state and local power has drawn criticism from across the political spectrum. Conservatives embrace states' rights and a new federalism, while progressives promote community empowerment and communitarianism. There seems to be an emerging national consensus that communities would be better off if they had more power to manage their own affairs. Despite the broad powers that U.S. local governments have, the federal government still stands in the way of their fully using them. Communities can move toward self-reliance much faster by removing these federal impediments, especially in the areas of home rule, trade, corporations, and banking.

REAL HOME RULE

Despite the many powers available to municipal governments, city attorneys—mindful of the costs and embarrassment of lawsuits—counsel local leaders to define them narrowly. Right now, communities are getting very mixed messages from Washington. Democrats talk about saving America's cities, but continue to favor large-scale federal programs that either legally quash or elbow out local initiatives. Republicans preach states' rights, but their 1994 Contract with America actually would have preempted state and local laws governing civil rights, consumer product safety, labor standards, and environmental protection. Were the federal government to hand over more power to states and localities—and mean it—recalcitrant local officials might feel more comfortable in undertaking the kinds of initiatives outlined in the previous chapter.

A serious commitment to the principles underlying the Tenth Amendment would prohibit the federal government from overriding community laws, except when Congress expresses a clear intent to preempt, or when simultaneous compliance with local and federal laws is impossible. Today, however, federal courts also will preempt state or local laws whenever they find federal policies "frustrated" or the federal government "occupying the field" of legislation.

In 1990, for example, the Supreme Court would not allow California to demand a higher minimum water flow in the South Fork of the American River than the Federal Energy Regulatory Commission (FERC) did, on grounds that it frustrated the purpose of the Federal Power Act.[2] California wanted a higher flow to protect fish, but FERC was more interested in optimizing operations of a hydroelectric facility. The Federal Power Act seemed to envision concurrent authority of the states over waterways: "Nothing contained in this chapter shall be construed as affecting . . . the laws of the respective States relating to the control, appropriation, use, or distribution of water used in irrigation or for municipal or other uses. . . ."[3] Even though there was no explicit language in the Act expressing Congress's desire to preempt state fish-conservation laws and Californians would have no difficulty obeying both federal and state regulations, the Supreme Court decided to strip California of authority over the flow of the American River. Justice O'Connor wrote: "Allowing California to impose significantly higher minimum stream flow requirements would disturb and conflict with the balance embodied in that considered federal agency determination."[4] This is the kind of subtle expansion of central authority that deters creative policymaking at both state and local levels. Congress should consider passing a Community Rights Act, in which it would narrow the grounds on which federal courts could preempt state and local legislation.

State governments also sometimes stand in the way of community empowerment. Each state is legally responsible for defining the powers of its communities, and even seemingly broad home-rule doctrines impose surprising limits on local policymaking. As noted in the previous chapter, courts in Pennsylvania prevented Pittsburgh from implementing a law requiring a local corporation to file an "economic impact statement" before departing because the ordinance was viewed as beyond the city's powers. A priority for community development must be to convince state governments to grant broader powers to municipalities. State-level Community Rights Acts should ensure that local governments have the power to act unless a specific state law expressly mandates otherwise.

One critically important power that needs to be expanded on behalf of communities is taxation. Communities look to higher levels of government for handouts because they don't have the powers of progressive taxation to fend for themselves. State governments could amend their Home Rule statutes to give municipalities the power to assess progressive income taxes. The U.S. government could push this kind of legislation by conditioning certain federal monies on a state's willingness to give its communities the right to enact such taxes. How differently community activists would be received in Washington if they wanted not more federal tax money, but more power to tax themselves so they could reduce transfer payments.

A clear congressional pronouncement on green taxes (which wouldn't cost a penny) could help spread them. Even if Congress cannot muster the courage to pass resource-based taxes, it should at least permit local governments to do so. There's a good argument that local governments already have this power. A community BTU tax, assessed evenhandedly on goods originating from either inside or outside the community, probably would not be found to be infringing on interstate commerce, in violation of the Commerce Clause of the U.S. Constitution. But, just to clear up any doubts, Congress might pass a resolution clarifying that it does not regard green taxes as interfering with commerce. This would immunize from court challenges communities implementing them.

Devolution may well proceed below city government to neighborhoods. Poverty is increasingly concentrated in the nation's biggest cities. As Harvard University sociologist William Julius Wilson writes: "[T]en cities accounted for three-fourths of the total rise of ghetto poverty during the 1970s. One-third of the increase was accounted for solely by New York City, and one-half by New York and Chicago together. By adding Philadelphia, Newark, and Detroit, two-thirds of the total increase is accounted for."[5] America's biggest cities seem to be its most economically dysfunctional.

The larger a political entity, the more difficulty a citizen has identifying with or caring about his or her neighbors. For people to have a meaning- ful *feeling* of community, they need to know, communicate, work with, and trust their neighbors. The larger a city gets, the more impersonal its social relations and the more bureaucratic its governance becomes. One recent study found that "voting turnout in all West European countries and states studied was highest in municipalities of less than 5,000 population, and scaled quite consistently downward through increasingly larger size cate- gories."[6] It concluded that "a movement toward smaller units might tend to result in a higher level of participation, at least if those units have impor- tant responsibilities."[7] This suggests the value of America's cities reorga- nizing themselves into smaller, more manageable neighborhoods—per- haps in the range of 5,000 to 10,000 people.

A United States with thousands of additional small communities, each financed with progressive taxes, each empowered to govern creatively, each with inhabitants who genuinely know their neighbors, would be a powerful incubator for community corporations. Smart national and state politicians should see this kind of devolution not as threatening their power, but as freeing their levels of government from social, economic, and political problems that must be solved primarily at the local level.

A NEW APPROACH TO TRADE

No area of power allocation requires a more radical rethinking than trade. A sensible, well-balanced relationship between the national government and communities is now giving way to an autocratic system in which global trade agencies can overrule community decisionmaking. And few community leaders are even dimly aware of the revolution under way.

Only a handful of advocates of self-reliance believe that communities should be permitted to place tariffs on outside goods. To make a local protectionist system work, goods-confiscating checkpoints would be needed at every community entrance. Such measures turn out to be either repressive or silly. If border policing is weak, smart producers gladly set up shops that sell foreign goods just past the borders, and smart consumers gladly frequent the border stores. Protectionism also carries a moral hazard. Fox, Arkansas, is a rural county where the antiliquor laws have remained in effect because of effective lobbying by its main church. A closer look, however, reveals that the county is hardly dry, since liquor stores on the borders do a thriving business. Rumor has it that the liquor stores contribute generously to the church's lobbying efforts.

The basis for the strategies discussed in the previous chapter (such as local investment, local purchasing, and local employment) should be enlightened consumer choice, not ham-fisted government coercion. Consumers should be free to save, buy, or hire as they see fit. In a self-reliant community they will see a value in local preferences, and make choices accordingly. And their local government will be proud to set a positive example with its own choices. The municipality might raise standards for business concerning wages, working conditions, environmental protection, and community ownership, but these would be applied in a nondiscriminatory way to all businesses operating in the community—local, national, and foreign.

The U.S. Constitution actually embraces this vision. Current court doctrines prohibit state or community governments from putting tariffs on outside goods, services, investors, and businesses, but allow localities to enact a wide range of *nondiscriminatory* laws that impinge on commerce. The key is that state regulations must be applied evenhandedly on local and nonlocal economic players. In 1978, for example, Maryland passed a law banning companies that produce and refine petroleum products from operating any retail service station within the state.[8] Exxon, an out-of-state corporation that faced the prospect of having to sell off 36 gas stations, challenged the law as an unconstitutional impediment on interstate commerce. The U.S. Supreme Court upheld the Maryland law, even though 95 percent of the companies excluded from operating gas stations were based outside the state.

Modern constitutional law also requires that state and local laws may infringe on commerce only if their purpose is to promote community health, safety, and welfare. The Supreme Court, following this doctrine, has invalidated several state laws limiting the length of trucks when the safety rationales for the laws were not clear.[9] But examples of judicial intolerance of state and local lawmaking are rare, and getting rarer all the time. In various cases the Supreme Court has viewed all of the following state or local goals as falling within the ambit of "health, safety, and welfare": "maximizing the financial return to an industry within [a state]"[10]; requiring "that produce packaged in the State be packaged in a particular kind of receptacle"[11]; protecting a state's "citizenry in matters pertaining to the sale of foodstuffs"[12]; "promoting conservation of energy and other natural resources and easing solid waste disposal problems"[13]; and legislating "against what are found to be injurious practices in their internal commercial and business affairs."[14] Any state or local government with competent counsel which can make a credible case about how a proposed law will serve public "health, safety, and welfare" can pretty much legislate as it pleases.

Another recent development in U.S. constitutional law is that state and local governments are now permitted to legislate on behalf of not only "health, safety, and welfare" but also local business interests, at least when they act in the capacity of a "market participant." This probably means that municipalities can invest, purchase, and hire locally.

All of these careful balances, however, were shattered by the recently signed "Uruguay Round" of the General Agreement on Tariffs and Trade. Now, as a result, a new World Trade Organization (WTO) is operating that places profound new restraints on state and local governments—but *none* on corporations. The new WTO gives private enterprises license to relocate factories and to sell products practically anywhere, and substantially limits the power of public institutions to regulate these transactions. It weakens the power of legal authorities at any level to guarantee the safety of goods and services. It forecloses many possibilities for public bodies to enter the marketplace as buyers, sellers, producers, or financiers. It promulgates new rules governing trade and product regulation without democratic decisionmaking or rudimentary due process. And it says virtually nothing about protecting workers, the environment, or communities. In short, it creates a global framework for crude, laissez-faire capitalism reminiscent of the depression-prone policies of Herbert Hoover.

Perhaps the most insidious feature of the WTO is that it systematically strips communities of powers they could otherwise use to protect themselves against the adverse effects of the global economy, and to promote community corporations. Here are some examples:

- *Product Regulation*—The WTO essentially sets ceilings, not floors, for local laws concerning product safety. The Agreement on the Application of Sanitary and Phytosanitary Measures, which governs the regulation of food and beverages, requires a national government to adopt international standards unless it can demonstrate a "scientific justification" for tougher standards.[15] The Agreement on Technical Barriers to Trade places similar rules on measures that regulate "all products, including industrial and agricultural products."[16] Unfortunately, the "scientific" standards and cost-benefit protocols recognized by the WTO are set by Codex Alimentarius and other bodies which are heavily influenced by the industries they are supposed to regulate.[17] Since the U.S. national government is obligated to press state and local governments to modify their laws to conform to international standards, the practical result is that looser international standards have the potential to displace stronger national, state, and local ones.

- *Targeted Subsidies*—The Agreement on Subsidies and Countervailing Measures bans communities from offering financial assistance to business. It prohibits not only subsidies per se but also loans, loan guarantees, tax abatements, guaranteed purchases, in-kind contributions, and price supports.[18] One part of the Agreement prohibits subsidies that cause "injury to the domestic industry of another Member," "nullification or impairment of benefits accruing directly or indirectly to other Members under the GATT 1994," or "serious prejudice to the interests of another Member."[19] "Serious prejudice" may be found if subsidies exceed 5 percent of the value of the firm, if subsidies cover operating losses of an industry or a firm (beyond a onetime bailout), if the government forgives a debt, or if the effect of a subsidy is to "displace or impede" the imports or exports of another Member or to create "significant price undercutting."[20] Since almost any subsidy can have *some* effect on foreign imports or exports, these provisions could prevent not only targeting local-government support for community corporations, but also possibilities for public ownership of factories, banks, stores, and services.

• *Selective Investment*—The WTO leaves some community investment choices intact, but not all. The General Agreement on Trade in Services allows public-employee pension funds to be invested locally. Selective investment of surplus city revenues, however, might be viewed as a prohibited subsidy. A subsidy, under the agreement, includes a "[g]overnment practice [that] involves a direct transfer of funds (e.g., grants, loans, and equity infusion)."[21]

• *Selective Contracting*—The WTO limits some state government purchasing and contracting decisions, though not those of local governments. The Agreement on Procurement sets out specific rules concerning the bidding, negotiating, and acceptance of public contracts. According to Article 3, Section 1, government agencies may not discriminate against foreign providers of products, suppliers, and services or against other signatories to the agreement. A strict interpretation of this provision would forbid "Buy American" rules. Had it been in effect during the 1980s and had South Africa been a signatory of the Agreement, it also would have outlawed the policies of various state agencies that did not allow firms tied to the apartheid system to bid on public contracts. Every country signing the Agreement on Procurement specifically lists "subcentral government entities" it deems covered by the agreement, and the United States thus far has convinced 39 state governments to sign on.[22] The Office of the U.S. Trade Representative has taken the position, unofficially at least, that unlisted states and state agencies are not covered, but that once a state signs in, it cannot change its mind and leave.[23]

• *Local Labeling*—The Agreement on Technical Barriers to Trade covers not only technical regulations and standards but also "packing, marking and labelling requirements."[24] Community labeling practices that induce consumers to purchase local goods could be found to contravene WTO's requirement that "products imported from the territory of any Member shall be accorded treatment no less favourable than that accorded to like products of national origin and to like products originating in any country."[25] Encouraging local production and consumption is not considered a legitimate objective of regulation. Other kinds of community labeling requirements that demanded identification of, for example, whether a product was made from recycled materials or from child labor also might be challengeable.

• *Local Currencies*—The General Agreement on Trade in Services states that "each Member shall accord to services and service suppliers of any other Member, in respect of all measures affecting the supply of services, treatment no less favourable than that it accords to its own like services and service suppliers."[26] A community-run currency system could be interpreted as a discriminatory banking service, should a local authority play a role in issuing currency or setting rules of exchange meant to induce community members to buy local (and not international).

• *Local Resource Conservation*—Only some kinds of community initiatives to promote sustainable use of natural resources are now acceptable under the WTO. Nondiscriminatory regulations and taxes are permitted, but subsidies or tax breaks for local-resource producers are not. Foreign aluminum or paper producers could challenge local subsidization of a recycling program on the grounds that it was adversely affecting their exports. Canadian exporters of oil, gas, or electricity could attack U.S. community-conservation programs or publicly owned utilities. Foreign food exporters might be able to convince U.S. courts to invalidate local government expenditures designed to induce consumers to buy local grains, fruits, and vegetables.

No one can say for sure whether the WTO will operate in the onerous ways suggested above. Like any statute, a treaty must be interpreted by courts and dispute-resolution bodies at the international, national, state, and local levels. Technically, only a member country can bring a complaint against a U.S. local law. If a WTO panel decides that the law is impermissible under the treaty, the United States can appeal the decision. If an appeal fails, the federal government has 60 days to decide whether to repeal the law or to face trade sanctions.

These checks and balances, under closer scrutiny, turn out to be illusory. WTO panels are made up of trade experts who, true to their neoclassical philosophies, have little or no sympathy toward an economics of place. It's telling that one of the first decisions to be handed down by the WTO held that U.S. environmental standards on gasoline cleanliness placed unjustifiable burdens on imports of more-polluting Venezuelan and Brazilian gasoline.[27] Decisions can be appealed only if the more than 120 other signatory nations *unanimously* agree to reverse. In other words, appeals are virtually impossible.

The Clinton Administration helped sell the Uruguay Round to Congress by emphasizing that no U.S. law can be overturned by a foreign country or corporation using a U.S. court. Only the U.S. Trade Representative can do so, with the permission of the President of the United States. This is technically true, but doesn't much matter. If, say, several aluminum producers convince an aluminum exporting country to challenge New York City for subsidizing its recycling industry, will the President of the United States risk tariffs on all U.S. imports of aluminum? Recent history suggests that when it comes to global trade, federal bureaucrats are likely to be more sympathetic with the fantasy of a global free market than with the pesky pleadings of community groups.

Even if federal officials are sympathetic with community laws, global officials may not be. As this book goes to press, the WTO is moving to rule against state and local sanctions against firms doing business in Burma. In 1990, a brutal military junta called the State Law and Order Restoration Council (SLORC) annulled the election and threw leading democracy supporters, including the popularly elected leader, Suu Kyi, into prison. In 1996, the state of Massachusetts and more than a dozen cities decided to retaliate: They refused to enter contracts or purchase goods from companies with significant operations in Burma. Trade officials in Japan and the European Economic Community, whose companies were among those most affected, were fearful that these boycotts could spread to other states and cities, as the sanctions against South Africa did in the 1980s. They warned U.S. officials that if the United States didn't preempt these laws, a challenge would be filed before the WTO. Agents of the U.S. Trade Representative shuttled in and out of Massachusetts to convince then-governor William Weld to repeal the sanctions, but the state held firm. The U.S. government then imposed light sanctions on Burma, banning future investment in the country—but its real purpose may well have been to lay the groundwork for the federal government to quash the Massachusetts law, should the WTO render an anticommunity verdict.

This may be just a sneak preview of what's in store for state and local governments. A new, proposed Multilateral Agreement on Investment seeks to create another international institution within the 29-nation Organization for Economic Cooperation and Development (OECD) that's even more powerful than the WTO. If realized, it could wipe out many of the proposals for local government initiative discussed in Chapter 5. Municipal subsidies, bonds, loans, or tax abatements could not be restricted to community corporations. Banks, insurance companies, and pension funds could not be required to reinvest locally. Limitations on corporate mobility (such as mandatory notice periods before shutdown) would be invalid. And enforcement would be more onerous: Unlike the WTO, the MAI would permit corporations to file complaints against countries.

Even if the MAI never comes into force and the President ignores WTO rulings, state and local laws may be in trouble. U.S. judges have an alarming habit of deferring to free trade in unpredictable ways. If a case arises between private parties on one set of issues, a court might still use the WTO to make pronouncements even without the presence of the U.S. Trade Representative. In the 1971 case of *Bethlehem Steel v. Board of Commissioners,* for example, the California Court of Appeals invalidated the state's "Buy American" Act (which mandated that state and local government agencies purchase goods and enter contracts, if possible, with U.S. firms), partially on the ground that it violated GATT.[28] There was no explicit language in GATT at that time which banned government purchasing preferences, there were no special provisions in the national legislation that implemented GATT, and no declarations were made by the President or the State Department that Buy American Acts were contrary to U.S. foreign policy. Instead, the California court read between the lines of the treaty, shouted a few cheers for free trade, and wiped out the state law. We may be entering an era in which courts throughout the world err on the side of free trade, and interpret the WTO in ways least favorable to communities.

Just as trade itself is not inconsistent with local self-reliance, a global trade agreement *could* be constructed that would prove friendly to communities. It would have to be built upon six principles, each of which would depart significantly from the WTO and MAI regimes.

The first principle would be to set minimum standards for corporate behavior concerning product safety, worker rights and wages, and environmental protection. International guidelines mandating the disclosure of crucial pieces of corporate information, such as its history of plant closures, also would be helpful. Over time, international rules might move in the direction of the social democracies and outlaw monopolistic and oligopolistic behavior, hold trustees and managers criminally liable for egregious acts, and require that a certain percentage of seats on every board be held by labor and community representatives. The central tenet of most trade agreements—that corporations should be freed, and public institutions constrained—needs to be reversed. Corporate charters should be seen not as natural rights that live in perpetuity, but rather as public privileges contingent upon responsible behavior by corporations in every community they affect.

A second principle is that standards enunciated by trade agreements should be floors, not ceilings, for regulation. Any nation, state, or locality that wishes to enact higher minimum wages, tougher environmental standards, or more rigorous information-disclosure requirements should be free to do so. The only trade test should be the one posed by the Commerce Clause of the U.S. Constitution: Are the regulations being applied evenhandedly to foreign and domestic firms? If so, the regulation should stand.

A third principle is that selective investment and selective contracting by public bodies should be left entirely free of the rule of the Commerce Clause. Just as corporations, nonprofits, churches, and individuals may decide where to invest, with whom to contract, and what to purchase, so should states and municipalities. It seems perverse that neoclassical economists touting the central importance of "choice" would deny legitimate political authorities the ability to make market choices.

A fourth principle is to allow government subsidies, except in the rare instance when they are being used purposefully to destroy international competition. Some economists have long pointed out that Americans should applaud decisions by other nations to subsidize their industries. Every foreign subsidy means cheaper products for American consumers, and the opportunities to consume more or to invest the savings in our own industries. If the Japanese want to sell $10 television sets, why refuse to buy them? The popular counterargument—that as soon as the Japanese wipe out the U.S. television industry, they'll raise prices and gouge American consumers—overlooks the fact that whenever television prices exceed competitive levels, American investors once again will have incentives to set up television manufacturers. Only in instances where it is very costly to set up a competitive television factory (where economies of scale are very large) will Japanese subsidies successfully squelch competition. And it makes more sense to outlaw these very specific instances of predatory behavior through global antitrust laws than to eliminate all public interventions in the marketplace.

Subsidies are essential tools for responsible governance, especially where markets fail. Moreover, if a national, state, or local government wishes to support certain industries, provide incentives for certain kinds of research and development, or underwrite certain types of consumption, it should be free to do so. Whether the costs of such subsidies are worth the benefits ought to be up to each community. As the next section underscores, many subsidies not only are foolish but also may have adverse economic and ecological consequences. Yet the massive injections of government capital into industry in China, Japan, Singapore, South Korea, and Taiwan—all of which have grown into formidable global competitors—suggests that subsidies, especially if carefully targeted and time-limited, can have important economic payoffs. Every elected government should be permitted to make its own mistakes.

A fifth principle is that community self-reliance should be seen as a legitimate objective of government regulation, just as local health, safety, morality, and environmental protection are (or should be). If communities use labels and local currency to make it easier for their citizens to identify and purchase local goods, they are not really infringing on trade. They are simply helping consumers to make market choices with full information about the origin of the goods. Moreover, public investments that enable local resources to be used more efficiently or to be recycled do not forbid imports of energy, water, or food; they merely make it unnecessary and unattractive for consumers to rely on such imports.

A sixth principle is that no national or international rules of trade should be adopted unless communities are part of the process. A system of fair representation would ensure that the voices of all the people, and not just those of special interests, are heard. All decisionmaking would be open. Dispute-resolution procedures would respect standards of due process, with reasonable opportunities for appeal.

It is certainly possible to conceive of a global trade regime that comported with these six principles. This kind of agreement would eliminate tariffs and most other barriers to trade, and create a code of conduct for corporations, yet still allow communities to shape their own economies. The regime produced under the Uruguay Round, however, does none of these things. It amounts to a corporate bill of rights that respects none of these principles. A major task for communities seeking self-reliance, therefore, must be to lobby national officials to undo the Uruguay Round, to derail the MAI, and to enact an alternative global trade regime that *protects* community power.

RETHINKING CORPORATIONS

Today the U.S. government also stands in the way of community self-reliance not only with its blind endorsement of free trade but in its lackadaisical treatment of corporations. Most Americans would be stunned to learn that national officials are helping U.S. corporations to move overseas. In numerous federal agencies, from the Export–Import Bank to the Overseas Product and Investment Corporation, are staff, grants, and loans dedicated to assisting U.S. business set up factories and offices abroad. Nowhere is this policy more self-destructive than in the U.S. tax code.

Under current IRS law, a U.S.-based corporation must treat as expenses all the state and local taxes it pays. It can deduct them from its taxable income. If, for example, a corporation with $1 billion in taxable net income pays $100 million in state and local taxes, $900 million is taxable. At the current upper-level corporate tax rate of 35 percent, the total federal tax bill would be $315 million. If the same corporation were based in Seoul and paying $100 million in taxes to South Korea, however, it could treat the foreign payment as a credit against U.S. taxes. The corporation would pay the U.S. government 35 percent on $1 billion of net income, or $350 million, and then be able to deduct $100 million from the tax bill. Its total federal taxes would be $250 million—or $65 million less than if it stayed in the United States!

Corporate tax law also facilitates mobility by allowing deductions for moving expenses. But why should the federal government allow corporations to take a deduction for delivering a devastating blow to a community? The practice seems especially perverse in the face of how many new burdens in terms of unemployment compensation, welfare checks, and so on the departure places on the federal treasury. A corporate tax system supportive of communities would disallow deductions for moving—and might even add penalties for doing so.

The entire system of corporate subsidies and tax exemptions in the United States strangles community economies. The Cato Institute estimates that the government annually gives corporations $51 billion in direct subsidies and another $53 billion through various tax breaks. Many of these subsidies undermine local self-reliance. Farm price supports and water subsidies give large-scale agribusiness an edge over community-supported agriculture. Depletion allowances and insurance liability limits that benefit the oil, gas, coal, and nuclear industries slow down the transition to community exploitation of renewable energy sources. Below-market sales or leases of publicly owned land, forests, and minerals encourage overexploitation for export, rather than sustainable use for local consumption. A comprehensive end to corporate welfare would be a tremendous boon for community corporations.

Perhaps no subsidies are more damaging to local self-reliance than those for transportation. Without them, local production for local markets would become a more economic choice for communities. But shipping of goods over long distances today is quite affordable, thanks to cheap oil and cheap transport. A recent study found that the federal, state, and local governments spend more than $3 billion a year to build, maintain, operate, and oversee highways in just New Jersey.[29] Various agencies bring in offsetting revenues through tolls, gas taxes, licensing fees, and traffic fines, but the net subsidy is still $700 million per year. Extrapolated to the United States as a whole, the national highway subsidy totals about $25 billion annually. This does not take into account the "external" environmental costs of accidents, congestion, air pollution, traffic noise, and vibration damage. The New Jersey study estimated these in the range of $23.5 billion a year. The World Resources Institute, employing a somewhat different methodology, estimates that the annual federal subsidy to cars and trucks is $300 billion a year, more than 30 times federal aid to cities.[30] Strip away subsidies to oil, roads, and transport vehicles, impose green taxes on these activities to internalize the environmental costs, and suddenly long-distance trade is no longer such a great bargain. Once Americans start paying the full costs of hauling people and goods halfway around the world, community corporations will find the economics of local production more and more attractive.

Would any politician dare tinker with energy and transportation subsidies? Recent history gives reason for pessimism. When President Clinton proposed a modest tax on gasoline in his first budget package in 1993, interest groups went ballistic and Congress killed the measures almost immediately. Yet a remarkable left–right consensus is emerging to strip away corporate welfare. The Green Scissors Coalition, spearheaded by the National Taxpayers Union Foundation, a conservative antigovernment group, and Friends of the Earth, a liberal environmental group, recently identified $33 billion of annual government subsidies to mining, logging, fishing, farming, arms, and energy-production industries that were simultaneously wasteful of taxpayer dollars and destructive of the environment.[31]

One way to proceed, which some members of Congress are proposing, is to set up a panel of experts analogous to the Base Realignment and Closure Commission. Recognizing that the end of the Cold War necessitated the mothballing of many redundant military bases but that politics as usual would make it impossible to close them one at a time, Congress appointed a bipartisan panel of experts to come up with a list of sensible targets for shutdown. The agreed-upon rule governing the Commission's recommendation was that Congress had to vote only once, thumbs up or down (and without the possibility of amendment), on the entire package. The tactic enabled a majority of politicians to tell their constituents that even though the local base was on the list, the policy was fair because everyone across the country was being asked to make equal sacrifices. A similar commission should be set up concerning corporate welfare. Put every pork-fed industry on the list (oil, gas, coal, nuclear, tobacco, agriculture, livestock, timber, sugar, helium, chemicals, automobiles, utilities, defense), and let's put the whole thing to a vote.

No bipartisan consensus yet exists on how to handle environmental costs. Many politicians have found a variety of clever excuses to resist internalizing them. Some seize upon the inevitable uncertainty about how to count unusual costs, like lung cancers from air pollution, as a reason not to count them at all. Others argue that future deaths, injuries, and ecological damage should be discounted like future cash gifts, at a rate of 5 percent to 10 percent a year, which essentially assumes that anyone killed a generation from now is worthless. Still others are willing to pretend that if the market does not recognize the costs, they simply do not exist.

Over the past two decades, environmentalists have gained enough economic sophistication to counter these arguments. They have convinced a growing number of utility regulatory agencies to demand "full-cost accounting," which attempts—however crudely—to set prices of electricity that internalize environmental costs. If these efforts continue, more and more businesses will find it economical to use renewable resources, to recycle nonrenewable resources, and to eliminate waste and pollution. If states and communities wish to stimulate the creation of new community corporations, they will continue to move more aggressively than the federal government to ensure that prices reflect full costs.

To the extent that federal tax breaks are still given to business, they might be restricted exclusively to community corporations. In 1996, Senate Majority Leader Tom Daschle of South Dakota and Senator Jeff Bingaman of New Mexico proposed creating the A-Corporation, which would qualify for lower federal taxes and streamlined regulatory treatment.[32] In exchange, the company would have to create portable pension plans and invest in worker training. It would have to retain a unionized workforce or embrace other forms of worker participation in management. It could not use child or prison labor. At least half of its new investment and jobs would have to be in the United States. And it would have to require every local plant to enter a Community Responsibility Agreement, which would limit sudden departures. This proposal would be much stronger if it added community corporations to the list of A-rated businesses. Better still, limit coverage to *just* community corporations.

A more modest reform would amend the tax-code provisions that allow individuals who buy municipal bonds to deduct interest payments, and cost the federal treasury about $2 billion a year. These bonds now are used to support all kinds of corporations, including those that snap up the subsidy and move to Mexico. The federal government might restrict tax-exempt municipal bonds to community corporations.

The bottom line is that the federal government must replace its crazy quilt of preferences for some companies over others with a thoughtful preference for community corporations over globe-trotting ones. These legislative reforms can take place only if both conservatives and progressives rethink their positions. Principled conservatives need to acknowledge subtle ways in which the national government now rewards irresponsible corporate behavior, and strip away these perverse incentives. Principled progressives need to understand that the problem with government policy is not that it's probusiness but rather that it's anti–community business.

NEIGHBORHOOD BANKING

Another impediment to community self-reliance is national banking policy. After the collapse of commercial banks during the Great Depression, the U.S government began serious regulation of the industry under the Glass–Steagall Act of 1933, which provided insurance of $5,000 per depositor through the Federal Deposit Insurance Corporation (FDIC) in exchange for banks' conforming to certain patterns of responsibility. (Federal insurance has since risen to $100,000 per depositor.) Commercial banks had to maintain adequate reserves, limit interest payments, and use deposits exclusively for low-risk loans, not investments. In 1934, a similar system of federal insurance was extended to savings-and-loans and to consumer credit unions.

Federal insurance is the linchpin of modern banking. Without it, few Americans would be willing to place their hard-earned dollars into someone else's hands. And with fewer deposits, banks would be less able to help consumers purchase their houses and cars, send their children to private universities, and start their own businesses. Federal insurance not only made personal financial security and access to credit possible for Americans—it also amounted to a social compact. Banks were given federal support in exchange for serving the public good through judicious lending. Recent efforts to deregulate banks, however, have shattered the compact and created the potential for financial havoc.

A harbinger of the future is the debacle of the savings-and-loan (S&L) industry.[33] The original purpose of S&Ls was to help provide affordable housing loans to poor and middle-class Americans. In 1980, using the rhetoric of deregulation, Congress expanded federal insurance from $40,000 to $100,000 per depositor, encouraging wealthier Americans to place their money into insured accounts. The Reagan Administration allowed investment firms to create "brokered accounts," in which they too could place $100,000 chunks of money into thrifts. The 1982 Garn–St. Germain Act loosened restrictions on who could own S&Ls, what constituted prudent investments, and how much capitalization was necessary for operations. Unscrupulous investors across the country seized the opening, taking over or buying out existing S&Ls, or setting up their own. They redirected loans from housing to commercial real estate, junk bonds, and even stock purchases, all with the protection of federal insurance. And they discovered multiple ways to drain the assets of the S&L to finance personal business schemes, pay for political campaigns, and of course enrich themselves. When all is said and done, the bill on American taxpayers for this mess over the next generation will be as much as half a trillion dollars.

Deregulation has also brought commercial banking near the brink of disaster. Throughout the 1980s, multistate behemoths like Citicorp and Chase Manhattan nearly went under after carelessly investing depositors' money in Third World boondoggles, junk bonds, mergers, leveraged buyouts, and commercial real estate. To give just one example, banks nationwide poured nearly four times the value of their equity into expanding commercial office space, while the population grew by just a trickle. By the end of the decade the predictable result of oversupply occurred—real-estate markets crashed across the country.

Federal insurance should never be awarded to depositors unless the money is used in carefully circumscribed ways for the public good. There are two ways in which policymakers might apply this lesson. One possibility might be to deregulate all banking sectors except the community-development financial institutions (CDFIs). Federal insurance would be limited to banking institutions that were community owned and operated. Consumers would still be able to place their money in deregulated commercial banks, thrifts, and non–community credit unions—but at their own risk. Conservatives might like this proposal, because it would facilitate a wholesale deregulation of most of the banking industry, and relieve the federal government of regulatory and insurance costs. Progressives might see this to be a tremendous boost for improving the community sensitivity of existing banks and for establishing new neighborhood banks. Why should federal money be wasted on any other banks except those that are dedicated to strengthening community economies?

But this kind of radical policy change would be fair only if depositors in banks, thrifts, and non–community credit unions really understood that their savings were no longer secure. Few Americans today, however, appreciate the intricacies of banking law, and few banks and thrifts could be relied upon to share information with their customers that will scare them away. A better approach is to tighten the community-reinvestment obligations on these institutions and to extend them to other institutions.

Tom Schlesinger of the Financial Markets Center has proposed placing currently unregulated financial institutions under federal control in a way that would benefit community. He points out that between 1978 and 1993, the share of all financial services comprising banks, thrifts, and credit unions fell from 57 percent to 34 percent.[34] Americans are increasingly placing their money in mutual funds, pension funds, and other collective investment instruments (the number of mutual-fund accounts grew from 17.5 million in 1981 to 95.2 million in 1993).[35] Meanwhile, businesses now tap finance companies, like General Electric Capital and HFC, for nearly half their short-term loans, which in turn are underwritten through sales of commercial paper to money-market mutual funds.[36] In recent years, new markets have flourished through the creation and trading of mortgage-backed and asset-backed securities, swaps, futures, and derivatives. Compared to current oversight of banks, the federal regulations governing these financial activities are practically nil.

Schlesinger recommends establishment of a National Reinvestment Fund that would place community obligations on all private financial institutions. Premiums assessed on everything from banks to pension funds would be used, in part, to provide seed capital for new CDFIs. The Fund would be administered primarily by the 12 districts of the Federal Reserve System. Why the Fed? Because, Schlesinger argues, promotion of community development was a central part of its original mission when it was created in 1913. The final report of the House Banking and Currency Committee that created the Fed declared:

> *Local control of banking, local application of resources to necessities, combined with Federal supervision and limited by Federal authorities to compel the joint application of bank resources to the relief of dangerous or stringent conditions in any locality, are the characteristic features of the plan as now put forward.*[37]

The Fed itself might be overhauled to promote community development. Under current banking law, it influences lending by banks by adjusting interbank discount rates and reserve requirements. The lower the Fed's discount rate, the more commercial banks can borrow, and the lower the interest rate they in turn will set for customers. Economist Norman

Kurland has suggested that the Fed set two interest rates: a higher tier for credit for consumption, and a lower tier for credit for productive investment.[38] Using the lower rate, the Fed could enact "An Industrial Homestead Act" which would help individuals, employees, and communities obtain low-interest capital to invest in community corporations.

Federal insurance for depositors is not the only subsidy to financial institutions that ought to be either tied to community or cut. Consider all the other national programs related to finance. In 1993, the total face value of all federal loans, loan guarantees, insurance programs, and government-sponsored financial enterprises was over $7 trillion.[39] Nearly half of this sum went to insure commercial banks, thrifts, and credit unions. Of the $151 million allocated to direct loans, about half went to rural areas through the Farm Service Agency and the Rural Electrification Administration, and the rest went to small business, commercial exports, foreign aid, and weapons sales abroad. Federal loan guarantees totaled $700 million, primarily to support student loans, small businesses, and home mortgages through the Federal Housing Administration and the Veterans Administration. Government-sponsored enterprises, with a value exceeding $1.2 trillion, included Freddie Mac, Fannie Mae, Federal Home Loan Banks, and Sallie Mae. (The annual burden on the federal budget to maintain these programs is, of course, substantially smaller than these figures—whatever is needed to cover defaults and administration.)

Careful reevaluation of these programs through the prism of community self-reliance would lead to many of them being axed. Programs that finance the sale of commercial and military products abroad would be eliminated, because they are grounded in an export-promoting model of economic development rather than import substitution. Home and student loan programs might be limited to community banks. Retirement-fund insurance, as well as tax deductions for IRAs and Keoghs (which totaled more than $392 billion between 1995 and 1999), might be limited to Americans who place their funds in institutions that reinvest locally.[40]

COMMUNITY LOBBYING

None of these changes in federal law will come easily. Municipal governments should learn from private corporations how to press national and international bodies to act with greater sensitivity to local interests.[41] They should orchestrate citizen pressure through education, debates, films, newspapers, and letter-writing campaigns. They should set up lobbying offices in Washington and in key international cities like Brussels, Geneva, and Tokyo. They should try to unseat politicians who are unsympathetic to the community agenda, and organize political action committees (PACs) for procommunity candidates.

Perceptions about the propriety of lobbying today are ironic: The leaders of private corporations (which are nonpolitical institutions) have no qualms about trying to influence national politics, while mayors heading local governments (which are political institutions) are inclined to steer clear of appearing partisan. Seeing themselves as subservient to national policies and as lacking the "competence" to address international concerns, many local officials are reluctant to express their opinions over key issues like the WTO, corporate taxes, and banking law.

A recent survey in the United States revealed that the country's 36,000 municipalities have deployed a total of 116 registered lobbyists in Washington, D.C.[42] Most U.S. cities see no need to hire lobbyists because they expect their advocacy to be performed by the National League of Cities (NLC) and the U.S. Conference of Mayors, which receive millions of dollars of municipal dues, in part to support their lobbying operations. But the NLC has only nine lobbyists, and the U.S. Conference of Mayors eight.[43] With the attention of these lobbyists split on hundreds of issues, it's easy to see how they can become overwhelmed.

The existing organizations of cities also have very little familiarity with, or sympathy for, alternatives to neoclassical economics. One can probably count on two hands the number of state or local officials with even the dimmest knowledge about the WTO. The economics "experts" of the National Governors Association, U.S. Conference of Mayors, National League of Cities, and National Association of Counties have been unable to move beyond uncritical boosterism of international trade.[44] If communities are ever to have the powers to cope with globalization, to create sustainable and self-reliant economies, and to govern in a meaningful way, they will need to send their own lobbyists to push the federal government to help—or at the very least to stay out of the way.

Communities should not expect federal politicians to make the changes outlined in this chapter without a fight. Lobbying is slow, difficult, and expensive. It means finding allies in other communities and interest groups willing to support specific political changes. It means being willing to stand up, engage in unpleasant political battles, and lose a few. But unless communities voice their positions, they may wake up one not-so-fine morning to find, as the Greater London Council and six other Labour-run metropolitan authorities did in the mid–1980s, that the national government had summarily abolished them.

Making History[1]

"It's the economy, stupid!" This shopworn slogan, which originally hung in the war room of Governor Bill Clinton's presidential campaign headquarters in 1992, still looms large in the consciousness of every politician. Americans vote their pocketbook, because the health of the economy goes to their perceptions about security, self-worth, and the future. Senator Bob Dole ridiculed Clinton's mantra as "condescending" in his acceptance speech at the Republican National Convention in 1996, but went on to make a 15 percent across-the-board tax cut the centerpiece of his own campaign. Why? Because it's the economy, stupid!

Today, politicians across the ideological spectrum push economic policies with only slightly more scientific support than the reptilian elixirs once sold from the backs of covered wagons. Supply-siders like Dole's running mate, Jack Kemp, are convinced that massive deregulation and deep tax cuts will spur business investment and economic growth. Moderates like former Senator Warren Rudman, who chairs an independent balanced-budget crusade called the Concord Commission, aim to stimulate growth by cutting the deficit and keeping interest rates low. Keynesians like Senators Ted Kennedy and Tom Harkin push the federal government to stimulate the economy by investing in infrastructure, technology, education, and employment. House Minority Leader Richard Gephardt and his whip, Representative David Bonior, advocate responsible trade, which would have the U.S. government impose tougher rules on importers to protect American wages and incomes.

What's striking about these proposals is that they come from the toolbox known as *macroeconomics.* Each is accompanied by a set of national policies—on budgets, investments, taxes, interest rates, public jobs, and trade rules. These also are the policies most removed from the American people. Few of us ever have the privilege of voting directly on federal budget priorities, investments, or tax rates. We are left to watch our TV sets as the leaders of two remarkably similar parties parrot the latest backroom compromises. A committee of the Fed, not accountable to even the President or Congress, meets in closed-door sessions and makes decisions about interest rates. Trade agreements are negotiated in secret, and railroaded through Congress on a "fast track"—without debate or amendment. No wonder so many of us feel uninvolved, uncertain, and uneasy over our economic future.

Any strategy of change that depends primarily on macroeconomics—especially if our goal is community self-reliance—is a dead end. The gridlock afflicting Washington today, with one party controlling Congress and the other controlling the White House, is not likely to break apart soon. Too many commercial interests are committed to preserving business as usual, and too many politicians are addicted to campaign contributions from these interests. Activists on the left or right who seek major political change through reform of national law and policy are kidding themselves. Newt Gingrich's Contract with America, the most coherent articulation of a conservative reform agenda since World War II, was buried within months. Whatever liberals come up with, whether it's a new NAFTA, a national-investment program, or a public-jobs program, is likely to meet a similar fate. Democratic control of Congress and the White House from 1992 to 1994 couldn't deliver health care reform when a clear majority of the public favored it. Even if a miraculous consensus coalesces on Capitol Hill about a new macroeconomic solution, it will ring hollow as long as the American people are reduced to spectators. A country committed to participatory democracy deserves better.

A more promising field of economics for "small-d" democrats is *microeconomics,* the nuts and bolts of consumer and producer behavior: How should firms be organized? Who should own them? What should they produce? With what technology? What should consumers buy? From whom? Microeconomics doesn't depend on the actions of faraway politicians and policymakers. It puts ordinary citizens in the driver's seat. Most of us never will have much influence over what happens in Washington, but we always will have enormous say over what happens in our local economies. As producers we decide what to make, how to make it, and which corporate form to use in so doing. As consumers we decide what to buy, and where to open checking accounts. As investors we decide how to target our pension funds and savings. As voters we decide which of our neighbors to entrust with political power, and we maintain face-to-face contact with them once they're in office.

The late Tip O'Neill used to say that all politics is local. Perhaps it's more accurate to say that all *meaningful* politics is local. The community is the most accessible instrument for collective political expression, because it is where citizens are most likely to overcome forces of corruption, money, and apathy, and to become engaged in a democratic process. It also is where people have the greatest influence over their economic and political relationships—where even small gestures can improve the quality of daily life. Most importantly, it is where policymaking has a human face.

Two detectives from the D.C. Metropolitan Police Department recently came to my institute to discuss what could be done to reverse the epidemic of crime and handgun killings afflicting Washington. Their conclusion after working to solve hundreds of murders? *Someone has to care.* Too many young people now grow up in poor, single-parent families in which love is either tough or nonexistent. With local economies collapsing, the institutions that might have helped (schools, churches, police, civic associations) are in total disarray. Cities have gotten to be so large, and their inhabitants so mobile, that personal contact and trust are virtually extinct.

One detective, an Italian-American who grew up in the hard-edged neighborhoods of Jersey City, reflected on a black man he'd arrested. As he locked the handcuffs, the young criminal cursed about not having a straight way to make a living. The officer, perhaps acting more out of guilt than compassion, called a friend who ran a local auto-repair shop and asked him to give the young man a job when he got out of jail. The young man got a second chance. A miracle happened. Someone cared.

Real caring begins at home. The President, the U.N. Secretary General, the CEO of General Motors, and the like cannot possibly care about the masses they claim to represent, because caring requires a *personal* relationship. This, in a nutshell, is why community matters. A community in which people know and care about each other is the basic building block for all other civilized activities, whether commercial, political, social, or spiritual. If we cannot care about our neighbors, we will never develop the capacity to care about our nation or world. And there is no better expression of caring than to create a local economy which meets the basic needs of every one of our neighbors, and to help other local economies throughout the world do likewise.

TEN STEPS TOWARD COMMUNITY SELF-RELIANCE

Enough philosophy. Your city budget is in the red, key companies are skipping town, vital public services are shutting down, civic institutions are disintegrating, citizens are feeling hopeless. What can you do? Where can you begin?

Throughout this book there are dozens of ideas already working in communities worldwide: Locally owned and operated for-profits, nonprofits, cooperatives, and public enterprises are demonstrating how business can be anchored in a community. New kinds of community corporations are meeting local needs for energy, food, water, and materials. Special banks, credit unions, and microloan funds are providing new sources of local finance. Local currency systems are inducing residents to prefer local goods and services. And local governments are accelerating the transition to homegrown economics by carefully targeting municipal grants, tax abatements, investments, contracts, privatization, and hiring. None of these efforts is a panacea, and any undertaken in isolation from the others is destined to have no more than a modest impact. It's crucial to view these initiatives as a package in which each policy reinforces the others.

The watchword of the Mondragon cooperatives is "We build the road as we travel," and every sustainable community must find its own way. Yet innovations in community economics, taken together, do suggest 10 reliable basic steps.

(1) A COMMUNITY BILL OF RIGHTS

Imagine a plaque on the wall of Cleveland's City Hall with the following words:

We, the people of Cleveland, seek to create a better city for our children by attracting outside business, marketing our wares internationally, and securing as much federal money as possible. We will create a good business climate by keeping wages and environmental protection to a minimum. We will endorse free trade in every forum, even if it reduces our ability to control our economy. And we will make sure our representatives in Washington bring back more than our fair share of pork.

I suspect that most Cleveland residents, if they thought about these words long enough, would summarily impeach the mayor and recall the city council.

The principles governing economic life today are a disgrace. Throughout the country, local politicians favor low-cost goods over high-quality living, multinational corporations over locally owned business, dependence on the global economy over independence through self-reliance, and federal pork over local power. These principles, priorities, and policies thrive—not because they represent what the American people want, but because they are invisible. A first step toward community self-reliance is to open up every nook and cranny of the local economy to scrutiny and discussion.

Market economics is fundamentally about choice—not just consumer and producer choice, but also political choice. What do we want to produce? How? Where? What kinds of goods and services truly are necessities? What should be our standard for worker rights and wages? Is it enough that companies meet the minimal environmental and public-safety standards required by federal and state law, or should we demand more? Should we and all our neighbors be entitled to a living wage, a pension, and a health-care plan? What kinds of ownership structures are best for the community? Most of us have strong feelings about these questions, even though we rarely have been able to express them in public.

An important first step for a community committed to self-reliance is a public conversation. The entire community, and especially its local entrepreneurs, should participate in a series of meetings that culminates in a statement of economic principles and practices—a Community Bill of Rights. This document should elucidate what constitutes community-friendly business and consumer behavior, and be distributed to every household. A citizen board might review the performance of local business, and each year award Good Community-keeping Seals of Approval to responsible firms (and strip Seals from irresponsible ones). Appearing prominently on qualifying goods, store windows, and service providers' stationery, these emblems can influence people's buying, banking, and investing decisions, and give local business a powerful incentive to comply with the Bill of Rights.

To earn the seal, a business might be required to file a comprehensive public report on its performance each year. Ralph Estes, an accounting professor at American University, outlines the kinds of data every business might disclose, in his recent book *Tyranny of the Bottom Line.*[2] What's the salary differential between the best- and worst-paid employees? Is the workforce unionized, and to what extent do employees otherwise have decision-making power? What are the major inputs for production like land, energy, water, steel, concrete, and so forth, and how many of these are imported from outside the community? What are the annual levels of discharge of pollutants and wastes, and what's being done to reduce them? What campaign contributions and lobbying expenditures did the company make? How many lawsuits against the company were filed in courts, how many fines imposed by government agencies, and how many complaints lodged with the Better Business Bureau? What percentage of the ownership of the company rests in the hands of community residents?

The existence of product-rating systems such as *Consumer Reports* and Green Seals suggests that participation of local government is not necessary. Still, the city council could help. It might hold hearings, ratify the Bill of Rights, and pay for the printing and circulation of the document. It might also underwrite the review board, make formal board appointments, and publish a list of community-friendly companies (as Paul Glover's bimonthly newspaper, *Ithaca Money,* does). Every year the council might hold new hearings to consider amendments.

A Community Bill of Rights accomplishes several goals. It enables residents to assert, fundamentally, that ends come before means—that businesses are welcome only if they serve the community. It creates a set of public norms about commercial behavior that protects the public and provides fair notice to corporations. A business's faithfulness to the Bill of Rights, while voluntary, carries consequences. Every time a citizen considers making a purchase, entering a contract, opening a bank account, or investing in securities, he or she will have the list of qualifying companies in mind. Community-friendly corporations will get a commercial advantage over unfriendly ones, and unfriendly ones will be inclined to go elsewhere.

There are precedents for this kind of community goal-setting, though none has dealt with corporate responsibility. Since 1994, Chattanooga, Tennessee, has held a series of public meetings where residents have visualized how they want the city to change. After the 1993 Midwest floods wiped out the city of Pattonsburg, Missouri, 250 homeless residents decided to adopt a Charter of Sustainability, and to ensure that reconstruction efforts proceeded with ecological principles in mind. They rebuilt their homes with the best orientation for capturing solar energy, expanded wetlands to treat pollution through natural biological processes, and installed a methane-recovery system at nearby pig farms. These efforts followed the technocratic vision of sustainability laid out by the President's Council on Sustainable Development and were silent on corporate mobility. Nevertheless, they demonstrated the potential for a community articulating a Bill of Rights.

(2) THE STATE OF THE CITY REPORT

Scholars and politicians debate endlessly over the appropriate scale of a viable economy. Most influential economists, from Adam Smith to Karl Marx, have seen the nation-state as the appropriate unit of planning. Jane Jacobs touted the economic strengths of big cities. Urban planners in academia focus increasingly on regions and "edge cities." To take too rigid a position on this question, however, inevitably neglects those unfortunates who live in unprioritized communities like small towns, ghettos, or mining regions. As Chapter 3 underscored, even small communities have the opportunity to generate their own electricity, grow their own food, recycle water and wood, fabricate local assets into clothing and shelter, create viable service economies, and participate in larger producer networks. The Mondragon cooperatives began in the 1940s in a town with 8,000 people, and even after its spectacular economic success the population has expanded to only 25,000. The potential to create a viable, self-reliant local economy rests in settlements as small as 1,000 inhabitants, perhaps even a few hundred. Who can possibly know until more experiments are tried? As Wess Roberts argues, "Anyone who doesn't make mistakes isn't trying hard enough.">³ To write off *any* community as economically unviable seems premature, unimaginative, and mean-spirited.

Virtually every community in America has a gold mine which econo- mists have yet to discover. Among its veins and other deposits may be found unemployed human resources, underused civic institutions, and dis- carded economic assets. In a wonderful workbook entitled *Building Communities from the Inside Out,* John P. Kretzmann and John L. McKnight of the Neighborhood Innovations Network at Northwestern University show, step by step, how a community can find, assess, and har- ness these resources.⁴ Many kinds of human assets now lie fallow: the inventiveness of the young; the forgotten skills of retirees; the lively minds of the physically disabled; the survival instincts of welfare mothers and the homeless; and the unmarketed talents of local artists. There are underuti- lized associations that make up civil society, especially in America's small- est communities. Drive down the local highway and note who has "adopt- ed" each mile: groups of writers, musicians, artists; the Chamber of Commerce; Elks, Kiwanis, Moose, and Rotary Clubs; youth groups like the 4-H Club, Girl Scouts, and Junior League; soccer clubs and Little League teams; PTAs and after-school groups; women's health clinics and Planned Parenthood chapters; local committees of Democrats and Republicans; liberal and conservative social-cause groups; charities like the United Way; neighborhood watches; ad-hoc organizing committees for special events at Christmas or July 4th; and nonprofit institutions that serve public purpos- es like churches, hospitals, and community colleges. Finally, tally the inan- imate assets that have been all but written off: empty buildings, idle machinery, vacant lots, abandoned industrial sites (known as "brown- fields"), wasted energy, and inefficiently used water.

A community might collect this information in an annual *State of the City Report.* The process of coming together periodically to inventory local strengths can be a powerful unifying exercise for a community. If distrib- uted to every household and business, the study can become a conversa- tion piece kept ready on coffee tables and in waiting rooms alike. Additional copies might be placed in schools and public libraries, or on a home page on the World Wide Web. What's needed is not just a snapshot of assets, but a motion picture of trends. The process of preparing the *State of the City Report* year after year will enable a community to chart what's getting better and worse—and what to do next.

Elizabeth Kline, a professor at Tufts University, has developed a set of community indicators to measure economic security, ecological integrity, quality of life, and political empowerment.[5] To gauge economic security, Kline recommends that a community monitor pensions, savings accounts, loans, inflation rates, wages, taxes, and income distribution. Since the local ecology is an integral part of economic security, she also suggests an inventory of consumption: Are local renewable resources (energy, trees, fish, wildlife, agricultural land, and water) being used sustainably? Are nonrenewable resources like petroleum and copper being replaced by renewables? To assess ecological health, Kline recommends that a community measure wetland areas, soil erosion, species diversity, and water supplies. The community should also monitor buildups of garbage, toxic wastes, and air and water pollution. Quality-of-life indicators of course include rates of longevity, divorce, hunger, homelessness, illness, and crime. Finally, there are indicators of empowerment. Here, Kline would have a community look at the number of community gardens, participation rates in elections and in city-council meetings, and progress toward gender and racial equity in various professions. Indicators are quantitative, but the choice of what and how to measure are inherently subjective. Kline and other advocates of indicators, like the San Francisco–based Redefining Progress, encourage communities to adapt this generic list to local values and needs.

A handful of U.S. cities have moved from theory to practice. Sustainable Seattle, a program launched in 1980, keeps track of more than 100 indicators in surrounding King County.[6] In Jacksonville, Florida, residents decided on 74 key indicators, and have set a series of community goals to reach by the year 2000.[7] Jacksonville grassroots groups have used the indicators to press elected officials to clean up local rivers and to prioritize public expenditures on reducing student dropout rates.[8]

Thus far, indicators seem to do better at measuring environmental performance than self-reliance or social progress. Over time, communities should develop input–output models of their own economies, to uncover exactly where the dependencies are: To what extent are savings and pension funds being reinvested in the community? Which natural resources are being imported? What nonlocal inputs of production might provide the basis for high-value-added industries? What's the community balance of trade? Are the best students moving away? Much of the data necessary to answer these questions will actually be in the annual reports filed by local businesses.

Several cities actually have undertaken these kinds of import–export analyses, and found them extremely useful.[9] In 1979, a nonprofit called Community Economics analyzed ownership, income, and expenditure patterns in Oakland, California. It uncovered three types of leakage from the local economy that helped explain the persistence of poverty in the city: $43 million per year flowing to absentee landlords in rent payments; $40 million going to outside banks for interest payments on mortgages; and $150 million in consumer expenditures being made at stores outside city limits. Eight years later, Chester, a small town in Pennsylvania south of Philadelphia, looked at its own possibilities for import substitution. With assistance from the Rodale Institute and the Presbyterian Church, the community produced a four-volume study documenting the tiny percentage of purchases of energy, food, and banking services being made inside the community that was depriving residents of the benefits of any economic multiplier. Overall, only 16 cents of each dollar earned by a resident of Chester came from local business, and a remarkable 87 cents of every dollar expended went to proprietors outside the community. The Community Renewal Project at the Rocky Mountain Institute has used this type of analysis to help small, rural towns revive themselves.

(3) ANCHOR CORPORATIONS

If done well, the *State of the City Report* will highlight ripe business opportunities in three ways. First, unmet needs suggest new markets for local business. Entrepreneurs, once they see neighbors who are hungry and malnourished, might build greenhouses or enter the business of urban agriculture. As Harvard Business School Professor Michael Porter points out, these demands are especially attractive to new businesses because they are so poorly met today. "[A]lthough the median household income in inner-city Baltimore is 39% lower than that of the rest of the city," he writes, "the aggregate spending power is nearly the same, and the estimated retail spending per establishment is *two-thirds greater* in the inner city than in the rest of the city."[10]

Second, unused or underutilized resources suggest promising inputs for production. Piles of discarded wooden pallets are the raw materials for the Bronx-based Big City Forest, which cuts, refurbishes, and polishes the wood into gorgeous furniture. Second-hand chairs, couches, desks, toys, and computers—all so old that even Goodwill won't touch the stuff—are regarded as invaluable by Urban Ore in Berkeley, California, which specializes in restoring, repairing, and reselling these abandoned products.

Finally, *every* dependency is an opportunity for community corporations. Consumers who discover that the electricity they're using is being transmitted from coal plants hundreds of miles away may be willing to spend another penny or two per kilowatt–hour for local generation alternatives. The Sacramento Municipal Utilities District (SMUD) launched a "green pricing" program in 1994 in which residential users were invited to pay a surcharge of $6 per month to have a 4-kilowatt photovoltaic array attached to their roof and plugged into the community grid.[11] More than 2,000 customers thus far have volunteered.

A community that has committed itself to the goal of self-reliance in its Bill of Rights will, of course, provide a more receptive home for these import-replacing businesses. A community that aims to meet most of its food needs with locally grown produce will entice entrepreneurs to set up a farmers' market or specialized grocery stores. If consumers are willing to pay a slightly higher price for locally made bread, business people will naturally open up neighborhood bakeries.

Nothing is more persuasive than a good example. A generation ago, recycling was an oddball way for Boy Scouts to make a few bucks by collecting and reselling old newspapers. But once a handful of successful recycling operations appeared across the country, imitators proliferated. Today, the recycling business grosses more than $30 billion, and more than 4,000 companies have joined a business association called the National Recycling Coalition.[12] Despite continued pronouncements by unimaginative politicians, cynical journalists, and companies that have invested in incineration, all of whom argue that the economics of recycling will never work, 200 U.S. cities are now making money by recycling more than half of their solid wastes.[13]

The existence of even one or two successful community corporations— using local inputs, producing quality goods, operating in harmony with the environment, selling to local consumers, treating workers well, delivering profits to local shareholders—should inspire others to follow. As the late Kenneth Boulding once said, anything that exists is possible.[14] These new firms will create new jobs, pump up local purchases by employees, and enlarge the local tax base. As they increase the demand for inputs to production, new firms will be motivated to set up shop. Jane Jacobs suggests that

> *an import-replacing city does not, upon replacing former imports, import less than it otherwise would, but shifts to other purchases in lieu of what it no longer needs from the outside. Economic life as a whole has expanded to the extent that the import-replacing city has everything it formerly had,* plus *its complement of new and different imports.*[15]

Community self-reliance does not mean isolation. It means expanding the economic base to produce necessities for residents and to focus existing resources on more value-added industries. It means an economy better insulated from sudden shifts in the price and supply of imports. It means striving to keep a growing share of the economic multiplier at home. The process of import replacing *never* ends. As soon as one set of dependencies are met, new dependencies take their place. But each new dependency is less and less vital to the survival of the whole community. New dependencies invariably open up new local business opportunities, provided there are local entrepreneurs prepared to seize them.

(4) COMMUNITY-FRIENDLY BUSINESS SCHOOLS

Few of us have experience running a business, but then again, neither did the Spanish priest who started Mondragon. If you already have the impulse to serve your community, if you volunteer for a soup kitchen or give to a local charity, consider refocusing those good intentions into starting a community corporation. If you're not up to the task yourself, ask others with business experience to become partners in a new venture.

An important lesson from Mondragon is the central role of training. Many of us who only have a liberal-arts education and limited financial resources have the potential to become good businesspeople. Communities need training institutions that can give us the special skills and confidence to succeed. You might encourage your adult-education programs and community colleges, as Milwaukee does, to emphasize accounting and management instead of bridge and tennis. High schools might be given community funding to beef up vocational training programs. Local nonprofits might set up training schools. In 1994, my institute set up the Social Action and Leadership School for Activists, SALSA, which has provided night classes on running nonprofits for more than 1,500 adults annually in the Washington area.

The transformation of business schools and university economics departments is another imperative. These institutions now celebrate personal profit over community service. Lewis Mumford once observed that industrial society transformed all seven deadly sins except sloth "into a positive virtue. Greed, avarice, envy, gluttony, luxury, and pride [are] the driving forces of the new economy."[16] A startling study at Cornell University found that graduate students in economics, when given an opportunity to contribute to charity, donated less than half what other graduate students did.[17] Their charitable impulse actually declined as they logged more years of training, and scraped bottom when they became professors.

Economics and business need to become professions with the highest principles of charity and public service. And its practitioners should meet the highest standards of professional and ethical conduct. It's absurd for states to require would-be doctors, lawyers, and accountants to pass strenuous, multiday examinations before conferring a license to practice, while the would-be businessperson only needs to write a check for $200 to be granted the privilege of running a corporation. A community might design a business ethics exam to ensure that only firms run by individuals committed to community welfare could receive the Good Community-keeping Seal.

(5) COMMUNITY FINANCE

An important innovation of Mondragon was to link business creation, training, and banking. Even if promising markets and dedicated entrepreneurs are available, *no* business can get started without capital. According to the U.S. Small Business Administration, one out of four new small businesses fail within two years, and nearly 70 percent fail within eight, primarily because of undercapitalization.[18]

Nearly all of us have savings and checking accounts, credit cards, IRAs, and Keoghs at institutions which we chose on the basis of convenience, rates of return, and friendliness—but not community loyalty. Anyone interested in the future who continues this practice is throwing good money away. Even if your current bank scores well by Community Reinvestment Act criteria, chances are good it's not financing community corporations.

There are many ways to localize banking, as Chapter 4 suggested. One option is to persuade your existing bank (whether a commercial bank, a savings-and-loan, or a credit union) to set up a special division that invests locally and allows civic-minded customers to place their savings in that account. Another is to convince your neighborhood association to start a community credit union. The U.S. National Credit Union Administration has certified and insured credit unions with total assets as small as $100,000. If you have difficulty raising enough capital to qualify for federal insurance, you might press your city council to buy equity shares, move payrolls into the bank, or offer either a loan or a loan guarantee.

Once a community bank hangs out a shingle and announces that credit is available for community corporations, local entrepreneurs naturally will step forward. If they don't, the bank should find and train them, perhaps through microenterprise programs. Or, it might set up a special community-development fund in which no-interest loans are exchanged for equity shares and some management responsibility, as Mondragon does. A community bank can support corporate borrowers by encouraging all its depositors to do business with them. It might send a monthly flyer to its customers, with advertisements. Or it might set up an internal trading system among all loan recipients, as the Economic Circle does in Switzerland.

As community corporations expand, so will the need for local investors. A concerted effort must be made to convince your neighbors to transfer their pensions and other assets from global stocks and bonds to local ones, and from mutual funds with no preference for place to local mutual funds targeting local businesses. An important ally in redirecting pension funds might be labor. The trade unions in Canada created investment funds in the provinces of Quebec, Ontario, British Columbia, and Manitoba that now invest $3.1 billion in worker-friendly small and medium-sized local businesses.[19] Municipal-employees' unions in the United States might press to have their pension funds similarly restructured and reinvested locally.

You may be nervous about experimenting with your investments if they are essential, as they are for most Americans, for your children's education and your own retirement. This may be the one area where even the most community-minded of us may be reluctant to sacrifice even a percentage point or two from our rate of return.

Risk, however, is not unique to local investment. Most of us forget that virtually *all* of our investments are now at risk—and uninsured. If the stock market were to crash tomorrow, your long-term financial security could be shattered. And so the real question is whether you regard the current casino economy, rife with speculation and based on exploitation of low-wage workers and collapsing ecosystems, as more risky over the long term than a revitalized local economy. Even if your retirement monies do well in conventional investment funds, it's worth asking how useful are they if your retirement must be spent in a community that's falling apart.

Mainstream financial analysts argue that any restrictions on a universe of investments, whether the preference is for socially responsible or community–friendly corporations, will lower the rate of return. Evidence is mounting, however, that socially responsible portfolios perform as well as irresponsible ones.[20] For example, John Guerard, Jr., director of quantitative research at Vantage Global Advisors, compared the performance of a 1,300-stock universe with a screened universe of 950 socially responsible companies. A dollar invested in the unscreened portfolio in 1987 would have grown to $2.77 by the end of 1994. A dollar invested in the socially responsible portfolio would have grown to $2.74—a statistical dead-heat.

Does risk nevertheless increase when geographical restrictions are imposed? Perhaps. But the remarkable success of Mondragon, in which worker pension funds were reinvested in member cooperatives, should give pause to skeptics. So should the experience of the Quebec Solidarity Fund, mentioned above, which invests strictly in business based in the province. A survey in 1992 found that 87 percent of the Fund's investors, who included both union members and other investors, were satisfied with the rate of return.

Even if geographic limits are ultimately found to impose some risk, there is an intriguing solution. Self-reliant communities could create national—perhaps even global—partnerships with one another. They could pool some of their pension portfolios and invest in one another's community corporations. This would diversify investment options and lower risk, yet in a way that continues to benefit locally owned and operated business.

(6) COMMUNITY CURRENCY

Local purchasing goes hand-in-hand with local investing, and nothing facilitates it better than local money. LETS, Ithaca's HOURS, and other systems demonstrate that designing, managing, and recruiting participants for a community currency is a terrific organizing project. It raises awareness about who lives in the community, which citizens are committed to self-reliance, and what and where goods and services are locally available. It strengthens relationships between local business and consumers. It heightens public appreciation that every purchase is a civic act.

No business should receive a Good Community-keeping Seal unless it accepts local currency. (This requirement is not really punitive, as long as the business is permitted to accept other currencies inside and outside the community.) The underlying principle is simple: Any business that refuses to take local currency is refusing to participate in a communal effort to enhance the local multiplier, and deserves to be shunned. If you won't support the community, the community will no longer support you.

Organizers might try to convince the local government to accept tax payments in local currency. This, in turn, would push that government to make sure that more of its payroll checks were issued in local currency, and that more of its contracts and purchases were with local businesses. Municipal-employees' unions might even ask for wage hikes in the community currency.

The administration of a community currency system provides an important opportunity for members of the community to discuss the local economy and plan its development. Debates over rules of entry (Should the system involve only firms with the Good Community-keeping Seal?) raise important political questions about the meaning of local self-reliance. Deciding on the right money supply democratizes and demystifies choices now made in secret by the economists at the Federal Reserve Board, who care far more about keeping national inflation low than about creating jobs and stabilizing communities.

(7) A COMMUNITY-FRIENDLY CITY HALL

All of the above steps can be taken by individuals and organizations acting unofficially. There is no law in the United States that prevents citizens, working together, from framing a set of principles, awarding seals, compiling a *State of the City Report,* starting locally owned businesses and banks, training community-minded entrepreneurs, waging an invest-local campaign, and issuing a community currency. For each and every one of these initiatives, the participation of local government is not necessary—even though it can add expertise, legitimacy, and funding.

Still, as Chapter 5 detailed, a local government committed to community self-reliance can accelerate the rate of transformation. It can make sure that the only beneficiaries of local investment, contracts, purchases, and bond finance are community corporations. It can help match local-input suppliers and workers with local producers. It can set up scholarship funds that encourage the best and brightest to return home after college. It can restructure taxes on income, wealth, and resources to favor community corporations.

These make up the platform that local politicians should be asked to endorse. Forget the Toyota package and the Wal-Mart deal. Don't get distracted by Jurassic stadium projects or convention centers. Stop letting politicians get away with overlooking the local economic agenda by grandstanding about crime or welfare moms. Remember: It's the economy, stupid!

If your mayor or city-council members refuse to start making the kinds of economic stands that make a difference, consider running against them. Few of the half-million local elected officials in America are professional politicians. Most are volunteers who also are practicing lawyers, doctors, teachers, business owners, assembly-line workers, or activists. It doesn't take a lot of money to win a city-council seat (though, until serious campaign-finance reform occurs, *some* fund-raising is necessary). And, in a medium-size city, a dedicated candidate running for, let's say, a 10,000-person ward, can actually meet most of the constituents by going to churches and businesses, standing at busy intersections and rail stations, and walking each precinct, door-to-door.

(8) POLITICAL REFORM

A community that begins the transformation to self-reliance will soon encounter powerful enemies. Multinational firms that find themselves losing local markets and special governmental privileges can be expected to retaliate. They will lobby state and national governments to take away local-government powers, and continue to use trade treaties and friendly courtrooms, wherever possible, to circumvent the inconveniences of democracy. But their most likely—and dangerous—reaction will be to tighten their grip on local governments. As long as America remains committed to a free market in political power, in which votes and influence can be sold to the highest bidder, multinational firms with huge financial coffers may be able to lobby, campaign, cajole, and bribe politicians away from community self-reliance. The central principle of politics in this country has been transformed from one person/one vote to $1/one vote.

Americans have among the lowest rates of participation in elections in the developed world. While three out of four eligible northern European voters casts a ballot in their national elections, only one out of two eligible American voters participates in presidential elections.[21] Of nine western democracies recently studied, the United States also had the lowest rate of citizen participation in municipal elections, and the largest gap between municipal and national participation rates.[22] It is no secret that Americans are becoming increasingly frustrated with their political system and dropping out.

The widely held perception is that voting doesn't matter. Journalist William Greider writes: "What the disenchanted are saying, what I have heard them say in many different places, is that the politics of elections seem pointless to them—no longer connected to anything that really matters."[23] If elections and policies can be bought by the rich, if the choice of candidates is always between Tweedledum and Tweedledee, if those elected seem to do very little anyway—why bother? Political reform, therefore, is an essential step in creating community self-reliance.

At least four different kinds of reform would be helpful. First, serious campaign-finance restrictions could help dispel the cynical conviction that politics is only for the wealthy. As long as money is an ever more important part of American politics, poor people will be reluctant to run for office or otherwise participate in the political system. One day, a wiser Supreme Court might reconsider the principles of *Buckley v. Valeo,* which equated the unconstrained ability to spend money on political campaigns with the First Amendment's freedom of speech.[24] Until then, local governments should consider creating systems of public financing of election campaigns, which a candidate could opt out of (as *Buckley* requires), but at the price of public humiliation.

A second problem is America's tired political parties. The strong showing of Ross Perot's candidacy for president in 1992 (the best third-party showing since 1912) suggests growing public disillusionment with the two-party system. Unlike their European brethren, America's political parties do not stand for well-defined, coherent ideologies. Foreigners who observe American politics are amazed at how small the differences are between

Republicans and Democrats. The national leaders of both parties today, for example, oppose income redistribution for the poor, military budget cuts, single-payer health care, stronger rights for labor unions, and campaign finance reform. Both parties are dominated by globe-trotting businesses and the wealthy, with grassroots organizations on both right and left marginalized. The emergence of new political parties could sharpen the positions of existing parties, increase the likelihood that at least one party would represent the interest of communities, and make public debate more informative and engaging. The fact that most local elections are nonpartisan actually makes it easier for candidates to align themselves with embryonic parties and win.

A third valuable reform is term limits, which hold the promise of ending the monopolistic control of political offices by a relatively small professional class of politicians. The longer a politician stays in office, the more likely will he or she be captured by special interests. Term limits increase the probability of newcomers, nonprofessionals, and poor people to run for office. Grassroots voices can also be better heard at the polls if citizens have the power to place initiatives on the ballot, and if they have the option to vote for "none of the above" (which would require parties to go back and choose different candidates).

A final key to citizen empowerment is to create ways for people to participate between elections. Communities might create, as Berkeley has, a wide network of citizen-run commissions on different policy issues affecting the community. These commissions might have the power to make small grants, and to place pieces of legislation before city councils. If members of the commissions are elected, they enhance the kinds of checks and balances within city government that can help prevent insularity and corruption.

(9) A LOBBY FOR LOCALISM

Chapter 6 suggested many ways in which communities have a critical stake in regional, state, national, and international policy-making. Local elected officials have to steer the devolution revolution so that they are given real powers over the local economy, and not just more responsibilities without the revenue-raising capacity to pay for them. They need to push the national government to reorient the nation's trade policies away from the centralized autocracy of the World Trade Organization and toward the nuanced principles of American federalism. They must convince Congress to abolish welfare for corporations and banks that have no loyalty to communities.

Today, a local elected official who shuttles to Washington and back is vulnerable to charges of junketeering and not attending to the local potholes. This kind of political thinking is obsolete. If local politicians don't reset the federalist agenda, the captains of community-destroying corporations will. Literally thousands of lobbyists for multinational business are working the corridors of power in Washington, New York, Brussels, and Geneva.

Framing the agenda for community lobbyists is an opportunity for public discussion, input, and planning. The city council—or perhaps a subsidiary body—can hold a set of annual hearings on the community's national and international agenda. It should then invest in professional lobbyists (or at least part of a lobbyist's time) to fight for this agenda on a regular basis.

(10) INTERLOCALISM[25]

Practitioners of community self-reliance must be vigilant against parochialism and isolationism. A community that pulls back from the world cannot assume its serious responsibilities as a part of the world. For too long we have equated responsible global citizenship with economic interdependence. As political scientists point out, however, economic interdependence is constructive only if power among the players is balanced.[26] Interdependence that surrenders power to outsiders carries long-term economic costs and creates the potential for serious conflict. Few communities in today's world have power over the footloose corporations driving globalization. Increased economic interdependence in this context ensures increased dependence, vulnerability, and exploitation.

A more responsible course for a globally minded community is to move toward local self-reliance, and to help other communities worldwide do likewise. How? By transferring innovations in technology and policy that foster self-reliance, especially to the poorest communities in the world that desperately need a new approach to sustainable development. More than 2,000 communities from wealthy countries in the Northern Hemisphere actually have some kind of relationship with an equal number of communities in the Southern Hemisphere. Americans call these relationships "sister cities"; Europeans call them "linkings" and "twinnings." Sometimes they exist only in name, but often they include exchanges of culture, information, technology, finance, expertise, and policy. The best of these relationships don't do this for private profit, but for the public good.

Too many participants in these city-to-city relationships talk the talk of community self-reliance, and walk the walk of mobile capital. U.S. mayors who support sister-city relationships, as well as the leaders of the organization that backs these ties (Sister Cities International), proclaim new contracts for export-oriented businesses to be measures of success. A better measure would be to what extent municipal partners, working together, can *reduce* their dependence on trade.

The city-state of Bremen in Germany, for example, has been spreading biogas technology to help communities become more self-reliant on energy. Since 1979, it has cosponsored three biogas conferences, financed a technical newsletter called "Biogas Forum," and supported demonstration projects through the Bremen Overseas Research and Development Association (BORDA). Over the 1980s, it spent over $300,000 to spread biogas digesters in communities in Mali, Ethiopia, and Tanzania.

Through the Canadian International Development Agency, 22 Canadian cities have taught African civic officials the technical skills needed to design better water and transportation systems. Each participating Canadian city is expected to provide three city administrators or technicians to work briefly in Africa, and to host two or more professionals from its African partner community for three weeks.

To fight deforestation in rain forests, Europeans have pushed municipalities at home and abroad to find local substitutes for tropical timber. Two-thirds of the communities in the Netherlands have adopted an official policy to reduce consumption of tropical timber in municipal building projects "whenever possible." Thanks to letter-writing by cooperative mayors, the campaign gradually spread to other municipalities in Europe and Japan.

Over 150 European municipalities, including 75 from the Netherlands and 20 from Austria, are fighting global warming through the Climate Alliance. Participating northern cities have committed themselves to cutting carbon-dioxide emissions in half by the year 2010 through energy conservation, mass transit, and selective purchasing (they will not, for example, buy products that contain chlorofluorocarbons or tropical hardwood). These cities also are providing financial and legal assistance to South

American communities, primarily those of indigenous peoples, to survey, demarcate, and protect the Amazon rain forest.

All these examples demonstrate how the quest for self-reliance doesn't inevitably lead to isolation. Nothing will spread procommunity economics faster than collaboration among cities committed to the joint pursuit of self-reliance. Communities around the globe need to share information about what's working in community banking, local currencies, urban agriculture, renewable-energy production, and so forth. The International Council of Local Environmental Initiatives (ICLEI), based in Toronto, now has 266 cities, each paying an average of $2,000 in dues to share state-of-the-art technology and policy-making for ecological protection. The United Towns Organisation (UTO) in Paris and the International Union of Local Authorities (IULA) in The Hague are promoting interlocal collaboration on sustainable development. Other global networks of cities are fighting for human rights, arms control, and corporate responsibility. As more communities plug into the World Wide Web and use other forms of telecommunications, this kind of global information-sharing and collaborating should become easier and cheaper.

THE NEW GLOBAL VILLAGE

In a world of increasingly self-reliant communities, there will still be trade and globe-trotting corporations, though the trade will be in less-essential goods and services, and these corporations will have less power over people's lives. One of the continuing challenges for communities will be how to manage these external forces. Those who have worried for many years about capital mobility have hoped to create a global corporate code of conduct. The idea circulated around the anterooms of the United Nations for years, and became a standard demand in proclamations by nonaligned and Third World countries. The U.N. Center for Transnational Corporations even drafted such a code. But global corporations fought back with a vengeance. *The Wall Street Journal* and other conservative media pilloried these efforts, and under U.S. leadership the U.N. Center was dismantled. The result is that global institutions are now promoting corporate freedom through the WTO, rather than corporate responsibility through the United Nations.

Even if the centralized approach to corporate responsibility is moribund, it's possible to conceive of a social charter drafted and implemented at the grass roots level. Imagine hundreds of communities worldwide coming together, formulating a standard code of conduct for corporations, setting up a central clearinghouse of information on corporate behavior, and agreeing to invest in, or purchase products from, responsible corporations. There could be a global Good Community-keeping Seal, which a consortium of communities and nongovernmental organizations (NGOs) might award to corporations that were responsible to their work force, their community base, and ecosystems.

A self-reliant community might ultimately strive to trade only with other communities committed to adhering to this global grading system. Global trade would continue, but only among partners committed to a community-centered vision of commerce. One consequence of this strategy could be the emergence of two global blocs of communities, each following different economic paradigms and each doing business with different corporations. The "neoliberal bloc" of communities might benefit from cheaper goods and higher rates of return off their investments, but also would have to endure deteriorating working conditions, environmental collapse, and community instability. The "socially responsible bloc" might wind up paying higher prices, but would enjoy a higher quality of life. Even though the communities and corporations in the latter bloc would start out in the minority, over time—as more workers in the neoliberal bloc lost jobs and pay; as problems from pollution and unsafe products multiplied; as ecology, labor, and social-change organizations emerged to respond to these problems—more and more neoliberal communities and corporations would probably begin to choose a better quality of life over obsolete notions of economic efficiency. The mere existence of an alternative bloc would give politicians and activists committed to a new economics of place a concrete goal for organizing.

The beginnings of such interlocal collaboration can already be seen in the emerging "fair trade" movement, in which buyers in developed countries purchase goods directly from producers in poor countries.[27] In the Netherlands, more than 300 communities and 11 (of 12) provincial governments are buying "solidarity coffee" from small coffee growers in countries like Guatemala and Nicaragua, at a slightly higher price to ensure that the growers receive enough income to make a decent living. By circumventing middlemen, who usually take a huge share of the profits, fair traders are able to sell coffee beans to mainstream roasters and distributors at a competitive price. Shoppers can identify solidarity coffee because it bears the "Max Havelaar" seal of approval. In just four years, solidarity coffee captured over 2 percent of the coffee market in the Netherlands and, along with solidarity tea and cocoa, is being introduced into Belgium, France, Germany, Luxembourg, Switzerland, and the United Kingdom.

There are now 500 "Third World shops" in Germany, 300 Wereldwinkels ("world shops") in the Netherlands, and 20 "Third World houses" in Denmark, many of which receive financial support from local authorities. These stores sell crafts, clothing, and other goods from poor countries, with little or no markup in price. Items are purchased from people or cooperatives in the Third World that pay livable wages and provide decent working conditions. Displays and literature inside the shops help educate customers about the makes of the goods, and profits are sometimes used to support education about the global economy. Such shops also can be found in the United States, though much of the fair trade business here is transacted by mail order through companies like One World Trading and Pueblo to People.

A global bloc of socially responsible communities, cemented through fair trade and institutionalized with dues from member cities, would help resolve many of the remaining challenges of going local. To provide the diminishing number of goods associated with large economies of scale, this new international organization could broker the formation of flexible manufacturing networks. It could create a geographically dispersed and diversified pension portfolio that invested in community corporations. It could convert local currencies on a fairer basis than the International Monetary Fund and mainstream banks now do. It could create a new Global Green Bank, which might provide seed capital for community credit unions and microcredit funds worldwide. And it could lobby the WTO and other international agencies for revision or repeal of anticommunity rules. The universe of possible interlocal initiatives is limited only by our imaginations.

THE LILLIPUTIAN STRATEGY

Can a twenty-first–century economy be localized? Skeptics might recall the history of the Great Leap Forward. In 1958, Mao Tse-tung and the Communist Party of the People's Republic of China dragged millions of reluctant farmers down the path of industrialization by ordering 25,000 communes to set up their own factories. Thousands of small-scale plants were hastily assembled across the countryside to churn out steel, cement, fertilizer, energy, and machinery with jerry-rigged technologies but without central coordination, and minus needed support and parts. Chaos ensued, and the Soviet Union promptly decided to withdraw its technicians from China. The images of the Great Leap that endure today are of dilapidated plants standing idle.

Since nowhere in this book is there a recommendation that government forcibly confiscate and convert existing corporations into community-owned structures, the analogy to the Great Leap is largely irrelevant. Community corporations should be formed voluntarily, not by government edict; they should be tailored to the needs of each community, not to a central ideology; they should be driven by the realities of desubsidized marketplace, not in spite of them. Moreover, even as small community corporations serve local needs, larger community corporations or networks of community corporations will continue to produce and deliver complex goods, such as computers and airplanes, that communities cannot efficiently produce for themselves. Community corporations are tools for moving toward self-reliance, not a totalitarian organizing principle for every part of the economy.

But the Great Leap does raise an important question: Can community action really set a nation's economic agenda? Or the world's? The forces of mobile corporations seem so huge, so global, so intractable, that anything done at the local level may seem trivial—like fighting a drought with an eyedropper. But no corporation can exist without customers and investors. Take away either, and even the most powerful firm collapses. Our own powers to buy goods or own stock are the Achilles' heels of the commercial behemoths now destroying communities.

I began my own journey in politics 20 years ago while campaigning against nuclear power. At the time, the spread of nuclear power and its "externalities" (radioactive wastes, meltdowns, spent-fuel accidents, weapons proliferation) seemed inevitable. Seventy nuclear-power plants were in operation, and electric utilities were projecting the need to build as many as one reactor *a day* by the turn of the century. Tens of thousands of protestors tried to stop a $100 billion-plus nuclear industry. They threw themselves in front of tractors and got themselves arrested at reactor construction sites. They fought dozens of court battles challenging the health-, safety-, and environmental analyses, and insisted on modifications in design. They placed referenda on ballots and presented bills in state legislatures to shut down power plants.

In the end, however, these initiatives didn't really matter. Something far more subtle, unexpected, and powerful all but destroyed the nuclear industry: People stopped buying more electricity. As Americans began finding and eliminating energy inefficiencies, projections of electrical demand plummeted. Utilities were left to figure out not whether the next power plants should be nuclear, but whether any additional power plants were needed at all.

There's an important lesson in all this. Why exhaust ourselves in fighting badly behaved corporations? If enough of us create our own corporations based on a new vision of social responsibility, and if we choose to buy and invest only in these firms, other corporations will either adapt or die. If we create even a small number of self-reliant communities in which every resident has a decent job that produces basic necessities for one and all, other communities will visit, learn, and follow. We have far more power than we realize.

Major turning points in human history have been defined by critical struggles. The Renaissance was a struggle between those who embraced myth and superstition, and those who sought empirical truth. The eighteenth and nineteenth centuries witnessed a struggle between monarchs who clung to power by birthright, and democrats who believed in the natural rights of all people to self-governance. The twentieth century has seen a struggle over the definition of progress, between social engineers who sought to conquer nature and ecologists who sought to achieve balance with it. The great struggle of the twenty-first century will be between those who believe in cheap goods and those who believe in place. This is a struggle that defies easy ideological definition. Advocates of cheap goods now dominate the major political parties, and run nearly every City Hall in the country. But across the political spectrum are dissidents who worry about the costs to nature, to families, and to communities. They are asking whether the future of civilization and humanity must be defined by an unlimited need to consume.

Most of us know in our hearts that there's far more to life than the next sale at the mall. We long for deeper connections with our families, our neighbors, and our natural environment. We're desperate for a sense of place in which we can nurture culture and take pride in our history. We work long hours to bequeath to our children and grandchildren the kinds of home-grown economies that keep delivering prosperity. Why just wonder about what's possible in your backyard? Why just dream about a past long gone, or a future far away? Why not get started *today?*

A p p e n d i x
Around the World Economy in 80 Ways

GENERAL—Throughout the English-speaking world are important think tanks—or, more accurately, *do* tanks—that collect case studies of community-scale economic innovations, propose new policies empowering localities, and help communities conduct their own experiments. Each is involved with many of the 80 approaches to economic self-reliance that follow. If you want to learn more about how to "go local" in your own community, there's no better place to start than to join these institutions, subscribe to their newsletters, and read their publications. You will never think about economics in the same way.

ACTION CANADA NETWORK
4 Jeffrey Ave.
Ottawa, ON K1L 0E2
Canada
613-746-5256
Fax: 613-233-6776
Web: www.web.net/~actcan

AKTIE STROHALM
Oudegracht 42
3511 AR Utrecht
Netherlands
Phone: 31-30-(2)314-314
Fax: 31-30-(2)343-986
E-mail: info@strohalm.nl
Web: www.strohalm.nl

COMMUNITIES BY CHOICE
433 Chestnut Street
Berea, KY 40403-1510
E-mail: contactdonna@communities-by-choice.org
Web: www.communities-by-choice.org

CO-OP AMERICA
Suite 600
1612 K St., NW
Washington, DC 20006
800-58-GREEN

Fax: 202-331-8166
E-mail: info@coopamerica.org
Web: www.coopamerica.org

E.F. SCHUMACHER SOCIETY
140 Jug End Rd.
Great Barrington, MA 01230
Phone: 413-528-1737
Fax: 413-528-4472
E-mail: efssociety@aol.com
Web: www.schumachersociety.org

GAIA FOUNDATION
18 Well Walk
London NW3 1LD
44-020-7435-5000
Fax: 44-020-7431-0551
E-mail: gaia@gaianet.org
Web: www.gaianet.org

INSTITUTE FOR ECONOMICS & ENTREPRENEURSHIP
Village Foundation
Suite 700
1600 Duke St.
Alexandria, VA 22314
703-548-3200
Fax: 703-548-5296
E-mail: shuman@igc.org
Web: www.villagefoundation.org

INSTITUTE FOR LOCAL SELF-RELIANCE
2425 18th St., NW
Washington, DC 20009-2096
202-232-4108
Fax: 202-332-0463
E-mail: nseldman@ilsr.org
Web: www.ilsr.org

NEW ECONOMICS FOUNDATION
Cinnamon House
6-8 Cole St.
London SE1 4YH
United Kingdom
44-020-7407-7447
Fax: 44-020-7407-6473
E-mail: info@neweconomics.org
Web: www.neweconomics.org

ROCKY MOUNTAIN INSTITUTE/ECONOMIC RENEWAL PROGRAM

1739 Old Snowmass Creek Rd.
Snowmass, CO 81654-9199
970-927-3851
Fax: 970-927-4178
E-mail: kinsley@rmi.org
Web: www.rmi.org

APPROPRIATE TECHNOLOGY—*No* technology is inevitable. A smart community will promote, subsidize, and deploy technologies that strengthen self-reliance, and stigmatize, regulate, and even ban those that weaken it. In *Small Is Beautiful*, E.F. Schumacher calls technologies that are friendly to communities, workers, and the environment *intermediate* or *appropriate*. To discern whether a technology meets these criteria requires some kind of democratic evaluation. Richard Sclove of the Loka Institute and Andrew Kimbrell of the International Center for Technology Assessment have studied community-based experiments around the world that facilitate citizen input in public and private choices of technology. See also *Renewable Energy*.

INTERNATIONAL CENTER FOR TECHNOLOGY ASSESSMENT
666 Pennsylvania Ave., SE
Washington, DC 20003
202-547-9359
Fax: 202-547-9429
E-mail: info@icta.org
Web: www.icta.org

LOKA INSTITUTE
P.O. Box 355
Amherst, MA 01004
413-559-8560
Fax: 413-559-5811
E-mail: loka@loka.org
Web: www.loka.org

BANKING REFORM—Two of the most thoughtful experts on bank reform who are committed to community empowerment are Tom Schlesinger of the Financial Markets Center and Jane D'Arista of Morin Center for Banking and Financial Law Studies. See also *Community Development Financial Institutions* and *Community Reinvestment Act*.

FINANCIAL MARKETS CENTER
P.O. Box 334
Philomont, VA 20131
540-338-7754
Fax: 540-338-7757
E-mail: tom@mindspring.com

Web: www.fmcenter.org

MORIN CENTER FOR BANKING AND FINANCIAL LAW STUDIES
Boston University School of Law
765 Commonwealth Ave.
Boston, MA 02215
617-353-3023
Fax: 617-353-2444
E-mail: banklaw@bu.edu
Web: www.bu.edu/law/banking

BARTER—There is a long history of businesses tiptoeing around the global monetary system through barter arrangements. A clearinghouse on socially responsible firms that practice this is Hank Monrobey & Associates. A web site on barter industry organizations worldwide is www.barter.net/bnworld.htm. Readers can learn more about Olaf Egeberg's neighborhood barter directory by contacting his McGee St. Foundation.

HANK MONROBEY & ASSOCIATES
P.O. Box 15656
Ann Arbor, MI 48106-5656
313-426-6929
Fax: 313-426-6935
E-mail: monrobey@ix.netcom.com
Web: www.monrobey.com

BIOREGIONALISM—Bioregionalists believe that the best way to structure a community—economically, socially, and politically—is around an ecosystem like a river basin, a bay, or a desert. The leading U.S. advocate of bioregionalism is Peter Berg, director of the Planet Drum Foundation, who publishes a magazine called *Raise the Stakes* and books on the Bay Area bioregion, such as *Reinhabiting a Separate Country: A Bioregional Anthology of Northern California* and *A Green City Program for the San Francisco and Beyond*. New Society Publishers, based in Canada, has a helpful book on the subject entitled *Home: A Bioregional Reader*. The Bioregional Development Group in Britain demonstrates the potential commercial applications of bioregional thinking its recent report, "Bioregional Fibres," which suggests how a regional paper and textile industry can be built on locally harvested hemp and flax. See also *Permaculture*.

BIOREGIONAL DEVELOPMENT GROUP
Sutton Ecology Centre
Honeywood Walk, Carshalton
Surrey SM5 3NX
United Kingdom
44-181-773-2322
Fax: 44-181-643-6419

E-mail: info@bioregional.com
Web: www.bioregional.com

NEW SOCIETY PUBLISHERS
P.O. Box 189
Gabriola Island, BC V0R 1X0
Canada
250-247-9737
Fax: 250-247-7471
E-mail: info@newsociety.com
Web: www.newsociety.com

PLANET DRUM FOUNDATION
P.O. Box 31251
San Francisco, CA 94131
415-285-6556
Fax: 415-285-6563
E-mail: planetdrum@igc.org
Web: www.planetdrum.org

BOYCOTTS—Purchasing decisions by consumers, businesses, and officials help determine which businesses are welcome and ought to thrive, and which ones are unwelcome and ought to fail. Reports on current boycotts can be found in *Boycott Action News* (a supplement to *Co-op America Quarterly*) and the AFL-CIO's *Label Letter* (to which only AFL-CIO members can subscribe). Simon Billenness, a senior analyst with Trillium Asset Management Co., has become a one-man clearinghouse on state and local boycotts against firms involved in Burma. Another good source is INFACT, which led the global boycott against Nestle for marketing synthetic infant formula to Third World mothers. See also *Selective Purchasing* and *Socially Responsible Investment.*

BOYCOTT ACTION NEWS
c/o Co-op America (see above)
Web: www.coopamerica.org/boycotts/bancover.htm

INFACT
46 Plympton St.
Boston, MA 02118
617-695-2525
Fax: 617-695-2626
E-mail: infact@igc.org
Web: www.infact.org

LABEL LETTER
Union Label & Trades Dept.
AFL-CIO
815 16th St., NW

Washington, DC 20006
202-628-2131
Fax: 202-638-1602
E-mail: ulstd@unionlabel.org
Web: www.unionlabel.org

TRILLIUM ASSET MANAGEMENT CO.
711 Atlantic Ave.
Boston, MA 02111
617-423-6655
Fax: 617-482-6179
E-mail: sbillenness@trilliumvest.com
Web: www.trilliumvest.com

CAMPAIGN FINANCE REFORM—If you want to get money out of elections, and help end the dominance of multinational corporations in community politics, two organizations that can help are the Center for Responsive Politics and Public Campaign. See also *Democratic Reform.*

CENTER FOR RESPONSIVE POLITICS
Suite 620
1320 19th St., NW
Washington, DC 20036
202-857-0044
Fax: 202-857-7809
E-mail: info@crp.org
Web: www.opensecrets.org

PUBLIC CAMPAIGN
Suite M-1
1320 19th St., NW
Washington, DC 20036
202-293-0222
Fax: 202-293-0202
E-mail: inform@publicampaign.org
Web: www.publicampaign.org

CARBOHYDRATE ECONOMY—The Institute for Local Self-Reliance (listed above) has published numerous reports, papers, and newsletters showing the technical feasibility and economic attractiveness of replacing petrochemicals with biochemicals derived from agricultural and forestry waste.

CAR REDUCTIONS—Tired of automobiles claiming half the land of your community, making the air less breathable, contributing to noise pollution, maintaining U.S. dependence on foreign oil, and taking a big bite out of your municipal and personal budget? You might set up a car-sharing program, so that members of the community can use and maintain a smaller number of automobiles more efficiently. A handbook on a dozen car-sharing experiments worldwide is available from the International Ecotechnology Research Centre in Britain. See also *Mass Transit*.

INTERNATIONAL ECOTECHNOLOGY RESEARCH CENTRE
Cranfield University
Bedford MK43 0AL
United Kingdom
44-1234-754-097
Fax: 44-1234-750-163
E-mail: s.cousins@cranfield.ac.uk
Web: www.cranfield.ac.uk/sims/ecotech

COMMUNITARIANISM—Despite their economic blindspots, communitarians have useful insights about how to solve practical social, political, and civic problems facing communities. If you're interested in following and participating in their discourse, you can subscribe to *The Responsive Community* from the Communitarian Network, run by Amitai Etzioni at George Washington University.

COMMUNITARIAN NETWORK
Suite 703
2130 H St., NW
Washington, DC 20052
202-994-7997
Fax: 202-994-1606
E-mail: comnet@gwu.edu
Web: www.gwu.edu/~ccps

COMMUNITY CORPORATIONS—Information about community owned and operated corporations is scarce. The Wisconsin Policy Research Institute, a conservative state think tank, has a wonderful report on the Green Bay Packers. The National Center for Economic and Security Alternatives has a series of publications on alternative forms of corporate ownership (*A Third Way: Innovation in Community-Owned Enterprise* by Jeff Shavelson is particularly good). Other clearinghouses and advocates for community ownership are Co-Op America (see above), SEEDCO, and the Village Retail Services Association (ViRSA) in the United Kingdom. See also *Worker Ownership*.

NATIONAL CENTER FOR ECONOMIC AND SECURITY ALTERNATIVES
Suite 330
2000 P St., NW
Washington, DC 20036
202-835-1150
Fax: 202-835-1152
E-mail: info@ncesa.org

Web: www.ncesa.org

SEEDCO
915 Broadway
New York, NY 10010
212-473-0255
Fax: 212-473-0357
E-Mail: info@seedco.org
Web: www.seedco.org

VILLAGE RETAIL SERVICES ASSOCIATION
The Little Keep
Bridport Rd.
Dorcester, Dorset DT1 1SQ
United Kingdom
44-1305-259-383
Fax: 44-1305-259-384
Web: www.virsa.org

WISCONSIN POLICY RESEARCH INSTITUTE
P.O. 487
Thiensville, WI 53062
262-241-0514
Fax: 262-241-0774
E-mail: wpri@pitnet.net
Web: www.wpri.org

COMMUNITY DEVELOPMENT CORPORATIONS (CDCs)—Community development corporations (CDCs) are nonprofits with a mission to build low-income housing, and support entrepreneurship in poor communities. If you're interested in starting a CDC, the Local Initiatives Support Corps offers grants and low-interest loans. The National Congress for Community Economic Development serves as a clearinghouse. Avis C. Vidal has written an excellent study, *Rebuilding Communities: A National Study of Urban CDCs*, which is available from the Community Development Research Center at the New School for Social Research.

COMMUNITY DEVELOPMENT RESEARCH CENTER
Graduate School of Management and Urban Policy
New School for Social Research
66 Fifth Ave.
New York, NY 10011
212-229-5462
Fax: 212-229-5404
Web: www.newschool.edu/milano/cdrc.htm

LOCAL INITIATIES SUPPORT CORPORATION
Suite 1100

1825 K St., NW
Washington, DC 20006
202-739-0882
Fax: 202-785-8030
E-mail: info@liscnet.org
Web: www.liscnet.org

NATIONAL CONGRESS FOR COMMUNITY ECONOMIC DEVELOPMENT
Suite 325
1030 15th St., NW
Washington, DC 20005
202-289-9020
Fax: 202-289-7051
E-mail: kalder@ncced.org
Web: www.ncced.org

COMMUNITY DEVELOPMENT CREDIT UNIONS—Credit unions are banking cooperatives owned and operated by their own members. Most are linked to workplaces, churches, or civic organizations, but about 300 are connected to geographically defined communities. Providing networking and assistance to these banks is the National Federation of Community Development Credit Unions. One of the best examples is the Self-Help Credit Union of Durham, North Carolina, which received a $50 million boost from the Ford Foundation in 1999. Other clearinghouses in the United States and the United Kingdom are noted below. See also *Community Development Financial Institutions.*

ASSOCIATION OF BRITISH CREDIT UNIONS LTD.
Hollybak House Hanover St.
Manchester M60 OA5
United Kingdom
44-0161-832-3694
Fax: 44-0161-832-3706
E-mail: info@abcul.org
Web: www.abcul.org

NATIONAL FEDERATION OF COMMUNITY DEVELOPMENT CREDIT UNIONS
10th Floor
120 Wall St.
New York, NY 10005-3902
212-809-1850
Fax: 212-809-3274
E-mail: email@natfed.org
Web: www.natfed.org

NATIONAL FEDERATION OF CREDIT UNIONS
Units 1.1 and 1.2
Howard House Commercial Centre
Howard Street

North Shields
Tyne and Wear NE30 1AR
United Kingdom
Phone: 44-191-257-2219
Fax: 44-191-258-2921

SELF HELP
301 W. Main St.
Durham, NC 27701
919-956-4400
Fax: 919-956-4600
Web: http://www.self-help.org

WORLD COUNCIL OF CREDIT UNIONS
Suite 300
805 15th St., NW
Washington, DC 20005-2207
202-682-5990
Fax: 202-682-9054
E-mail: info@woccu.org
Web: http://www.woccu.org

COMMUNITY DEVELOPMENT FINANCIAL INSTITUTIONS—CDFIs provide loans locally for community development, often to poor people. They include community-friendly commercial banks (like South Shore in Chicago or ASN in the Netherlands), thrifts, credit unions, microenterprise funds, and community-development loan funds. Three excellent sources of information are the National Association of Community Development Loan Funds in Philadelphia, the Self Help Association for a Regional Economy (SHARE) in western Massachusetts, and the Woodstock Institute in Chicago. A number of listserves now link community bankers, including ones focused on community-development banking (Community DevelopmentBanking@cornell.edu), development finance (DevFinance@lists.acs. ohio-state.edu), and microenterprise (Microenterprise@listserve.aol.com). See also *Community Development Credit Unions*.

ALGEMENE SPAARBANK VOOR NEDERALND (ASN N.V.)
Postbus 30502
2500 GM Den Haag
Netherlands
070-35-69-333
Fax: 070-36-17-948

CDFI COALITION
2nd Floor
924 Cherry St.
Philadelphia, PA 19107-2411

215-923-5363
Fax: 215-923-4755
E-mail: cdfi@cdfi.org
Web: www.cdfi.org

SELF HELP ASSOCIATION FOR A REGIONAL ECONOMY
140 Jug End Rd.
Great Barrington, MA 01230
413-528-1737
Fax: 413-528-4472
E-mail: efssociety@aol.com
Web: members.aol.com/efssociety/share.html

SOUTH SHORE BANK
7054 S. Jeffrey Blvd.
Chicago, IL 60649
800-NOW-SSBK
Fax: 773-753-5699
E-mail: deposits@sbk.com
Web: www.sbk.com

WOODSTOCK INSTITUTE
Suite 550
407 South Dearborn
Chicago, IL 60605
312-427-8070
Fax: 312-427-4007
E-mail: woodstock@woodstockinst.org
Web: www.woodstockinst.org

COMMUNITY DEVELOPMENT PLANNING—Even though most mainstream groups promoting "community development" are addicted to two of the most toxic economic elixirs, attracting multinational corporations and pursuing export-led growth, they nevertheless are useful sources of information about what's happening in specific communities, in government policymaking, and in academic debates. Most have a handful of decent staff who quietly try to promote economic self-reliance when their superiors are not looking. Among the organizations with a somewhat more progressive viewpoint are the National Neighborhood Coalition, the Planners Network, the Resource Renewal Institute (which promotes "Green Plans"), and the Urban Institute. See also *Community Development Corporations*.

AMERICAN PLANNING ASSOCIATION
1776 Massachusetts Ave., NW
Washington, DC 20036
202-872-0641
Fax: 202-872-0643
E-mail: membership@planning.org

Web: www.planning.org

COMMUNITY DEVELOPMENT PROGRAM
225 Gentry Hall
University of Missouri - Columbia
Columbia, MO 65201
573-882-8393
Fax: 573-882-5127
E-mail: Hughesco@missouri.edu
Web: ssu.agri.missouri.edu/commdev

NATIONAL COUNCIL FOR URBAN ECONOMIC DEVELOPMENT
Suite 700
1730 K St., NW
Washington, DC 20006
202-223-4735
Fax: 202-223-4745
E-mail: cued@urbandevelopment.com
Web: www.cued.org

NATIONAL DEVELOPMENT COUNCIL
Suite 300
51 East 42nd St.
New York, NY 10017
212-682-1106
Fax: 212-573-6118

NATIONAL ECONOMIC DEVELOPMENT AND LAW CENTER
Suite 815
2201 Broadway
Oakland, CA 94612
510-251-2600
Fax: 510-251-0600
E-mail: nedlcsearch@igc.org
Web: www.nedlc.org

NATIONAL NEIGHBORHOOD COALITION
Suite 410
1875 Connecticut Ave., NW
Washington, DC 20009
202-986-2096
Fax: 202-986-1941
E-mail: nncnnc@erols.com
Web: www.neighborhoodcoalition.org

NEIGHBORHOOD REINVESTMENT CORPORATION
Suite 800
1325 G St., NW
Washington, DC 20005

202-220-2300
Fax: 202-376-2618
E-mail: nrti@nw.org
Web: www.nw.org

PLANNERS NETWORK
Pratt Graduate Center for Planning and the Environment
379 DeKalb Ave
Brooklyn, NY 11205
718-636-3461
Fax: 718-636-3709
E-mail: pr-net@pratt.edu
Web: www.pratt.edu/arch/gcpe/index.html

PUBLIC TECHNOLOGY INC.
Suite 800
1301 Pennsylvania Ave., NW
Washington, DC 20004
800-852-4934
Fax: 202-626-2498
E-mail: gold@pti.nw.dc.us
Web: pti.nw.dc.us

RESOURCE RENEWAL INSTITUTE
Fort Mason Center, Pier One
San Francisco, CA 94123
415-928-3774
Fax: 415-928-6529
E-mail: info@rri.org
Web: www.rri.org

URBAN INSTITUTE
Suite 401
2100 M St., NW
Washington, DC 20037
202-833-7200
Fax: 202-223-3043
E-mail: paffairs@uip.urban.org
Web: www.urban.org

COMMUNITY FOOD SYSTEMS—Organizations and programs promoting community self-reliance in food expanded dramatically in recent years, in part because of major financial commitments made by funders like the W.K. Kellogg Foundation's Integrated Food Systems Program. Important clearinghouses include the Campaign for Sustainable Agriculture, the Sustainable Agriculture Network at the U.S. Department of Agriculture, the Wallace Institute, and the World Campaign for Sustainable Agriculture. Interest has been especially keen in direct marketing relationships between farms and nearby consumers, which are called CSAs or Community Supported Agriculture. Some of the best introductory material to CSAs, such as *Basic Formula to Create Community Supported Agriculture*, written by the late Robin Van En, is available from the E.F. Schumacher Society (see above). Other newsletters and reports are published by the Common Food Security Coalition in California, the Hartford Food System (which has attracted impressive support from local and state officials), and the Bio-Dynamic Farming & Gardening Association. Since most urban farmers run city-based CSAs, also check out the references in *Urban Agriculture*, as well as those in *Permaculture*, *Rural Development*, and *Sustainable Forestry*.

BIO-DYNAMIC FARMING & GARDENING ASSOCIATION
P.O. Box 550
Kimberton, PA 19442
215-983-3196
Fax: 800-516-7797

COMMUNITY FOOD SECURITY COALITION
P.O. Box 209
Venice, CA 90294
310-822-5410
Fax: 310-822-1440
E-mail: asfisher@aol.com
Web: www.foodsecurity.org

HARTFORD FOOD SYSTEM
509 Wethersfield Ave.
Hartford, CT 06114
860-296-9325
Fax: 860-296-8326
E-mail: hfood@erols.com

INTEGRATED FOOD SYSTEMS PROGRAM
W.K. Kellogg Foundation
One Michigan Ave. East
Battle Creek, MI 49017-4058
616-968-1611
Fax: 616-969-2693
E-mail: oran.hesterman@wkkf.org
Web: www.wkkf.org

INTERNATIONAL ALLIANCE FOR SUSTAINABLE AGRICULTURE
1701 University Ave., SE
Minneapolis, MN 55414
612-331-1099
Fax: 612-379-1527
E-mail: iasa@mtm.org

NATIONAL CAMPAIGN FOR SUSTAINABLE AGRICULTURE

P.O. Box 396
Pine Bush, NY 12566
914-744-8448
Fax: 914-744-8477
E-mail: campaign@magiccarpet.com
Web: www.sustainableagriculture.net

SUSTAINABLE AGRICULTURE NETWORK
U.S. Department of Agriculture
Room 304
10301 Baltimore Blvd.
Beltsville, MD 20705
301-504-6425
Fax: 301-504-6409
E-mail: san@nal.usda.gov
Web: www.sare.org

WALLACE INSTITUTE FOR ALTERNATIVE AGRICULTURE
Suite 117
9200 Edmonston Rd.
Greenbelt, MD 20770
301-441-8777
Fax: 301-220-0164
E-mail: wagpol@access.digex.net
Web: www.hawiaa.org/wagpol.html

WORLD SUSTAINABLE AGRICULTURE ASSOCIATION
Suite 512
2025 I St., NW
Washington, DC 20006
202-293-2155
Fax: 202-293-2209
E-mail: wsaadc@igc.org
Web: www.igc.apc.org/wsaala/wsaa.html

COMMUNITY FRIENDLY TRADE—The most articulate critics of neoliberal trade policies have been the environmental and labor groups who showed their strength on the streets of Seattle in December 1999. The leading organizations, listed below, appreciate the adverse impacts of trade on communities and work on alternative models of economic development. Most have excellent newsletters that provide updates on trade negotiations or disputes. Remarkably, nearly all the mainstream organizations listed under *Community Development Planning* have been cheerleaders for community-destructive trade.

ALLIANCE FOR RESPONSIBLE TRADE
Fourth Floor
927 15th St., NW

Washington, DC 20005
202-888-1566
Fax: 202-898-1612
E-mail: dgap@igc.org
Web: www.igc.org/dgap

CITIZENS TRADE CAMPAIGN
P.O. Box 77077
Washington, DC 20013-7077
202-546-4611
Fax: 202-547-7392
Web: www.tradewatch.org

COALITION FOR JUSTICE IN THE MAQUILADORAS
530 Bandera Rd.
San Antonio, TX 78228
210-732-8957
Fax: 210-732-8324
E-mail: cjm@igc.org

FOCUS ON THE GLOBAL SOUTH
c/o CUSRI
Chulalongkore University
Prachuabmoh, Phyathai Rd.
Bangkok 10330
Thailand
662-218-7363
Fax: 662-255-9976
E-mail: admin@focusweb.org
Web: www.focusweb.org

INSTITUTE FOR AGRICULTURE AND TRADE POLICY
2105 1st Ave. South
Minneapolis, MN 55404
612-870-0453
Fax: 612-870-4846
E-mail: iatp@iatp.org
Web: www.iatp.org

INSTITUTE FOR POLICY STUDIES
Global Economy Program
Suite 1020
733 15th St., NW
Washington, DC 20005
202-234-9382
Fax: 202-387-7915
E-mail: jcavanagh@igc.org
Web: www.ips-dc.org

INTERNATIONAL FORUM ON GLOBALIZATION
Bldg. 1062, Fort Cronkite
San Francisco, CA 94965
415-229-9350
Fax: 415-229-9340
Email: ifg@ifg.org
Web: www.ifg.org

PUBLIC CITIZEN/GLOBAL TRADE WATCH
1600 20th St., NW
Washington, DC 20009
202-588-1000
Fax: 202-547-7392
E-mail: gfwinfo@citizen.org
Web: www.citizen.org/gtw

SIERRA CLUB
408 C St., NE
Washington, DC 20002
202-547-1141
Fax: 202-547-6009
E-mail: dan.seligman@sierraclub.org
Web: www.sierraclub.org

THIRD WORLD NETWORK
228 Macalist Rd., 10400
Panang
Malaysia
60-4-3226-6728
Fax: 60-4-3226-4505
E-mail: tun@igc.org
Web: www.twinside.org.sg

COMMUNITY LAND TRUSTS—CLTs are plots of land owned, governed, and maintained by a collective of occupants, in which an individual shareholder, if he or she decides to leave, must resell his or her share back to the collective. The Institute for Community Economics, one of the pioneers of the concept, publishes the *CLT Handbook* and *Profiles of CLTs*. Another promoter is Asset Democracy in the United Kingdom.

ASSET DEMOCRACY
The Old School
29 Bailbrook Lane
Swainswick, Bath BA1 7AN
United Kingdom
01-225-333-688
E-mail: Assetdem1@aol.com

INSTITUTE FOR COMMUNITY ECONOMICS
57 School St.
Springfield, MA 01105-1331
413-746-8660
Fax: 413-746-8862
E-mail: iceconomic@aol.com

COMMUNITY REINVESTMENT ACT—The CRA mandates that U.S. banks, thrifts, and credit unions reinvest a portion of their deposits locally. ACORN, a neighborhood organizing network with more than 600 chapters nationwide, has used the CRA successfully to pry open bank lending to low-income and minority borrowers. Detailed analysis on how communities actually use the CRA, what more they can do, and why Congress should strengthen the law is available from the Center for Community Change and the National Community Reinvestment Coalition.

ACORN
739 Eighth St., SE
Washington, DC 20003
202-547-2500
Fax: 202-546-2483
E-mail: dcacorndc@acorn.org
Web: www.acorn.org

CENTER FOR COMMUNITY CHANGE
1000 Wisconsin Ave., NW
Washington, DC 20007
202-342-0567
Fax: 202-333-5462
E-mail: info@communitychange.org
Web: www.communitychange.org

NATIONAL COMMUNITY REINVESTMENT COALITION
Suite 540
733 15th St., NW
Washington, DC 20005
202-628-8866
Fax: 202-628-9800
E-mail: pnotaro@ncrc.org
Web: www.ncrc.org

CONVERSION—If your community is dependent on a military base or weapons factory, two organizations can help you kick the Cold War habit: the Center for Economic Conversion in California and the National Commission for Economic Conversion and Disarmament in Washington, D.C.

CENTER FOR ECONOMIC CONVERSION
222 View St.
Mountain View, CA 94041-1344
650-968-8798
Fax: 650-968-1126
E-mail: cec@igc.org
Web: www.conversion.org

NATIONAL COMMISSION FOR ECONOMIC CONVERSION AND DISARMAMENT
c/o Institute for Policy Studies
Suite 1020
733 15th, NW
Washington, DC 20005
202-234-9382, ext. 214
Fax: 202-387-7915
E-mail: ncecd@igc.org
Web: www.webcom.com/ncecd

COOPERATIVES—Co-ops are businesses owned by their members or workers. Co-op America (listed above) puts out a *National Greenpages*. Other clearinghouses are the Co-op Resources & Service Project, the National Cooperative Business Association, and the Canadian-based Centre for the Study of Cooperatives.

CENTRE FOR THE STUDY OF COOPERATIVES
101 Diefenbaker Place
University of Saskatchewan
Saskatoon, Saskatchewan S7N 5B8
Canada
306-966-8509
Fax: 306-966-8517
E-mail: coop.studies@usask.ca
Web: www.coop_studies.usask.ca

CO-OP RESOURCES & SERVICE PROJECT
3551 White House Place
Los Angeles, CA 90004
213-738-1254
Fax: 213-386-8873
E-mail: crsp@igc.org
Web: www.ic.org/laev

NATIONAL COOPERATIVE BUSINESS ASSOCIATION
Suite 1100
1401 New York Ave., NW
Washington, DC 20005
202-638-6222
Fax: 202-638-1374

E-mail: ncba@ncba.org
Web: www.cooperative.org

CORPORATE ACCOUNTABILITY—Communities have many tools at their disposal to make corporations more accountable. A nice summary of who's doing what is "Minding Our Business: The Role of Corporate Accountability in Sustainable Development," available from Integrative Strategies. Ralph Estes' Center for Public Policy is pushing for corporations to disclose more data in their annual reports. Other groups monitoring corporate behavior include Corporate Watch, the Data Center, the Interfaith Center on Corporate Responsibility (which publishes the *Corporate Examiner*), the Center for the Study of Responsive Law (which has an excellent magazine, the *Multinational Monitor*), and the Transnational Research and Action Center. Another good periodical is *Dollars and Sense*. If you want to learn how to study businesses in your own backyard, the Food and Allied Service Trade Department of the AFL-CIO publishes two useful guides: *Manual of Corporate Investigation* and *Basic Organizing Research for Private Companies*. Several noteworthy organizations have dedicated themselves to rethinking the kinds of public responsibilities state governments should exact from private corporations before awarding them a license to do business. Richard Grossman's Program on Corporations, Law, and Democracy has books, pamphlets, and papers advocating national rechartering of corporations.

CENTER FOR ADVANCEMENT OF PUBLIC POLICY
Suite 1010
733 15th St., NW
Washington, DC 20005
Phone: 202-797-0606
Fax: 202-265-6245
E-mail: capp@essential.org
Web: www.essential.org/capp

CORPORATE WATCH
P.O. Box 29344
San Francisco, CA 94129
415-561-6567
Fax: 415-561-6493
Web: www.corpwatch.org

DATA CENTER
464 19th St.
Oakland, CA 94612
510-835-4692
Fax: 510-835-3017
E-mail: datacenter@datacenter.org
Web: www.igc.org/datacenter

DOLLARS AND SENSE
1 Summer St.

Somerville, MA 02143
617-628-8411
Fax: 617-628-2025
E-mail: dollars@igc.org
Web: www.igc.org/dollars

FOOD & ALLIED SERVICE TRADE DEPT.
AFL-CIO
Room 408
Washington, DC 20006
202-737-7200
Fax: 202-737-7208
E-mail: fast3@fastaflcio.org
Web: www.fastaflcio.org/fasthome.htm

INTERFAITH CENTER ON CORPORATE RESPONSIBILITY
Room 566
475 Riverside Dr.
New York, NY 10115
212-870-2295
Fax: 212-870-2023
E-mail: info@iccr.org

INTEGRATIVE STRATEGIES FORUM
Suite 600
1612 K St., NW
Washington, DC 20006
202-872-5339
Fax: 202-331-8166
E-mail: jbarber@igc.org

MULTINATIONAL MONITOR
P.O. Box 19405
Washington, DC 20036
202-387-8030
Fax: 202-234-5176
E-mail: monitor@essential.org
Web: www.essential.org

PROGRAM ON CORPORATIONS, LAW, AND DEMOCRACY
P. O. Box 246
S. Yarmouth MA 02664-0246
508-398-1145
Fax: 508-398-1552
E-mail: people@poclad.org
Web: www.poclad.org

TRANSNATIONAL RESEARCH AND ACTION CENTER
P.O. Box 29344

San Francisco, CA 94129
E-mail: corpwatch@corpwatch.org
Web: www.corpwatch.org

CORPORATE SUBSIDIES—If you're mad about corporate welfare, three unlikely allies are doing excellent work to identify and purge it: the libertarian Cato Institute, Essential Information (an arm of Ralph Nader's), and Friends of the Earth (which spearheads the Green Scissors Coalition). The best single document on state and local subsidies, *No More Candystore*, written by Greg LeRoy, was originally published by the Federation for Industrial Retention and Renewal and is now available from the Preamble Center. LeRoy also publishes periodic reports on state and local corporate subsidies through Good Jobs First.

CATO INSTITUTE
1000 Massachusetts Ave., NW
Washington, DC 20001
202-842-0200
Fax: 202-842-3490
E-mail: cato@cato.org
Web: www.cato.org

GOOD JOBS FIRST
1311 L St., NW
Washington, DC 20005
202-737-4315
Fax: 202-638-3486
E-mail: goodjobs@ctj.org
Web: www.ctj.org/itep/gjf.htm

GREEN SCISSORS CAMPAIGN
c/o Friends of the Earth
Suite 300
1025 Vermont Ave., NW
Washington, DC 20005
202-783-7400
Fax: 202-783-0444
E-mail: foe@foe.org
Web: www.foe.org

PREAMBLE CENTER
Suite 203
2040 S St., NW
Washington, DC 20009
202-387-2935
Fax: 202-234-0981
E-mail: rhealey@preamble.org
Web: www.preamble.org

DEMOCRATIC REFORM—A critical requisite for economic self-reliance is healthy self-governance. The Center for Living Democracy gathers and publishes success stories involving community groups in their newspaper *Doing Democracy*. The Center for Voting and Democracy helps communities adopt proportional representation as a means of expanding participation. See also *Campaign Finance Reform*.

CENTER FOR LIVING DEMOCRACY
289 Fox Farm Rd.
Brattleboro, VT 05301
802-254-1234
Fax: 802-254-1227
E-mail: info@livingdemocracy.org
Web: www.livingdemocracy.org

CENTER FOR VOTING AND DEMOCRACY
6930 Carroll Ave., Suite 901
Takoma Park, MD 20912
301-270-4616
Fax: 301-270-4133
E-mail: cvdusa@aol.com
Web: www.igc.org/cvd

DEVOLUTION—A remarkable range of progressive and conservative groups believe in decentralizing government and political authority. On the left are advocates like David Morris of the Institute for Local Self-Reliance (noted above) and Kirkpatrick Sale. On the right are groups like the Federalist Society and the Cato Institute (see *Corporate Subsidies*). Two groups with publications that bring together a wide range of viewpoints are the E.F. Schumacher Society (noted above), and PEGS.

FEDERALIST SOCIETY
Suite 425
1015 18th St., NW
Washington, DC 20036
202-822-8138
Fax: 202-296-8061
E-mail: fedsoc@radix.net
Web: www.fed-soc.org

PEGS
Department of Government and Politics
University of Maryland
College Park, MD 20742
301-405-7799
Fax: 301-314-9690
E-mail: pegs@grpt.umd.edu
Web: www.bsos.umd.edu

ECO-BUILDING—If you're interested in living, working, or playing in eco-friendly buildings made from natural materials, often grown and processed nearby, the organizations below have numerous contacts. EcoDesign Resources in Canada also publishes the *EcoDesign Quarterly*.

CENTER FOR MAXIMUM POTENTIAL BUILDING SYSTEMS
8604 F.M. 969
Austin, TX 78724
512-928-4786
Fax: 512-926-4418
E-mail: center@cmpbs.org
Web: www.cmpbs.org

CENTER FOR RESOURCEFUL BUILDING TECHNOLOGY
P.O. Box 100
Missoula, MT 59806
406-549-7678
Fax: 406-549-4100
E-mail: crbt@montana.com
Web: www.montana.com/crbt

ECODESIGN RESOURCES SOCIETY
P.O. Box 3981, Main Post Office
Vancouver, BC V6B 3Z4
Canada
604-255-2049
Fax: 604-255-2079
E-mail: penner@infoserve.net
Web: www.ecodesign.bc.ca

EOS INSTITUTE
P.O. Box 4380
Laguna Beach, CA 92651
949-497-1896
E-mail: enviroproj@home.com

ENERGY SERVICE COMPANIES—The National Association of Energy Service Companies charts and promotes the development of ESCOs, which are small-to-medium-sized corporations that identify, design, finance, and implement energy-saving technical fixes. See also *Water-efficiency Service Companies*.

NATIONAL ASSOCIATION OF ENERGY SERVICE COMPANIES
Suite 800
1615 M St., NW
Washington, DC 20036
202-822-0950
Fax: 202-822-0955
Web: www.naesco.org

ENVIRONMENTAL JUSTICE—A growing number of organizations are helping communities ensure that environmental protection takes into account the special needs and interests of people of color. Carl Anthony of the Urban Habitat Program argues that it's "in the best interest of advocates of sustainable communities to make this racial content explicit, and to anticipate and shape these consequences so that the outcomes are socially and environmentally constructive." Clearinghouses include the National Environmental Justice Action Council, the Poverty & Race Research Action Council, and EcoNet's Environmental Justice Home Page (www.igc.org/envjustice). A new magazine that focuses on environmental justice is *ColorLines*.

COLORLINES
Suite 319
4096 Piedmont Ave.
Oakland, CA 94611-5221
510-653-3415
Fax: 510-653-3427
E-mail: colorlines@arc.org
Web: www.arc.org/Pages/ArcColorlines.html

COMMUNITIES FOR A BETTER ENVIRONMENT
Suite 506
500 Howard St.
San Francisco, CA 94105
415-243-8373
E-mail: cbesf@igc.apc.org
Web: www.igc.org/envjustice

POVERTY & RACE RESEARCH ACTION COUNCIL
Suite 200
3000 Connecticut Ave., NW
Washington, DC 20008
202-387-9887
Fax: 202-387-0764
E-mail: info@prrac.org
Web: www.prrac.org

URBAN HABITAT PROGRAM
P.O. Box 29908
Presidio Station
San Francisco, CA 94129
415-561-3333
Fax: 415-561-3334
E-mail: uhp@igc.org
Web: www.igc.org/uhp

FAIR TRADE—Fair traders link poor farmers and artisans in the Third World (now called, less paternalistically, the South) with wealthier consumers in the North, thereby eliminating profiteering by distributors, middlemen, and wholesalers. Many of the best practitioners, such as Oxfam, Twin Trading, and Traidcraft, are based primarily in Europe. The Fair Trade Federation serves as a clearinghouse for dozens of practitioner companies, which include the U.S.-based Fair Trade Foundation, Global Exchange, One World Trading, and Pueblo to People.

FAIR TRADE FEDERATION
P.O. Box 698
Kirksville, MO 63501
660-665-8962
E-mail: ftfok@fairtradefederation.com
Web: www.fairtradefederation.com

FAIR TRADE FOUNDATION
65 Landing Rd.
Hagganum, CT 06441
860-345-3374
Fax: 860-345-4922

GLOBAL EXCHANGE
2840 College Avenue
Berkeley, CA 94705
510-548-0370
Fax: 510-548-0371
E-mail: berkeleystore@globalexchange.org
Web: www.globalexchange.org

INTERNATIONAL FEDERATION FOR ALTERNATIVE TRADE
30 Murdock Rd.
Bicester, OXON OX6 7RF
United Kingdom
44-1869-249-819
Fax: 44-1869-246-381
E-mail: cwills@ifat.ork.uk
Web: www.ifat.org

ONE WORLD TRADING
227 Ewing Rd.
Pittsburgh, PA 15205
412-921-7208
E-mail: kurtlarcin@hotmail.com

OXFAM
274 Banbury Road
Oxford OX2 7DZ
United Kingdom
44-1865-313-600
Fax: oxfam@oxfam.org.uk
Web: www.oxfam.org.uk/buy.htm

PUEBLO TO PEOPLE
P.O. Box 2545
Houston, TX 77252
713-956-1172
Fax: 713-956-8443
E-mail: info@pueblo_to_people.com
Web: www.pueblo_to_people.com

TRAIDCRAFT
Kingsway
Gateshead
Tyne & Wear NE11 0NE
United Kingdom
44-0191-491-0591
Fax: 44-0191-482-2690

TWIN TRADING
1 Curtain Street, 3rd floor
London EC2A 3JX
United Kingdom
44-171-375-1221
Fax: 44-171-375-1337
Email: info@twin.org.uk
Web: www.twin.org.uk

FLEXIBLE MANUFACTURING NETWORKS—If you're interested in helping local businesses produce complex goods without being tempted to desert the community—by working in informal networks with other small businesses in nearby communities—you should contact ACEnet.

ACENET
94 N. Columbus Rd.
Athens, OH 45701
614-592-3854
Fax: 614-593-5451
E-mail: jholley@tmn.com
Web: www.seorf.ohiou.edu/~acenet

GEORGE TAXES—Economist Henry George first laid out his principles for community-friendly land taxation in *Progress and Poverty* in 1879. The three institutes listed below promote and study use of these taxes. See also *Green Taxes* and *Income and Wealth Taxes*.

CENTRAL RESEARCH GROUP, INC.
P.O. Box 4112, Patroon Station
Albany, NY 12204-0112

518-462-5068
Fax: 518-462-3921
E-mail: hwbatt@yahoo.com

HENRY GEORGE FOUNDATION
Suite 212
8775 Cloud Leap Court
Columbia, MD 21045
410-740-1177
Fax: 410-740-3279
E-mail: hgeorge@smart.net
Web: www.smart.net/~hgeorge

ROBERT SCHALKENBACH FOUNDATION
149 Madison Ave., Suite 601
New York, NY 10016
212-988-1680
Fax: 212-988-1687
E-mail: schalkenba@aol.com

GRASSROOTS ORGANIZING—To change the direction of the local economy requires a critical mass of community residents demanding such change. Enter community organizers. If you want to organize your own neighbors, you can turn to the following groups for information, assistance, training, and inspiration:

CIVIC PRACTICE NETWORKS
Center for Human Resources
Heller Graduate School
Brandeis University
60 Turner St.
Waltham, MA 02154
617-736-4890
Fax: 617-736-4891
E-mail: cpn@tiac.net
Web: www.heller.brandeis.edu

GRASSROOTS ECONOMIC ORGANIZING (GEO) NEWSLETTER
R.R. Box 124A
Stillwater, PA 77878
800-240-9721
E-mail: wadew@epix.net
Web: www.geonewsletter.org

HIGHLANDER RESEARCH AND EDUCATION CENTER
1959 Highlander Way
New Market, TN 37820
423-933-3443

Fax: 423-933-3424
E-mail: hrec@igc.org
Web: www.hrec.org

NATIONAL ASSOCIATION OF COMMUNITY ACTION AGENCIES
Suite 500
1100 17th St., NW
Washington, DC 20036
202-265-7546
Fax: 202-265-8850
E-mail: info@nacaa.org
Web: www.nacaa.org

NATIONAL ORGANIZERS ALLIANCE
715 G St., SE
Washington, DC 20003
202-543-6603
Fax: 202-543-2462
E-mail: noa@igc.org
Web: www.noacentral.org

GREEN TAXES—The policy arguments for moving tax burdens from labor and capital onto natural resources and pollution have been spearheaded by Robert Repetto and his associates at the World Resources Institute. Other organizations with lively web sites on the subject are the Banneker Center, the International Institute for Sustainable Development, the Organization for Economic Cooperation and Development, and the Wuppertal Institute (which publishes the *Bulletin of Ecological Tax Reform*). See also *George Taxes* and *Income and Wealth Taxes*.

BANNEKER CENTER
5465 High Tide Court
Columbia, MD 21044
410-740-0969
E-mail: banneker@progress.org
Web: www.progress.org/banneker/shift.html

INTERNATIONAL INSTITUTE FOR SUSTAINABLE DEVELOPMENT
6th Floor
161 Portage Ave. East
Winnipeg, Manitoba R3B 0Y4
Canada
204-958-7700
Fax: 204-958-7710
E-mail: info@iisd.ca
Web: www.iisd.ca

ORGANIZATION OF ECONOMIC COOPERATION AND DEVELOPMENT

Suite 250
2001 L St., NW
Washington, DC 20036-4922
202-785-6323
Fax: 202-785-0350
Web: www.oecd.org/env/online.htm

WORLD RESOURCES INSTITUTE
10 G St., NE, Suite 800
Washington, DC 20002
202-729-7600
Fax: 202-729-7610
E-mail: lauralee@wri.org
Web: www.wri.org

WUPPERTAL INSTITUTE FOR CLIMATE, ENVIRONMENT, AND ENERGY
Doppersberg 19
42103 Wuppertal
Germany
49-20-22-49-20
Fax: 49-20-22-49-2108
E-mail: info@wupperinst.org
Web: www.wuppertal-forum.ed/wuppertal_bulletin

HAZARDOUS MATERIALS MONITORING—One way in which communities have held businesses accountable is by monitoring their releases of pollution and toxic wastes. Corporations are required to file toxic release inventories with the Environmental Protection Agency, which provide communities with a lever for pressing local firms to reduce pollution. Then OMB Watch aims to protect and expand these legal mandates for corporate disclosure, and the Environmental Research Foundation helps activists use them with newsletters, reports, and a computerized database called Remote Access Chemical Hazards Electronic Library. The Center for Health, Environment, and Justice and the Silicon Valley Toxics Coalition also keep track of grassroots anti-toxics campaigns across the country.

CENTER FOR HEALTH, ENVIRONMENT, AND JUSTICE
Box 6806
Falls Church, VA 22040
703-237-CCHW
Fax: 703-237-8389
E-mail: cchw@essential.org
Web: www.essential.org/cchw

ENVIRONMENTAL RESEARCH FOUNDATION
P.O. Box 5036
Annapolis, MD 21403-7036
410-263-8944
E-mail: erf@igc.apc.org

Web: www.monitor.net/rachel

OMB WATCH
1742 Connecticut Ave., NW
Washington, DC 20009
202-234-8494
Fax: 202-234-8584
E-mail: ombwatch@ombwatch.org
Web: www.ombwatch.org

SILICON VALLEY TOXICS COALITION
760 North First St.
San Jose, CA 95112
408-287-6707
Fax: 408-287-6771
E-mail: svtc@igc.org
Web: www.svtc.org/svtc

HOUSING—Home ownership has long been an important tool for community development. From the homesteads granted to pioneers willing to move West, to the low-interest loans given today to the poor by the U.S. Department of Housing and Urban Development (HUD), policymakers have understood that homeowners take special care to protect and enhance the value of their property. Those interested in following national programs promoting homeownership can subscribe to the McAuley Institute's *Housing Gazette* and order various publications from HUD. In the United Kingdom, groups like the Community Self-Build Agency and the Walter Segal Self-Build Trust (which publishes a magazine called *You Build*) follow community efforts to mobilize townspeople to design, build, and finance new housing.

COMMUNITY SELF-BUILD AGENCY
Unit 26, Finshury Business Centre
40 Bowling Green Lane
London EC1R 0NE
United Kingdom
44-171-415-7092
Fax: 44-171-415-7142
E-Mail: csbigloo@dircon.co.uk

MCAULEY INSTITUTE
Suite 310
8300 Colesville Rd.
Silver Spring, MD 20910
301-588-8110
Fax: 301-588-8154
E-mail: hn0331@handsnet.org
Web: www.mcauley.org

U.S. DEPT. OF HOUSING AND URBAN DEVELOPMENT
Washington, DC 20410-0001
202-708-1422
Fax: 800-245-2691
E-mail: Candis_B_Harrison@hud.gov
Web: www.hud.gov

WALTER SEGAL SELF-BUILD TRUST
Unit 213, 16 Baldwins Garden
London EC1N 7R5
United Kingdom
22-7831-5696
Fax: 22-7831-5697
E-mail: info@segalselfbuild.co.uk
Web: www.segalselfbuild.co.uk

INCOME AND WEALTH TAXES—An important tool but frequently overlooked aid to community development is the replacement of regressive taxes on property and sales with progressive taxes on income and wealth. The two national organizations producing a steady stream of books and studies on tax policy (though primarily focusing on national taxes) are Citizens for Tax Justice and the Economic Policy Institute. For materials documenting the widening gulf between rich and poor in the country, contact Share the Wealth, and Too Much. See also *George Taxes* and *Green Taxes*.

CITIZENS FOR TAX JUSTICE
1311 L St., NW
Washington, DC 20005
202-626-3780
Fax: 638-3486
E-mail: ctj@ctj.org
Web: www.ctj.org

ECONOMIC POLICY INSTITUTE
Suite 1200
1660 L St., NW
Washington, DC 20036
202-775-8810
Fax: 202-775-0819
E-mail: epi@epinet.org
Web: www.epinet.org

SHARE THE WEALTH
5th Floor
37 Temple Place
Boston, MA 02111
617-423-2148

Fax: 617-423-0191
E-mail: stw@stw.org
Web: www.stw.org

TOO MUCH
Suite 3C
777 United Nations Plaza
New York, NY 10017
800-316-2739 (Voice & Fax)
E-mail: cipany@igc.org

INDICATORS—If you're interested in developing formal indicators of your community's well-being, the main clearinghouses are the Integrative Strategies Forum, Redefining Progress, and a web site created by Maureen Hart. The most advanced effort under way is Sustainable Seattle. The New Economics Foundation has an excellent study on efforts in the United Kingdom called "Accounting for Change."

MAUREEN HART
P.O. Box 361
North Andover, MA 01845
508-975-1988
Fax: 508-975-2241
E-mail: mhart@tiac.net
Web: www.subjectmatters.com/indicators

INTEGRATIVE STRATEGIES FORUM
Suite 600
1612 K St., NW
Washington, DC 20006
202-872-5339
Fax: 202-331-8166
E-mail: jbarber@igc.org

REDEFINING PROGRESS
4th Floor
1 Kearny St.
San Francisco, CA 94108
415-781-1191
Fax: 415-781-1198
E-mail: info@rprogress.org
Web: www.rprogress.org

SUSTAINABLE SEATTLE
514 Minor Ave.
Seattle, WA 98109
206-622-3522
Fax: 206-622-3611

E-mail: sustsea@halcyon.com
Web: www.scn.org/sustainable

INTENTIONAL COMMUNITIES—There are more than 400 so-called intentional communities in the United States in which residents with common religious beliefs or lifestyle philosophies construct their own utopias, often supported by community-owned and -operated businesses. News from these communities is covered in *Communities Magazine*.

COMMUNITIES MAGAZINE
138 West Twin Oaks Rd.
Louisa, VA 23093
540-894-5798
Web: fic.ic.org/cmag/subscribe.html

INTERLOCALISM—Communities are increasingly reaching out to other communities worldwide to share technology and policy ideas that enhance economic self-reliance. The International Union of Local Authorities, based in the Hague, facilitates practical exchanges and assistance among cities. More than 300 communities interested in collaborating on global environmental protection are members of the International Council on Local Environmental Initiatives based in Toronto. A much larger number are involved in Local Agenda 21, a process launched at the United Nations Earth Summit in Rio de Janeiro in 1982 and promoted by the Citizens Network for Sustainable Development. See also *Fair Trade* and *North-South Development Cooperation*.

CITNET U.N. LIAISON OFFICE
Suite 206
73 Spring St.
New York, NY 10012
212-431-3922
Fax: 212-431-4427
E-mail: cca@igc.org

INTERNATIONAL COUNCIL FOR LOCAL ENVIRONMENTAL INITIATIVES
West Tower 16th Floor
Toronto, ON M5H 2N2
Canada
416-392-1462
Fax: 416-392-1478
E-mail: iclei@iclei.org
Web: www.iclei.org

INTERNATIONAL UNION OF LOCAL AUTHORITIES
P.O. Box 90646
2509 LP The Hague
Netherlands
31-70-324-4032

Fax: 31-70-350-0496
E-mail: iula@iula-hq.nl
Web: www.iula.org

INVENTORIES—Workbooks to help a community assess unused or under-used resources, from unemployed musicians to wasted water, are available from the Neighborhood Innovations Network at Northwestern University (*Building Communities from the Inside Out*) and the Rocky Mountain Institute (noted above) (*Economic Renewal Guide*).

NEIGHBORHOOD INNOVATIONS NETWORK
Center for Urban Affairs and Policy Research
Northwestern University
2040 Sheridan Rd.
Evanston, IL 60208
708-491-3518
Fax: 708-491-9916
E-mail: achambers@nwu.edu
Web: www.nwu.edu/IPR

LABELS—While there are no examples yet of cities awarding products Good Communitykeeping Seals of Approval, Green Seal does award its label to environmentally friendly products. In Canada the Environmental Choice Program awards its EcoLogo to more than 700 products and services.

ENVIRONMENTAL CHOICE PROGRAM
Suite 200
107 Sparks St.
Ottawa, Ontario K1A 0H3
Canada
613-952-9440
Fax: 613-247-2228
E-mail: ecoinfo@terrachoice.ca
Web: www.terrachoice.ca/ecologo.htm

GREEN SEAL
Suite 827
1001 Connecticut Ave., NW
Washington, DC 20036-5525
202-872-6400
Fax: 202-872-4324
E-mail: aweissman@greenseal.org
Web: www.greenseal.org

LABOR RIGHTS—Thousands of trade unions around the world promote labor rights at the local, state, national, and international level. If you want to see what kinds of policy initiatives are working, the journals listed below can be quite valuable. See also *Worker Ownership*.

ECONOMIC AND INDUSTRIAL DEMOCRACY
Sage Publications Ltd.
28 Banner St.
London EC1Y 8QE
United Kingdom
44-171-374-0645
Fax: 44-171-374-8741
E-mail: clive.parry@sagepub.co.uk
Web: www.sagepub.co.uk

LABOR NOTES
7435 Michigan Ave.
Detroit, MI 48210
313-842-6262
Fax: 313-842-0227
E-mail: labornotes@labornotes.org
Web: www.labornotes.org

LABOR RESEARCH REVIEW
Center for Labor and Community Research
Suite 14
3411 W. Diversey Ave.
Chicago, IL 60647
312-278-5418
Fax: 773-278-5918
E-mail: clcr@mindspring.com
Web: www.clcr.org

LIVABLE METROPOLITAN AREAS AND SMART GROWTH—One of the fastest growing sustainable-community movements in recent years, fueled by writers like Myron Orfield (*Metropolitics: A Regional Agency for Community and Stability*) and Neil Peirce, has been fierce opposition to sprawl. As suburbanites face ever longer and more irritating commutes to work, school, shops, and parks, and face more aesthetically deadening strip malls, they have finally come to realize that they solve their problems by working together with people living in the urban cores. The solutions of the movement, promulgated by the American Land Institute, Brooking Institution, the Center for Neighborhood Technologies, the National Congress for Community Economic Development, and PolicyLink, tend to focus on *regional* planning, tax-sharing, and governance. The entire discourse, however, assumes that regions are the basic building blocks for prosperous economies, and seems relatively uninterested in addressing the problem by creating local owned, import-replacing businesses in *both* the suburbs and urban neighborhoods. Other organizations active in the field are listed below. See also *New Urbanism*.

ALLIANCE FOR METROPOLITAN STABILITY
2105 First Ave.
Minneapolis, MN 55404
612-332-4471
Fax: 612-339-3481
E-mail: radam03@ibm.net

AMERICAN LAND INSTITUTE
Suite 714
534 SW 3rd St.
Portland, OR 97204
503-228-9462
Fax: 503-223-1475
E-mail: ngmlp@teleport.com

ATLANTA NEIGHBORHOOD DEVELOPMENT PARTNERSHIP
Suite 1700
34 Peachtree St.
Atlanta, GA 30303
404-522-2637
Fax: 404-523-4357
E-mail: andpi@andpi.org
Web: www.andpi.org

CENTER FOR NEIGHBORHOOD TECHNOLOGIES
2125 West North Ave.
Chicago, IL 60647
773-278-4800
Fax: 773-278-3840
E-mail: info@cnt.org
Web: www.cnt.org

CHICAGO METROPOLIS 2020
30 W. Monroe St., 18th Floor
Chicago, IL 60603
312-332-2020
Fax: 312-332-2626
E-mail: info@cm2020.org
Web: www.chicagometropolis2020.org

COLLINS CENTER FOR PUBLIC POLICY AND SMART GROWTH
150 SE 2nd Ave.
Miami, FL 33131
305-377-4484
Fax: 305-377-4485
E-mail: collins-info@collinscenter.org
Web: www.collinscenter.org

CENTER ON URBAN AND METROPOLITAN POLICY
Brookings Institution
1775 Massachusetts Ave., NW
Washington, DC 20036
202-797-6139
Fax: 202-797-2965
E-mail: brookinfo@brook.edu
Web: brook.edu

NATIONAL CONGRESS FOR COMMUNITY ECONOMIC DEVELOPMENT
Suite 325
1030 15th St., NW
Washington, DC 20005
202-289-9020
Fax: 202-289-7051
E-mail: meminfo@ncced.org
Web: ncced.org

POLICYLINK
101 Broadway
Oakland, CA 94607
510-663-2333
Fax: 510-663-9684
Web: www.policylink.org

SMART GROWTH NETWORK
c/o ICMA
Suite 500
777 North Capitol St., NE
Washington, DC 20002-4201
202-962-3591
Fax: 202-962-3500
E-mail: smartgrowth@icma.org
Web: www.smartgrowth.org

SPRAWL WATCH CLEARINGHOUSE
10th Floor
1100 17th Street, NW
Washington, DC 20036
202-974-5133
Fax: 202-466-2247
E-mail: allison@sprawlwatch.org
Web: www.sprawlwatch.org

LIVABLE WAGES—If you're interested in raising local living conditions, why not raise the minimum wage? Livable wage campaigns mounted by ACORN (see *Community Reinvestment Act*) have persuaded such cities as Baltimore, Los Angeles,

New York, Portland, San Jose, and St. Paul to do so. These local laws typically require that major contractors with the city pay all their employees a wage of at least $7 to $10.

LOCAL CURRENCIES—If you'd like to start your own local money system, the architects of the Ithaca Hours system have put together *A Home Town Money Starter Kit*, available for $25. You can follow experiments worldwide *Local Currency Nesw*, published by the E.F. Schumacher Society (see above). An on-line journal linking local currency practioners is the *International Journal of Community Currency Research* (www.geog.le.ac.uk/ijccr). If you are interested in the Local Exchange Trading Systems (LETS), its pioneer, Michael Linton, is reachable at Landsman Community Services, Ltd. A variety of other LETS resources are available on-line via the LETSystem Home Page (www.gmlets.u-net.com) and the publications of LETSlink UK (including a magazine, a *LETS Info Pack*, and *LETS Work: Rebuilding the Local Economy*). See also *Time Dollars*.

ITHACA HOURS
Box 6731
Ithaca, NY 14851
Phone: 607-272-3738
E-mail: ithacahours@lightlink.com
Web: www.ithacahours.org

LANDSMAN COMMUNITY SERVICES, LTD.
1600 Embleton Crescent
Courtenay, BC V9N 6N8
Canada
Phone & Fax: 250-338-0213
E-mail: lcs@mars.ark.com
Web: www.communityway.org

LETSLINK UK
56 Campbell Road, Southsea
Hants, PO5 1RW
United Kingdom
E-mail: lets@letslinkuk.org
Web: www.letslinkuk.demon.co.uk

LOBBYING—Most U.S. towns and cities lobby at the national level through the organizations listed under *Official Action*. These efforts are notable for their singular ineffectiveness, timidity, and conservatism. A more worthwhile network which educates state officials on new economic ideas is overseen by the Center for Policy Alternatives. Any municipality serious about changing national policy ought to consider mounting its own lobbying efforts, alone or with other communities. Training for effective lobbying is available at reasonable cost from the Advocacy Institute.

ADVOCACY INSTITUTE
Suite 400
1707 L St., NW
Washington, DC 20036
202-659-8475
Fax: 202-659-8484
E-mail: www.advocacy.org
Web: www.advocacy.org

CENTER FOR POLICY ALTERNATIVES
Suite 710
1875 Connecticut Ave., NW
Washington, DC 20009
202-387-6030
Fax: 202-986-2539
E-mail: info@cfpa.org
Web: www.cfpa.org

MAGAZINE RACK—The following magazines and journals contain essential news, proposals, analysis, and debate on community economics. Since most operate on a financial shoestring through paid subscriptions, a self-reliant community ought to feel duty-bound to make sure these magazines are widely read in City Hall, and available in public libraries.

ALTERNATIVES
c/o Environmental Studies
University of Waterloo
Waterloo, ON N2L 3G1
Canada
519-888-4567, ext. 6783
Fax: 519-746-0292
E-mail: alternat@ses.uwaterloo.ca
Web: www.fes.uwaterloo.ca/research

ECOLOGIST
c/o MIT Press
55 Hayward St.
Cambridge, MA 02142
617-253-2889
Fax: 617-577-1545
E-mail: ecologist@gn.apc.org
Web: www.gn.apc.org/ecologist

ECOLOGICAL ECONOMICS
International Society for Ecological Economics
P.O. Box 1589
Solomons, MD 20688

410-326-7263
Fax: 410-326-7354
E-mail: king@cbl.umces.edu
Web: www.ecoeco.org

GOVERNING
Suite 1300
1100 Connecticut Ave., NW
Washington, DC 20036
202-862-8802
Fax: 202-862-0032
E-mail: mailbox@governing.com
Web: www.governing.com

NEIGHBORHOOD WORKS
2125 W. North Ave.
Chicago, IL 60647
312-278-4800
Fax: 312-278-3840
E-mail: info@cnt.org
Web: www.cnt.org

PROGRESSIVE REVIEW
Suite 502
1312 18th St., NW
Washington, DC 20036
202-835-0770
Fax: 202-835-0779
E-mail: news@prorev.com
Web: prorev.com

RESURGENCE
Ford House, Hartland
Bideford, Devon EX39 6EE
United Kingdom
44-01237-441-293
Fax: 44-01237-441-203
Web: www.gn.apc.org/resurgence

SHELTERFORCE
National Housing Institute
Suite 311
439 Main St.
Orange, NJ 07050
973-678-9060
Fax: 973-678-8437
E-mail: nhi@nhi.org
Web: www.nhi.org

SOCIAL POLICY
Suite 620
25 W. 43rd St.
New York, NY 10036
212-642-2929
Fax: 212-642-1956
E-mail: agrten1@gc.cuny.edu
Web: www.socialpolicy.org

THIRD WORLD RESURGENCE & THIRD WORLD ECONOMICS
228 Macalister Rd.
10400 Panang
Malaysia
604-226-6159
Fax: 604-226-4505
E-mail: twnpen@twn.po.my
Web: www.twnside.org.sg

URBAN ECOLOGIST
Suite 900
Oakland, CA 94612
510-251-6330
Fax: 510-251-2117
E-mail: urbanecology@igc.org
Web: www.urbanecology.org

WHO CARES
Suite 412
1511 K St., NW
Washington, DC 20005
202-628-1691
Fax: 202-628-2063
E-mail: info@whocares.org
Web: www.whocares.org

YES!
P.O. Box 10818
Bainbridge Island, WA 98110-0818
206-842-0216
Fax: 206-842-5208
E-mail: yes@futurenet.org
Web: www.futurenet.org

MASS TRANSIT—If you're interested in replacing sprawl-inducing and smog-belching automobiles with community-friendly mass transit, you should contact the Transportation Action Network. You also can fight federal subsidies for roads and oil by disseminating the excellent reports on the subject by Komanoff Energy Associations and the World Resources Institute.

KOMANOFF ENERGY ASSOCIATES
Suite 412
270 Lafayette St.
New York, NY 10012
212-334-9767
Fax: 212-925-2151
E-mail: kea@igc.org

TRANSPORTATION ACTION NETWORK
10th Floor
1100 17th St., NW
Washington, DC 20036
202-466-2636
Fax: 202-466-2247
E-mail: stpp@trasact.org
Web: www.transact.org/stpp.htm

WORLD RESOURCES INSTITUTE
Suite 800
10 G St., NE
Washington, DC 20002
202-729-7600
Fax: 202-729-7610
E-mail: lauralee@wri.org
Web: www.wri.org

MICROENTERPRISE FUNDS—A great deal has been written on the world's most successful microenterprise fund, the Grameen Bank, including two outstanding books: Alex Counts' *Give Us Credit* (Times Book, 1996) and David Bornstein's *The Price of a Dream* (Simon & Schuster, 1996). Counts also discusses domestic U.S. microcredit programs such as the Women's Self-Employment Project. Peggy Clark at the Aspen Institute has prepared a number of directories and studies of U.S. microenterprise programs. The Grameen Bank also publishes its own newsletter called *Grameen Dialogue*.

ASPEN INSTITUTE
Suite 700
One Dupont Circle, NW
Washington, DC 20036-1133
202-736-5800
Fax: 202-466-4568
Web: www.aspeninstitute.org

GRAMEEN BANK

Mirpur, Section-2
Dhaka – 1216 Bangladesh
8802-9005257-68
E-mail: grameenbank@grameen.net
Web: www.grameen-info.org

WOMEN'S SELF-EMPLOYMENT PROJECT
Suite 400
20 North Clark St.
Chicago, IL 60602
Phone: 312-606-8255
Fax: 312-606-9215
E-mail: hn1578@handsnet.org

MODEL ECOVILLAGES—A few communities have integrated the best practices in ecological design, planning, and technology to create model neighborhoods. EcoVillages can be found in rural communities like Findhorn in the United Kingdom, college towns like Ithaca, and megacities like Los Angeles. Information about these efforts worldwide is available from the Global EcoVillage Network in Denmark. Two useful books are *The Restoration Development Project*, published by Ecocity Builders, and Joan Roelofs' *Greening Cities*, available from Keene State College.

ECOCITY BUILDERS
1678 Shattuck Ave., #66
Berkeley, CA 94709
510-649-1817
Fax: 510-649-1817
E-mail: ecocity@igc.org
Web: www.citizen-planners.org/ecocitybuilders

ECOVILLAGE AT ITHACA
Anabel Taylor Hall
Cornell University
Ithaca, NY 14853
607-255-8276
Fax: 607-255-9985
E-mail: ecovillage@cornell.edu
Web: www.ecovillage.ithaca.ny.us

FINDHORN FOUNDATION
The Park, Findhorn
Forres Moray IV36 0TQ
United Kingdom
Phone: 44-1309-691620
E-mail: communications@findhorn.org
Web: www.findhorn.org

GLOBAL ECO-VILLAGE NETWORK
Gaia Villages
Skyumevej 101
Snedsted 7752
Denmark
45-9793-6655
Fax: 45-9793-6677
E-mail: gen@gaia.org
Web: www.gaia.org

KEENE STATE COLLEGE
Dept. of Political Economy—2001
Keene, NH 03435-2001
603-358-2634
Fax: 603-358-2257
E-mail: jroelofs@keene.edu
Web: www.keene.edu

LOS ANGELES ECOVILLAGE
Cooperative Resources & Services Project
3551 White House Pl.
Los Angeles, CA 90004
213-738-1254
Fax: 213-386-8873
E-mail: crsp@igc.org
Web: www.ic.org/laev

MUNICIPAL FOREIGN POLICY—The 1980s witnessed a spectacular growth of U.S. state, county, and local government involvement in foreign policymaking. More than 900 localities passed resolutions supporting a "freeze" in the arms race; 197 demanded a halt to nuclear testing; 120 refused to cooperate with the Federal Emergency Management Agency's nuclear-war exercises; 126, plus 27 states, divested from firms doing business in South Africa; 86 formed linkages with Nicaragua and, along with grassroots activists, provided more humanitarian assistance to the Nicaraguan people than all the military aid Congress voted for the contras; 80, along with the U.S. Conference of Mayors, demanded cuts in the Pentagon's budget; 73 formed sister-city relationships with Soviet cities; 29 provided sanctuary for Guatemalan and Salvadoran refugees; 20 passed stratospheric protection ordinances phasing out ozone-depleting chemicals; and at least ten established funded offices of international affairs—essentially municipal state departments. If you'd like to learn more about this movement, contact the author, who ran a clearinghouse on these activities in the 1980s called the Center for Innovative Diplomacy (now defunct).

MICHAEL SHUMAN
c/o ProgressivePubs.com
3713 Warren St., NW
Washington, DC 20016

202-238-0010
Fax: 202-238-0011
E-mail: shuman@igc.org
Web: www.progressivepubs.com

NEW ECONOMICS—To win debates over your community's economic future, you may find it necessary to counter traditional economists with experts committed to new economic thinking. The institutes below all have outstanding analysts (the most prominent are noted in parentheses) skilled at deflating outmoded theories, graphs, and statistics of the dismal science. Several other outstanding scholars unaffiliated with any institution are noted as well. See also *Regional Think Tanks*.

JEREMY BRECHER
36 Yelping Hill Rd.
W. Cornwall, CT 06796

THE CENTER FOR LABOR AND COMMUNITY RESEARCH (DAN SWINNEY)
3411 W. Diverse, Suite 10
Chicago, IL 60647
773-278-5418
Fax: 773-278-5918
E-mail: clcr@mindspring.com
Web: www.mclr.com

CENTER FOR POPULAR ECONOMICS
P.O. Box 785
Amherst, MA 01004
413-545-0743
Web: www.ctrpopec.org

HAZEL HENDERSON
Box 5190
St. Augustine, FL 32085

HUMAN ECONOMY CENTER
P.O. Box 28
West Swanzey, NH 03469-0028
603-436-1565
E-mail: humanecon@igc.org

INSTITUTE FOR SOCIAL ECOLOGY (MURRAY BOOKCHIN)
P.O. Box 89
Plainfield, VT 05667
802-454-8493
E-mail: ise@sover.net
Web: ise.rootmedia.org

INTERNATIONAL SOCIETY FOR ECOLOGY AND CULTURE
(HELENA NORBERG-HODGE)
21 Victoria Sq.
Clifton, Bristol
United Kingdom
44-1803-868650
Fax: 44-1803-868651
E-mail: isec@gniapc.org
Web: www.isec.org.uk

SUSAN MEEKER-LOWRY
Catalyst
P.O. Box 1308
Montpelier, VT 05601

PEGS
Department of Government and Politics
University of Maryland
College Park, MD 20742
301-405-7799
E-mail: pegs@gvpt.umd.edu
Web: www.bsos.umd.edu/pegs/pegs.html

PROTECT THE LOCAL, GLOBALLY (COLIN HINES)
11 Park House Gardens
East Twickenham
Middlesex TW1 2DF
United Kingdom
44-171-892-5051
E-mail: chines@dial.pepex.com

RESEARCH FOUNDATION FOR SCIENCE, TECHNOLOGY, AND NATURAL RESOURCE
POLICY (VANDANA SHIVA)
A-60 Haus Khas
New Delhi 110016
India
91-11-665-003
Fax: 91-11-686-6795

UNIVERSITY OF MARYLAND (HERMAN DALY)
School of Public Affairs
Van Munching Hall
University of Maryland
College Park, MD 20742
301-405-6359/60
Fax: 301-314-9346
E-mail: hdaly@puafmail.umd.edu
Web: www.puaf.umd.edu

WORLDWATCH INSTITUTE (LESTER BROWN)
1776 Massachusetts Ave., NW
Washington, DC 20036
202-452-1999
Fax: 202-296-7365
E-mail: worldwatch@worldwatch.org
Web: www.worldwatch.org

NEW URBANISM—Coalescing around the philosophy, writings, and architectural work of Peter Calthorpe, Douglas Duany, Peter Katz, and Elizabeth Plater-Zyberk, the New Urbanists believe that design matters. Buildings should be made to be aesthetically pleasing as well as human-scale and comfortable, and neighborhoods should be constructed to support a close-knit community. No vital necessities should ever be more than a ten minute walk from home, which means that most activity-restricting and car-friendly zoning laws ought to be removed from the books. These views have been popularized through the entertaining writings of James Kunstler (*Geography of Nowhere* and *Home from Nowhere*) and promoted through the Congress for New Urbanism and other groups listed below. You can follow this movement through the *New Urban News*. See also *Livable Metropolitan Areas and Smart Growth*.

CONGRESS FOR NEW URBANISM
The Hearst Building
5 Third Street, Suite 725
San Francisco, CA 94103
415-495-2255
Fax: 415-495-1731
E-mail: cnuinfo@cnu.org
Web: www.cnu.org

NATIONAL TOWN BUILDERS ASSOCIATION
Suite 715
1400 16th Street, NW
Washington DC 20036
202-518-6300
Fax: 202-518-6398
E-mail: info@townbuild.com
Web: www.ntba.net

NATIONAL MAIN STREET CENTER
National Trust for Historic Preservation
1785 Massachusetts Avenue, NW
Washington, DC 20036 USA
202-588-6219
Fax: 202-588-6050
Web: www.mainst.org

NEW URBAN NEWS
P.O. Box 6515
Ithaca, NY 14851
607-275-3087
Fax: 607-272-2685
E-mail: newurban@aol.com
Web: www.newurbannews.com

THE SEASIDE INSTITUTE
P.O. 4730
Seaside, FL 32459
850-231-2421
Fax: 850-231-1884
E-mail: pbleiweis@theseasideinstitute.org
Web: www.theseasideinstitute.com

WORLD IDEA NETWORKS
P.O. Box 18224
Washington DC 20036
202-518-2800
Fax: 202-518-6398
E-mail: support@worldideanet.org
Web: www.worldideanet.org

NONPROFITS—For an excellent treatise on nonprofit businesses, see *New Social Entrepreneurs* by the Roberts Foundation and other papers written by its executive director, Jed Emerson. Since one virtue of nonprofits is that they can receive grants from foundations, it's important to be in touch with funders interested in community self-reliance. Four of the most important networks are: the Funders Network for Smart Growth and Livable Communities; the National Network of Grantmakers; the Environmental Grantmakers Network; and the Neighborhood Funders Group, an affinity group within the Council on Foundations.

ENVIRONMENTAL GRANTMAKERS NETWORK
c/o Environmental Data Research Institute
P.O. Box 22770
Rochester, NY 14692-2770
716-473-3090
Fax: 716-473-0968
E-mail: edri@eznet.net

FUNDERS NETWORK FOR SMART GROWTH AND LIVABLE COMMUNITIES
Suite 709
150 SE 2nd Ave.
Miami, FL 33131
305-377-4484

Fax: 305-377-4485
E-mail bstarrett@collinscenter.org
Web: www.fundersnetwork.org

NATIONAL NETWORK OF GRANTMAKERS
Suite 110
1717 Kettner Blvd.
San Diego, CA 92101
619-231-1348
Fax: 619-231-1349
E-mail: nng@nng.org
Web: www.nng.org

NEIGHBORHOOD FUNDERS GROUP
Suite 320
6862 Elm St.
McLean, VA 22101
703-448-1777
Fax: 703-448-1780
E-mail: nfg@nfg.org
Web: www.nfg.org

ROBERTS FOUNDATION
P.O. Box 29966
San Francisco, CA 94129-0906
415-561-6680
Fax: 415-561-6685
E-mail: info@redf.org
Web: www.redf.org

NORTH-SOUTH DEVELOPMENT COOPERATION—Nearly 4,000 municipalities are participating in North-South development cooperation through the efforts of Towns and Development, based in the Hague. One of the best practitioners, spending more than $1 per capita per year of municipal money on development cooperation, is the city-state of Bremen in Germany. Guidance on how best to structure such partnerships is available in *Towards A Global Village* (Pluto, 1994), from the web site of the People-Centered Development Forum (iisd1.iisd.ca/pcdf), and from various publications of the Institute for Food and Development Policy (formerly Food First). One promising idea for such partnerships is for a community in the North to set up and place seed money in a microcredit fund in the South. The city of Madison, Wisconsin, did just that with its partners in Managua, Nicaragua, and you can read the details in Carter Garber's report for North-South Center (Paper #23) on "Private Investment as a Financing Source for Microcredit." See also *Fair Trade, Interlocalism,* and *Municipal Foreign Policy.*

INSTITUTE FOR FOOD AND DEVELOPMENT POLICY
398 60th St.

Oakland, CA 94618
510-654-4400
Fax: 510-654-4551
E-mail: foodfirst@foodfirst.org
Web: www.foodfirst.org

NORTH-SOUTH CENTER
University of Miami
1500 Monza Ave.
Coral Gables, FL 33146-3027
305-284-6868
Fax: 305-284-6370
E-mail: ahmoss@miami.edu
Web: www.miami.edu/nsc

STATE OFFICE FOR DEVELOPMENT COOPERATION
Kirchenstrasse 4-5a
D-28195 Bremen
Germany
49-421-361-2194
Fax: 49-421-361-2648
E-mail: ghilliges@hva.bremen.de
Web: www.bremend-initiative.de

TOWNS AND DEVELOPMENT
Postbus 85615
2508 CH The Hague
Netherlands
31-70-362-3894
Fax: 31-70-364-2869

OFFICIAL ACTION—To learn what's happening in the mainstream (and, more often than not, what's being done wrong), check out the offical organizations linking governors, mayors, city council members, county supervisors, city/county managers, planners, and chamber of commerce executives.

AMERICAN CHAMBER OF COMMERCE EXECUTIVES
4232 King St.
Alexandria, VA 22302
703-998-0072
Fax: 703-931-5624
E-mail: webmaster@acce.org
Web: www.acce.org

INTERNATIONAL CITY/COUNTY MANAGEMENT ASSOCIATION
Suite 500

777 North Capitol St., NE
Washington, DC 20002-4201
202-289-4262
Fax: 202-962-3500
E-mail: info@icma.org
Web: www.icma.org

NATIONAL ASSOCIATION OF COUNTIES
440 First St., NW, Suite 800
Washington, DC 20001
202-393-6226
Fax: 202-393-2630
E-mail: info@naco.org
Web: www.naco.org

NATIONAL ASSOCIATION OF TOWNS AND TOWNSHIPS
Suite 208
444 North Capitol St.
Washington, DC 20001
202-624-3550
Fax: 202-624-3554
E-mail: natat@sso.org
Web: natat.org

NATIONAL GOVERNORS ASSOCIATION
Hall of the States
444 North Capitol St.
Washington, DC 20001-1512
202-624-5300
Fax: 202-624-5313
E-mail: webmaster@nga.org
Web: www.nga.org

NATIONAL LEAGUE OF CITIES
1301 Pennsylvania Ave., NW
Washington, DC 20004
202-626-3000
Fax: 202-626-3043
E-mail: Pa@nlc.org
Web: www.nlc.org

U.S. CONFERENCE OF MAYORS
1620 Eye St., NW
Washington, DC 20006
202-293-7330
Fax: 202-293-2352
E-mail: info@usmayors.org
Web: www.usmayors.org

WESTERN GOVERNORS ASSOCIATION
Suite 1705 S.
600 17th St.
Denver, CO 80202-5452
303-623-9378
Fax: 303-534-7309
E-mail: cmck@westgov.org
Web: www.westgov.org

PERMACULTURE—The word permaculture comes from *perma*nent agri*culture*, and describes an emerging discourse that integrates sustainable agriculture with environmentally friendly gardening, architecture, land-use planning, and business creation. The International Institute for Ecological Agriculture publishes papers in the field, and discussions can be found in a magazine called the *Permaculture Activist*. See also *Community Food Systems*.

INTERNATIONAL INSTITUTE FOR ECOLOGICAL AGRICULTURE
834 West California Way
Woodside, CA 94062
650-365-2993
Fax: 650-366-2241
E-mail: dblume@igc.org
Web: www.permaculture-institute.org

PERMACULTURE ACTIVIST
P.O. Box 1209W
Black Mountain, NC 28711
828-298-2812
Fax: 828-298-6441
E-mail: peactiv@metalab.unc.edu

PRODUCER COOPERATIVES—If you are interested in the two producer cooperatives discussed in the book, the Economic Circle (Wirtschaftsring) in Switzerland and Mondragon in Spain, you can contact them directly at the addresses below. Mondragon also has a newsletter, with English excerpts on the World Wide Web, called *TU Lankide*. You also can educate your community about Mondragon by showing films about the cooperative, available from the Canadian Cooperatives Association, or by going on tours of Mondragon led by the Intercommunity Justice and Peace Center of Cincinnati.

CANADIAN COOPERATIVE ASSOCIATION
Suite 601
415 Young St.
Ottawa, ON M5B 2E7
Canada
416-348-9666

Fax: 416-348-9283
E-mail: ccaont@ccaont.on.ca
Web: www.ccaont.on.ca

INTERCOMMUNITY JUSTICE & PEACE CENTER
215 East 14th St.
Cincinnati, OH 45210
513-579-8547
Fax: 513-579-0674
E-mail: IJPCCinti@aol.com
Web: http://hometown.aol.com/IJPCCinti/index.html

MONDRAGON CORPORACION COOPERATIVA
P. Jose Maria Arizmendiarrieta n. 5
Edificio LK 3
20500 Mondragon (Guipuzcoa)
Spain
34-43-779-300
Fax: 34-43-796-632
E-mail: info@mondragon.mcc.es
Web: www.mondragon.mcc.es

TU LANKIDE
Otalora - Azatza Auzoa
Aretxabaleta
20550 Gipuzkoa
Spain
Phone: 34-943-779-300
Fax: 34-943-796-632
E-mail: lankide@mondragon.mcc.es
Web: www.mondragon.mcc.es

WIRTSCHAFTSRING
Auberg 1
4002 Basel
Switzerland
Phone: 41-61-277-9111
Fax: 41-61-277-9239
E-mail: Roy.Davies@exeter.ac.uk
Web: www.ex.ac.uk/~RDavies/arian/wir.html

PRODUCTIVITY BANK—If your city council claims it's too broke to finance public innovations toward self-reliance, you might encourage the creation of a productivity bank. Philadelphia, for example, established a $20 million revolving loan fund that finances, among other things, recycling, conserving energy, and purchasing more-efficient police cars. Loans are repaid through savings over the lifetime of money-saving projects. Neil Seldman of the Institute for Local Self-Reliance (see above) has written an excellent paper on the subject entitled "Municipal Productivity Programs and Their Potential Application to Washington, D.C."

PUBLIC HEALTH—In recent years a literature has emerged using human health as a way of promoting community health, and vice-versa. One of the key organizations is the Coalition for Healthier Cities and Communities. Public health schools and institutes, many funded by the Robert Wood Johnson Foundation, have focused on the importance of smart community policymaking to ensure decent nutrition, preventative health care, safe drinking water, and high levels of sanitation. These analysts also suggest how careful reorganization of community health-care institutions like health maintenance organizations (HMOs) and hospitals can improve the overall functioning of the community. The Natural Step, based in Sweden but spreading in the United States, has turned this holistic view about human and community health into a global movement.

COALITION FOR HEALTHIER CITIES AND COMMUNITIES
E-mail: info@healthycommunities.org
Web: www.healthycommunities.org

NATURAL STEP
P.O. Box 29372
San Francisco, CA 94129
415-561-3344
Fax: 415-561-3345
E-mail: TNS@naturalstep.org
Web: www.naturalstep.org

ROBERT WOOD JOHNSON FOUNDATION
P.O. Box 2316
Princeton, NJ 08543-2316
609-452-8701
Fax: 609-987-8845
E-mail: mail@rwjf.org
Web: www.rwjf.org

RECYCLING & REUSE—The best materials on the state-of-the-art on recycling and reuse are available from the Institute for Local Self-Reliance (see above). The following groups also have useful studies and information.

FOREST FRIENDLY PAPER CAMPAIGN
Earth Island Institute
Suite 28
300 Broadway
San Francisco, CA 94133-3312
415-788-3666
Fax: 415-788-7324

E-mail: atwork@igc.org
Web: www.earthisland.org

MATERIALS FOR THE FUTURE FOUNDATION
Suite 222
Presidio Building 1016
Torney Ave.
P.O. Box 29091
San Francisco, CA 94129
415-561-6530
Fax: 415-561-6474
E-mail: mff@igc.org
Web: www.materials4future.org

NATIONAL RECYCLING COALITION
Suite 105
1727 King St.
Alexandria, VA 22314
703-683-9025
Fax: 703-683-9026
Web: www.nrc-recycle.org

REGIONAL THINK TANKS—Across the country are small think tanks promoting community, county, state, or regional self-reliance. Most produce a steady stream of books, studies, and newsletters. Check out the list below to see which are operating in or near your own area. If there's none nearby, you might consider starting one, perhaps through a local university or community college.

ALLIANCE FOR A SUSTAINABLE FUTURE
1042 Lime Kiln Pike
Ambler, PA 19002
215-641-9417
Fax: 215-283-0737
E-mail: thechelman@aol.com

CENTER FOR NEIGHBORHOOD TECHNOLOGY
2125 W. North Ave.
Chicago, IL 60647
773-278-4800
Fax: 773-278-3840
E-mail: info@cnt.org
Web: www.cnt.org

COALITION FOR JOBS AND THE ENVIRONMENT
P.O. Box 645
Abingdon, VA 24210
Phone and Fax: 540-628-8996

COMMONWEALTH INC.
1221 Elm St.
Youngstown, OH 44505
330-744-2667
Fax: 330-744-1819

COMMUNITY DEVELOPMENT ACADEMY
103 Whitten Hall
University of Missouri
Columbia, MO 65211
800-545-2604
Fax: 573-884-5371
E-mail: Hughesco@missouri.edu
Web: ssu.agri.missouri.edu/CommDev/default.htm

FEDERATION OF SOUTHERN COOPERATIVES
P.O. Box 95
Epes, AL 35460
205-652-9676
Fax: 205-652-9678
E-mail: fsc@mindspring.com
Web: www.federationsoutherncoop.com

INSTITUTE FOR ENVIRONMENTAL STUDIES
Ramapo College of New Jersey
505 Ramapo Valley Rd.
Mahwah, NJ 07430-1680
201-529-7742
Fax: 201-529-7508

JOBS AND ENVIRONMENT CAMPAIGN
1168 Commonwealth Ave.
Boston, MA 01234
617-232-5833
Fax: 617-232-3837

LOCAL GOVERNMENT COMMISSION
Suite 250
1414 K St.
Sacramento, CA 95814
916-448-1198
Fax: 916-448-8246
E-mail: info@lgc.org
Web: www.lgc.org

NOVA SCOTIA ENVIRONMENT & DEVELOPMENT COALITION
Suite 133
1657 Barrington St.

Halifax, NS B3J 2A1
902-422-4276
Fax: 902-423-9736
E-mail: ip-scn@ccn.cs.dal.ca
Web: http://cfn.cs.dal/ca/Environment/SCN/SCN_home.html

SUSTAINABILITY PROJECT
4 Gavilan Rd.
Sante Fe, NM 87505
505-466-2052 (Voice & Fax)

URBAN ECOLOGY
405 14th St., Suite 900
Oakland, CA 94612
510-251-6330
Fax: 510-251-2117
E-mail: urbanecology@urbanecology.org
Web: www.urbanecology.org

RENEWABLE ENERGY—Literally thousands of books and studies now exist on business opportunities that lie in transforming renewable resources like the sun, wind, and rivers into useful heat, motion, and electricity. An outstanding work on the state of the art is John J. Berger's *Charging Ahead: The Business of Renewable Energy and What It Means for America* (Henry Holt, 1997). Summaries of recent breakthroughs can be found in: *Energy Ideas*, published by the Government Purchasing Project; various materials of the Rocky Mountain Institute (see above); and the *World Directory of Renewable Energy Suppliers and Service*, from James and James Science Publishers. Useful web sites filled with resource materials have been set up by the American Solar Energy Society, the Center for Renewable Energy and Sustainable Technology (CREST), the Federal Energy Management Program, the Interstate Renewable Energy Council, the National Renewable Energy Laboratory, the Solar Energy Industries Association, and the Union of Concerned Scientists. See also *Energy Service Companies.*

AMERICAN SOLAR ENERGY SOCIETY
2400 Central Ave., G-1
Boulder, CO 80301
303-443-3130
Fax: 303-443-3212
E-mail: ases@ases.org
Web: www.ases.org

CENTER FOR RENEWABLE ENERGY AND SUSTAINABLE TECHNOLOGY
Suite 900
1200 18th St., NW
Washington, DC 20036
202-530-2202

Fax: 202-887-0497
E-mail: mkcampbell@repp.org
Web: solstice.crest.org

ENERGY EFFICIENCY AND RENEWABLE ENERGY CLEARINGHOUSE
P.O. Box 3048
Merrifield, VA 22116
800-363-3732
Fax: 703-893-0400
E-mail: DOE.erec@nciinc.com
Web: www.eren.doe.gov

GOVERNMENT PURCHASING PROJECT
Center for Study of Responsive Law
P.O. Box 19367
Washington, DC 20036
202-387-8030
Fax: 202-234-5176
E-mail: gpp@essential.org
Web: www.gpp.org

INTERSTATE RENEWABLE ENERGY COUNCIL
P.O. Box 1154
Latham, NY 12110-1156
518-458-6059
E-mail: IREC1@aol.com
Web: www.irecusa.org

JAMES AND JAMES SCIENCE PUBLISHERS
Waterside House
47 Kentish Town Rd.
London NW1 8NZ
United Kingdom
Phone: 44-171-387-8558

NATIONAL RENEWABLE ENERGY LABORATORY
1617 Cole Blvd.
Golden, CO 80401
303-275-3000
Fax: 303-275-4119
Web: www.nrel.gov

SOLAR ENERGY INDUSTRIES ASSOCIATION
Suite 260
1111 North 19th St.
Arlington, VA 22209
703-248-0702
Fax: 703-248-0714

E-mail: plowenth@seia.org
Web: www.seia.org

UNION OF CONCERNED SCIENTISTS
2 Brattle Square
Cambridge, MA 02238-9105
617-547-5552
Fax: 617-864-9405
E-mail: ucs@ucsusa.org
Web: www.ucsusa.org

U.S. DEPARTMENT OF ENERGY
Web: www.eren.doe.gov

RURAL DEVELOPMENT—The groups below publish books, studies, and newsletters that provide special guidance concerning the economic development of rural communities. S.U.R.E. Exchange also creates partnerships between urban and rural areas. See also *Community Food Systems*.

ACTION WITH COMMUNITIES IN RURAL ENGLAND
Somerford Court
Somerford Rd.
Cirencester, Glos. Gl7 1TW
United Kingdom
44-1285-653-477
Fax: 44-1285-654-537
E-mail: acre@acre.org.uk
Web: www.acreciro.demon.co.uk

CENTER FOR RURAL AFFAIRS
P.O. Box 406
Walthill, NE 68067
402-846-5428
Fax: 402-846-5420
Web: www.cfra.org

COMMUNITY AND RURAL DEVELOPMENT INSTITUTE (CARDI)
43 Warren Hall
Cornell University
Ithaca, NY 14853-7801
607-255-9510
Fax: 607-255-9984
E-mail: cardi@cornell.edu
Web: www.cals.cornell.edu/dept/cardi

MOUNTAIN APPALACHIAN CENTER FOR ECONOMIC DEVELOPMENT
433 Chestnut St.
Berea, KY 40403

606-986-2372
Fax: 606-986-1299
E-mail: dharker@maced.org
Web: www.maced.org

RURAL ACTION
P.O. Box 157
Trimble, OH 45782
614-767-4938
Fax: 614-767-4957
E-mail: Ratrimbl@ruralaction.org
Web: www.ruralaction.org

RURAL COMMUNITY ASSISTANCE CORPORATION
Suite 201
3120 Freeboard Drive
Sacramento, CA 95691
916-376-0507
Fax: 916-447-2878
E-mail: wfrench@rcac.org
Web: www.rcac.org

REGIONAL DEVELOPMENT AGENCY
141 Castle St.
Salisbury, Wiltshire SP1 3TP
United Kingdom
44-1722-336-255
Fax: 44-1722-654-537

SOUTHERN RURAL DEVELOPMENT INITIATIVE
128 East Hargett St., Suite 202
Raleigh, NC 27602
919-829-5900
Fax: 919-829-0504
E-mail: srdi@srdi.org
Web: www.srdi.org

S.U.R.E. EXCHANGE/GRASSROOTS RESOURCES, INC.
P.O.Box 11343
Takoma Park, MD 20913
301-588-7227

SEED BANKS—If you are interested in learning how your community can conserve its genetic resources and protect indigenous plants and trees, you should subscribe to *Seedling*, the quarterly newsletter of Genetic Resources Action International in

Barcelona, Spain. You also might consider introducing into your own ecosystem new, open pollinating seeds from the Heritage Seed Library or from Seeds of Change.

GRAIN
Jonqueres 16
08005 Barcelona
Spain
Phone: 343-310-5909
Fax: 343-310-5952
E-mail: grain@gn.apc.org

HERITAGE SEED LIBRARY
Genetic Resources Dept.
Henry Doubleday Research Association
Ryton Organic Gardens
Ryton-on-Dunsmore CV8 3LG
United Kingdom
Phone: 44-1203-303-507 ·
Fax: 44-1203-303-517
E-mail: enquir@hrda.org.uk
Web: www.hrda.org.uk

SEEDS OF CHANGE
621 Old Sante Fe Trail, #10
Santa Fe, NM 87501
505-983-8956
Fax: 505-438-7052
E-mail: gardener@seedsofchange.com
Web: www.seedsofchange.com

SELECTIVE PURCHASING—Selective purchases can be viewed as boycotts with panache, in which consumers, businesses, and officials carefully purchase as much as possible from community- friendly business. Useful information on which companies are worthy of your community's business can be found in *Shopping for a Better World*, published by the Council for Economic Priorities (though little weight is given to community ownership as a criterion of social responsibility). The Government Purchasing Project provides state, county, and local governments with contacts that facilitate the substitution of environmentally friendly products. See also *Boycotts* and *Socially Responsible Investment*.

COUNCIL FOR ECONOMIC PRIORITIES
30 Irving Pl.
New York, NY 10003
212-420-1133
Fax: 212-420-8988
E-mail: info@cepnyc.org
Web: www.cepnyc.org

GOVERNMENT PURCHASING PROJECT
P.O. Box 19367
Washington, DC 20036
202-387-8030
Fax: 202-234-5176
E-mail: GPP@essential.org
Web: www.gpp.org

SMALL BUSINESS INCUBATION—If you interested in helping local entrepreneurs get new businesses off the ground, you can find out from the contacts below how other communities have set up incubators. Community Information Exchange (see above) has a helpful report on the topic.

NATIONAL BUSINESS INCUBATION
20 East Circle Drive, Suite 190
Athens, OH 45701
740-593-4331
Fax: 740-593-1996
E-mail: webmaster@nbia.org
Web: www.nbia.org

PAUL TERRY & ASSOCIATES
185 Arkansas St.
San Francisco, CA 94107
415-255-0131
Fax: 415-255-1995
E-mail: pta@paulterry.com
Web: www.paulterry.com

SOCIALLY RESPONSIBLE BUSINESS—Most U.S. groups promoting socially responsible business are willing to take each company's word for it. Scanning the pages of Co-op America's *National Green Pages*, for example, one finds many firms that produce snake oil products, treat their employees poorly, or have little loyalty to any particular community. Nevertheless, networks of these businesses inevitably provide a forum for members to question one another's practices. These networks include Business Ethics, Businesses for Social Responsibility, and the Social Ventures Network. Net Impact has been attempting to organize simpatico business students around the country before Wall Street turns them in the wrong direction. In Canada, an independent organization called Ethicscan has reports on the social performance of 1,500 Canadian companies. *In Business* is a useful magazine for "eco-entrepreneurs."

BUSINESS ETHICS
Suite 110
52 S. 10th St.
Minneapolis, MN 55403

612-879-0695
Fax: 612-879-0699
E-mail: bizethics@aol.com
Web: www.business-ethics.com

BUSINESSES FOR SOCIAL RESPONSIBILITY
2nd Floor
609 Mission St.
San Francisco, CA 94105-3506
415-537-3506
Fax: 415-537-0889
E-mail: webmaster@bsr.org
Web: www.bsr.org

ETHICSCAN CANADA
Box 165
Postal Station S
Toronto, ON M5M 4L7
Canada
416-783-6776
Fax: 416-783-7386
E-mail: ethic@concentric.net
Web: www.ethicscan.on.ca

IN BUSINESS
The JG Press, Inc.
419 State Avenue
Emmaus PA, 18049
800-661-4905
E-mail: jgpress@jgpress.com
Web: www.jgpress.com

NET IMPACT
Third Floor
609 Mission St.
San Francisco, CA
415-778-8366
Fax: 415-778-8367
E-mail: mail@net-impact.org
Web: www.net-impact.org

SOCIAL VENTURES NETWORK
P.O. Box 29221
San Francisco, CA 94129
415-561-6501
Fax: 415-561-6435
Web: svn.org/home.html

APPENDIX **269**

SOCIALLY RESPONSIBLE EMPLOYMENT—If you're looking for work with a socially responsible business, information about job opportunities can be found in the publications of Access and Job Seeker, or the web site of ProgressivePubs.Com. Provocative publications on the future of work have been written by Jeremy Rifkin and his colleagues at the Foundation on Economic Trends. Of course, don't overlook the best job opportunity possible: to start your own community corporation and hire yourself as CEO.

ACCESS: COMMUNITY JOBS
Suite 838
1001 Connecticut Ave., NW
Washington, DC 20036
202-785-4233
Fax: 202-785-4212
E-mail: accesscntr@aol.com
Web: www.communityjobs.org

FOUNDATION ON ECONOMIC TRENDS
Suite 216
1660 L St., NW
Washington, DC 20036
202-466-2823
Fax: 202-429-9602
E-mail: office@biotechcentury.org
Web: www.biotechcentury.org

JOB SEEKER
Rt. 2, Box 16
Warrens, WI 54666
Phone & Fax: 608-378-4290
E-mail: jobseeker@tomah.com
Web: www.tomah.com

PROGRESSIVEPUBS.COM
3713 Warren St., NW
Washington, DC 20016
202-238-0010
Fax: 202-238-0011
Web: www.progressivepubs.com

SOCIALLY RESPONSIBLE INVESTING—User-friendly guides to socially responsible investment are available from Co-Op America (*The Social Responsible Financial Planning Handbook*), Good Money Publications (*Social Funds Guide*), the Social Investment Forum (*Social Investment Services Guide*), and Friends of the Earth (*Green Paycheck*). Newsletters on the subject are published by Clean Yield Asset

Management, Tillium Asset Management Company (*Insight*), Good Money Publications, and the Investor Responsibility Research Center. The *Greenmoney Journal* also reports news on SRI. CERES is attempting to develop specific guidelines for green investing. Trillium and the First Affirmative Financial Network have professional advisors who help clients make smart investment choices.

CERES
11 Arlington St., 6th Floor
Boston, MA 02116
617-247-0700
Fax: 617-287-5400
E-mail: muzila@ceres.org
Web: www.ceres.org

FIRST AFFIRMATIVE FINANCIAL NETWORK
Suite 200
1040 South 8th St.
Colorado Springs, CO 13736
800-422-7284
Fax: 719-636-1943
Web: www.firstaffirmative.com

FRIENDS OF THE EARTH
1025 Vermont Ave., NW
Washington, DC 20005
202-783-7400
Fax: 202-783-0444
E-mail: foe@foe.org
Web: www.foe.org

GREENMONEY JOURNAL
West 608 Glass Ave.
Spokane, WA 99205
509-328-1741
Fax: 509-328-9422
E-mail: editor@greenmoney.com
Web: www.greenmoney.com

INVESTOR RESPONSIBILITY RESEARCH CENTER
Suite 700
1350 Connecticut Ave., NW
Washington, DC 20036-1701
202-833-0700
Fax: 202-833-3555
E-mail: mkt@irrc.org
Web: www.irrc.org

SOCIAL INVESTMENT FORUM

1612 K St., NW, Suite 650
Washington, DC 20006
202-872-5319
Fax: 202-822-8471
E-mail: info@socialinvest.org
Web: www.socialinvest.org

SOCIAL INVESTMENT ORGANIZATION
Suite E-447
336 Adelaide St.
Toronto, ON M5A 3X9
Canada
416-360-6047
Fax: 416-360-6380
E-mail: sio@web.net
Web: www.mjra-jsi.com

TRILLIUM ASSET MANAGEMENT CO.
711 Atlantic Ave.
Boston, MA 02111-2809
617-423-6655
Fax: 617-482-6179
Web: www.trilliumvest.com

UK SOCIAL INVESTMENT FORUM
c/o Danyal Sattar
Holywell Centre
1 Phipp St.
London EC2A 4PS
United Kingdom
020-7749-4880
Fax: 020-4479-4881
E-mail: info@uksif.org
Web: www.uksif.org

SUSTAINABLE COMMUNITIES—As noted in the Introduction, the sustainable-communities movement tends to prioritize schmoozing, visioning, and technical-fixing over challenging multinational business or proposing coherent economic alternatives. Falling into this category are the publications and web sites of Concern, the Global Cities Project, the President's Council on Sustainable Development, the Sustainability Project, and the Joint Center on Sustainable Communities (a project of the National Association of Counties and the U.S. Conference of Mayors). Andy Euston, of the U.S. Department of Housing and Urban Development, has lists of community organizations taking similar initiatives.

CONCERN
1794 Columbia, NW

Washington, DC 20009
202-328-8160
Fax: 202-387-3378
E-mail: concern@igc.org
Web: www.concern.org

GLOBAL CITIES PROJECT
Center for the Study of Law and Politics
2962 Fillmore St.
San Francisco, CA 94123
415-775-0791
Fax: 415-775-4159
E-mail: epc@globalcities.org
Web: www.globalcities.org

JOINT CENTER FOR SUSTAINABLE COMMUNITIES
1620 Eye St., NW
Washington, DC 20006
202-861-6773
Fax: 202-429-0422
E-mail: peterson@usmayors.org
Web: www.usmayors.org/USCM/sustainable/index.html

PRESIDENT'S COUNCIL ON SUSTAINABLE DEVELOPMENT
730 Jackson Pl., NW
Washington, DC 20503
202-408-5296
Fax: 202-408-6839
E-mail: pcsd@igc.org
Web: www.whitehouse.gov/PCSD

SUSTAINABLE COMMUNITY DEVELOPMENT EXPLORATIONS
Room 7244
U.S. Department of H.U.D.
Washington, DC 20410
202-708-0614, ext. 4648
E-mail: andrew_euston@hud.gov
Web: www.hud.gov

SUSTAINABLE CONSUMPTION—Interested in improving the quality of life by consuming less? The New Road Map Foundation distributes the bestseller, *Your Money or Your Life,* by Joe Dominguez and Vicki Robin, and other publications with lots of practical suggestions. The Center for a New American Dream is a national clearinghouse on these questions, and the Northwest Environmental Watch is attempting to answer them for the Pacific Northwest. An outstanding report on "The Ethics of Consumption" is available from Institute for Philosophy and Public Policy at the University of Maryland. For more than a decade the Center for Energy and

Environmental Studies (CEES) at Princeton has documented how economic advancement is accompanied—and spurred—by more efficient consumption of fewer materials.

CENTER FOR ENERGY AND ENVIRONMENTAL STUDIES
Princeton University
Princeton, NJ 08544
609-258-5445
Fax: 609-258-3661
E-mail: cees@princeton.edu
Web: www.princeton.edu/~cees

CENTER FOR A NEW AMERICAN DREAM
6930 Carroll Ave., Suite 900
Takoma Park, MD 20912
301-891-3683
Fax: 301-891-3684
E-Mail: newdream@newdream.org
Web: www.newdream.org

INSTITUTE FOR PHILOSOPHY AND PUBLIC POLICY
School of Public Affairs
University of Maryland
College Park, MD 20742
301-405-6330
E-mail: sscwab@deans.umd.edu
Web: www.puaf.umd.edu

NEW ROAD MAP FOUNDATION
P.O. Box 15981
Seattle, WA 98115
Web: www.newroadmap.org

NORTHWEST ENVIRONMENT WATCH
Suite 1127
1402 Third Ave.
Seattle, WA 98101-2118
888-643-9820
Fax: 206-447-1880
E-mail: new@northwestwatch.org
Web: www.northwestwatch.org

SUSTAINABLE FORESTRY—If you're interested in learning how to harvest local trees for commercial use in sustainable ways, you should contact the institutes listed below. Many also have studies on how to reduce consumption of paper, pulp, and lumber through conservation and sustainable crops. Ohio Hempery is one of several groups advocating the development of the hemp and kanaff industry to replace wood-based paper with more sustainable alternatives.

ECOFORESTRY INSTITUTE
785 Barton Rd.
Glendale, OR 97442
541-832-2968
Fax: 541-832-2968
E-mail: ecoforest@pioneer-net.com

ECOFORESTRY INSTITUTE CANADA
P.O. Box 5070, Station B
Victoria, BC V8R 6N3
Canada
250-477-8479
Fax: 250-721-5579
Web: www.ecoforestry.ca

FOREST PARTNERSHIP
P.O. Box 426
Burlington, VT 05402
802-865-1111
Fax: 802-863-4344
E-mail: webmaster@forestworld.com
Web: www.forestworld.com

FOREST TRUST
P.O.Box 519
Santa Fe, NM 87504
505-983-8992
Fax: 505-986-0798
E-mail: foresttrust@igc.org

INSTITUTE FOR SUSTAINABLE FORESTRY
P.O. Box 1580
Redway, CA 95560
707-247-1101
Fax: 707-247-3555
E-mail: info@isf-sw.org
Web: www.isf-sw.org

OHIO HEMPERY, INC.
P.O. Box 18
Guysville, OH 45735
740-662-4367
Fax: 740-662-6446
E-mail: hempery@hempery.com
Web: www.hempery.com

RAINFOREST ALLIANCE/SMART WOOD PROGRAM
65 Bleecker St.
New York, NY 10012
212-677-1900
Fax: 212-677-2187
E-mail: canopy@cdp.org
Web: www.rainforestalliance.org

RAINFOREST ACTION NETWORK
Suite 500
221 Pine St.
San Francisco, CA 94104
415-398-4404
Fax: 415-398-2732
E-mail: rainforest@ran.org
Web: www.ran.org

ROGUE INSTITUTE FOR ECOLOGY AND ECONOMY
762 A St.
Ashland, OR 97520
503-482-6031
Fax: 503-482-8581
E-mail: info@rogueinstitute.org
Web: www.rogueinstitute.org

WILD IRIS FORESTRY
P.O. Box 1423
Redway, CA 95560
707-923-2344
E-mail: wip@isf-sw.org
Web: 222.isf.sw.org

TIME DOLLARS—If you'd like to adopt Time Dollars, you can find out who's doing what from the Time Dollar Institute, and download from the Institute's web site software for running your own Time Dollar system. Another system operating on similar principles is Womanshare in New York City.

TIME DOLLAR INSTITUTE
P.O. Box 42519
Washington, DC 20015
202-686-5200
Fax: 202-537-5033
E-mail: info@timedollar.org
Web: www.timedollar.org

WOMANSHARE
680 West End Ave.

New York, NY 10025
Phone: 212-662-9746
Fax: 212-662-9746
E-mail: wshare@aol.com

URBAN AGRICULTURE—If you'd like to cultivate unused land in your city, a key publication is *Urban Agriculture: Food, Jobs and Sustainable Cities*, published by the United Nations Development Programme. Other important overviews of the field have been written by Gail Feenstra at the Sustainable Agriculture Research and Education Program at U.C. Davis, Jac Smit of the Urban Agriculture Network, and Jerome Kaufman at the Department of Urban and Regional Planning at the University of Wisconsin. Some of largest and most enterprising local urban-ag programs are listed below. See also *Community Food Systems* and *Urban Forestry*.

AUSTIN SUSTAINABLE FOOD CENTER
434 Bastrop Hwy.
Austin, TX 78741
512-385-0080
Fax: 512-385-0082
E-mail: susfood@aol.com

CITIES FEEDING PEOPLE PROJECT
International Development Research Centre
250 Albert St.
P.O. Box 8500
Ottawa, ON K1G3H9
Canada
613-236-6163
Fax: 613-567-7749
E-mail: info@idrc.ca
Web: www.idrc.ca

COMMUNITY FOOD SECURITY COALITION
P.O. Box 209
Venice, CA 90294
310-822-5410
Fax: 310-822-1440
E-mail: asfisher@aol.com
Web: www.foodsecurity.com

D.C. COMMUNITY HARVEST
419 V St., NW
Washington, DC 20009
202-234-0591
Fax: 202-234-0592
E-mail: GoodFood4@aol.com

DEPT. OF URBAN AND REGIONAL PLANNING
University of Wisconsin
925 Bascom Mall
Madison, WI 53706
608-262-3769
E-mail: jlkaufma@facstaff.wisc.edu

DETROIT URBAN COOPERATIVE AGRICULTURE NETWORK
c/o Hunger Action
220 Bagley
Suite 326
Detroit, MI 48226
313-963-7788
Fax: 313-963-6819
E-mail: hn0144@handsnet.org

HARTFORD FOOD SYSTEM
509 Wethersfield Ave.
Hartford, CN 06114
860-296-9325
Fax: 860-296-8326
E-mail: hfood@erols.com

NATIONAL CAMPAIGN FOR SUSTAINABLE AGRICULTURE
P.O. Box 396
Pine Bush, NY 12566
914-744-8448
Fax: 914-744-8477
E-mail: campaign@magiccarpet.com
Web: www.sustainableagriculture.org

SAN FRANCISCO LEAGUE OF URBAN GARDENERS
2088 Oakdale Ave.
San Francisco, CA 94124
415-285-7584
Fax: 415-287-7586
E-mail: membership@slug-sf.org
Web: www.slug-sf.org

SUSTAINABLE AGRICULTURE RESEARCH AND EDUCATION PROGRAM
University of California at Davis
One Shields Ave.
Davis, CA 95616
530-752-8408
Fax: 530-754-8550
E-mail: gwfeestra@ucdavis.edu

URBAN AGRICULTURE NETWORK
1711 Lamont, NW

Washington, DC 20010
202-483-8130
Fax: 202-986-6732
E-mail: urbanag@compuserve.com
Web: www.cityfarmer.org

URBAN DEVELOPMENT—Most urban-development practitioners are stuck in old economic paradigms that are of little use to promoters of community self-reliance. Two exceptions are the Great Cities Institute at the University of Illinois at Chicago, and the Mega-Cities Project, which spreads policy innovations among the 18 cities of the world that now have populations exceeding 10 million. The Metro Futures Project at the University of Wisconsin also has an exceptionally visionary approach to the field.

GREAT CITIES INSTITUTE
University of Illinois at Chicago
Suite 400
412 South Peoria St.
Chicago, IL 60607
312-996-8700
Fax: 312-996-8933
E-mail: gcities@uic.edu
Web: www.uic.edu/cuppa/gci

MEGA-CITIES
695 Park Ave.
New York, NY 10021
212-659-3100
Fax: 212-650-3128
E-mail: nyc@megacities.org
Web: www.megacity.org

METRO FUTURES
Center on Wisconsin Strategy
8116 Social Science
University of Wisconsin-Madison
Madison, WI 53706
608-262-4266
Fax: 608-262-9046

NATIONAL COUNCIL FOR URBAN ECONOMIC DEVELOPMENT
Suite 915
1730 K St., NW
Washington, DC 20006
202-223-4735
Fax: 202-223-4745
E-mail: mail@urbandevelopment.com
Web: www.cued.org

URBAN FORESTRY—Greening cities is good for aesthetics, healthy lungs, and mental well-being. Tree People have undertaken remarkable reforestation efforts in one of the least tree-friendly cities in the world—Los Angeles. Common Ground and the Woodland Trust, both in the United Kingdom, have materials on how to develop profitable fruit orchards. See also *Sustainable Forestry* and *Urban Agriculture*.

COMMON GROUND
Seven Dials Warehouse
44 Earlah St.
London WC2H 9LA
United Kingdom
44-171-379-3109
Fax: 44-171-836-5741

TREE PEOPLE
12601 Mulholland Dr.
Beverly Hills, CA 90210
818-753-4600
Fax: 818-753-4625
E-mail: TreePeople@treepeople.org
Web: www.treepeople.org

WOODLAND TRUST
Autumn Park, Grantham
Lincolnshire NG31 6LL
United Kingdom
44-1476-581-111
Fax: 44-1476-590-808
E-mail: inquires@woodland-trust.org.uk
Web: www.woodland-trust.org.uk

WATER-EFFICIENCY SERVICE COMPANIES (WASCOS)—Guidebooks on the latest technologies for serious water conservation – and the vast economic savings resulting from them – are available from the Rocky Mountain Institute (see above) and the Global Cities Project (see Sustainable Communities). An electronic directory of dozens of WASCOs around the country helping communities realize these savings can be found on the Web (www.waterwise.org). See also *Energy Efficiency Companies*.

WOMEN'S BUSINESSES—The organizations below provide useful information, technical assistance, and loans to small businesses owned by women.

NATIONAL ASSOCIATION OF WOMEN BUSINESS OWNERS
Suite 1100
1511 K St., NW
Washington, DC 20005

202-638-5322
Fax: 301-220-1626
E-mail: national@nawbo.org
Webwww.wawbo.org

NATIONAL EDUCATION CENTER FOR WOMEN IN BUSINESS
Seton Hill College
Greensburg, PA 15601-1599
412-830-4625
Fax: 412-834-7131
E-mail: info@necwb.setonhill.edu
Web: www.necwb.setonhill.edu

NATIONAL WOMEN'S BUSINESS COUNCIL
Suite 5850
409 Third St., SW
Washington, DC 20024
202-205-3850
Fax: 202-205-6825
E-mail: debra.filtzer@sba.gov
Web: www.nwbc.gov

OFFICE OF WOMEN'S BUSINESS OWNERSHIP
U.S. Small Business Administration
6th Floor
409 Third St., SW
Washington, DC 20416
202-205-6673
Fax: 202-205-7287
E-mail: Marae.Versteeg@sba.gov
Web: www.sba.gov/womeninbusiness

WOMEN'S BUSINESS DEVELOPMENT CENTER
Suite 400
8 S. Michigan St.
Chicago, IL 60603
312-853-3477
Fax: 312-853-0145

WORKER OWNERSHIP—A bible for those interested in who's doing what in worker ownership is *When Workers Decide* (New Society, 1992), edited by Len Krimerman and Frank Lindenfeld. The Industrial Cooperative Association and the National Center for Employee Ownership serve as clearinghouses. Norm Kurland is carrying on the work of Louis Kelso, particularly around employee stock-ownership plans (ESOPs), at the Center for Economic and Social Justice. The International

Labor Rights Education and Research Fund tracks the development of labor standards at all levels of governance—local, state, national, and global. One successful promoter of worker-owned factories has been the Steel Valley Authority in the Pittsburgh area. See also *Community Corporations, Cooperative,* and *Labor Rights.*

CENTER FOR ECONOMIC AND SOCIAL JUSTICE
P.O. Box 40711
Washington, DC 20016
703-243-5155
Fax: 703-243-5935
E-mail: thirdway@cesj.org
Web: www.cesj.org

INDUSTRIAL COOPERATIVE ASSOCIATION (ICA GROUP)
Suite 1127
20 Park Plaza
Boston, MA 02116
617-338-0010
Fax: 617-338-2788
E-mail: icaica@aol.com
Web: www.ica-group.org

INTERNATIONAL LABOR RIGHTS EDUCATION AND RESEARCH FUND
Suite 920
733 15th St., NW
Washington, DC 20005
202-347-4100
Fax: 202-347-4885
E-mail: laborrights@igc.org
Web: www.laborrights.com

NATIONAL CENTER FOR EMPLOYEE OWNERSHIP
1736 Franklin St., 8th Floor
Oakland, CA 94612
510-272-9461
Fax: 510-272-9510
E-mail: nceo@nceo.org
Web: www.nceo.org

STEEL VALLEY AUTHORITY
1 Library Place
Duquesne, PA 15110
412-460-0488
Fax: 412-460-0487

YOUTH ENTREPRENEURSHIP—One way to develop community-friendly business is to train people to become entrepreneurs when their idealism is at its highest—in their youth. The Village Foundation (noted above) is launching a Team 2000 Program, in which it is teaming up two thousand senior executive to coach an equal number of young entrepreneurs in the inner city. Other programs with exciting youth entrepreneurship training programs are noted below:

CONSORTIUM FOR ENTREPRENEURIAL EDUCATION
1601 West Fifth Ave., PMB 199
Columbus, OH 43212
614-486-6538
Fax: 614-488-4667
E-mail: ashmoreC@aol.com
Web: www.entre-ed.org

ENTERPRISE AMBASSADOR USA
1750 NE 167th St.
North Miami Beach, FL 33162
954-262-5084
Fax: 954-262-3963
E-mail: eausa@face.nova.edu
Web: www.fgse.nova.edu/eausa

KIDS WAY
5589 Peachtree Rd.
Atlanta, GA 30341
888-KIDSWAY
Fax: 770-458-1170
E-mail: Yemag@kidsway.com
Web: www.kidsway.com

NATIONAL COALITION FOR EMPOWERING YOUTH ENTREPRENEURS
3597 Shannon Dr.
Baltimore, MD 21213
410-325-2439
Fax: 410-485-5774
E-mail: nceye@aol.com
Web: members.aol.com/nceye

NATIONAL FOUNDATION FOR TEACHING ENTREPRENEURHSIP
29th Floor
120 Wall St.
New York, NY 10005
212-232-3333
Fax: 212-232-2244
E-mail: nfte@nfte.com
Web: www.nfte.com

REGINALD F. LEWIS YOUTH ENTREPRENEURIAL INSTITUTE AND ACT-SO PROGRAM
National Association for the Advancement of Colored People

4805 Mt. Hope Drive
Baltimore, MD 21215
410-602-6924
Fax: 410-358-1607
E-mail: rlucas@naacpnet.org
Web: www.naacp.org

YOUNG ENTREPRENEURS ORGANIZATION
Suite 300
1321 Duke St.
Alexandria, VA 22314
703-519-6700
Fax: 703-519-1864
E-mail: tkerns@yeo.org
Web: www.yeo.org

Notes

Introduction

1. Robin Soslow, "Cleveland: A Special Report," *World Trade,* October 1992, p. 36.

2. *Ibid.*

3. Robin Tierney, "America's 10 Best Cities for International Companies," *World Trade,* October 1993, pp. 33–50.

4. Rosabeth Moss Kanter, *World Class: Thriving Locally in the Global Economy* (New York: Touchstone, 1995), p. 20.

5. Tierney, *supra* note 3, p. 38.

6. David J. Lynch, "Growing More Separate, More Unequal: Widening Gap Divides USA," *USA Today,* 23 September 1996, Money Section, p. 18.

7. Joel Achenbach, "The City That Came Back From the Dead," *Washington Post,* 26 October 1995, pp. C1–2.

8. Jay Weiner, "Public Ownership of Twins? Team, Governor Intrigued," *Minneapolis Star Tribune,* 21 September 1996, pp. A1, A20.

9. *Ibid.,* p. A20.

10. Daniel J. Alesch, "The Green Bay Packers: America's Only Not-for-Profit, Major-League Sports Franchise," (monograph) (Milwaukee, WI: Wisconsin Policy Research Institute, November 1995), p. 1.

11. Harvey J. Kaye and Isaac Kramnick, ". . . Take on the Happy Pack," *Washington Post,* Outlook Section, 26 January 1997, p. C4.

12. Quoted in Paul Starobin, "Rethinking Capitalism," *National Journal,* 18 January 1997, p. 106.

13. Milton Friedman, "The Social Responsibility of Business Is to Increase Its Profits," *New York Times,* Magazine Section, 13 September 1970, p. 125.

14. Robert B. Reich, "Who Is Them?" *Harvard Business Review,* March–April 1991, p. 77.

15. *Ibid.*

16. Alexis de Tocqueville, *Democracy in America* (New York: Perennial, 1988), p. 69.

17. Barry Bluestone, "Deindustrialization and Unemployment in America," *Review of Black Political Economy,* Fall 1988, p. 31.

18. Louis Uchitelle and N. R. Kleinfield, "The Price of Jobs Lost," in *The Downsizing of America* (New York: Times Books, 1996), p. 4.

19. Bennett Harrison and Barry Bluestone, *The Great U-Turn: Corporate Restructing and the Polarizing of America* (New York: Basic Books, 1988), p. 5.

20. *Ibid.*

21. Reich, *supra* note 14, p. 85.

22. Allen R. Myerson, "O Governor, Won't You Buy Me a Mercedes Plant?" *New York Times,* 1 September 1996, Sect. 3, pp. 1 and 10.

23. *Ibid.*

24. William Schweke, Carl Rist, and Brian Dabson, *Bidding for Business: Are Cities and States Selling Themselves Short?* (Washington, DC: Corporation for Enterprise Development, 1994), p. 23; and Greg LeRoy, "No More Candy Story" (monograph) (Washington, DC: Grassroots Policy Project/Federation for Industrial Retention and Renewal, 1994), p. 2.

25. E. S. Browning and Helene Cooper, "Ante Up: States' Bidding War Over Mercedes Plan Made for Costly Chase," *Wall Street Journal,* 24 November 1993, p. 1.

26. Donald L. Barlett and James B. Steele, *America: Who Really Pays the Taxes?* (New York: Touchstone, 1994), pp. 299–306.

27. Robert B. Reich, *The Wealth of Nations* (New York: Vintage, 1991), pp. 295–96.

28. Myerson, *supra* note 22.

29. LeRoy, *supra* note 24, p. 3.

30. Jim Edgar, "Are Economic Development Incentives Smart?" *State Government News,* March 1993, reprinted in LeRoy, *supra* note 24, p. 14.

31. National Governors Association, EDC-3, "Economic Growth and Development Incentives," reprinted in LeRoy, *supra* note 24, p. 129.

32. Richard J. Barnet and John Cavanagh, *Global Dreams: Imperial Corporations and the New World Order* (New York: Simon & Schuster, 1994), p. 294.

33. U.S. International Trade Commission, "U.S. Global Competitiveness: Steel Sheet and Strip Industry," Publication 2050 (Washington, DC). Also see Walter Russell Mead, "The Low-Wage Challenge to Global Growth: The Labor Cost–Productivity Imbalance in Newly Industrializing Countries" (monograph) (Washington, DC: Economic Policy Institute, 1990).

34. Harley Shaiken, "The First Three Years of NAFTA," Memo to Reps. Richard Gephardt and David Bonior, 26 February 1997.

35. Walter Russell Mead, "Examining American Free Trade," in Jonathan Greenberg and William Kistler, eds., *Buying America Back* (Tulsa, OK: Council Oak Books, 1992), p. 224.

36. Michael Weisskopt, "World Bank Official's Irony Backfires," *Washington Post,* 10 February 1992, p. A9.

37. Barry Bluestone and Bennett Harrison, *The Deindustrialization of America: Plant Closings, Community Abandonment, and the Dismantling of Basic Industry* (New York: Basic Books, 1982), pp. 63–72.

38. Harvey Brenner, *Estimating the Costs of National Economic Policy: Implications for Mental and Physical Health and Clinical Aggression,* Report prepared for the Joint Economic Committee (Washington, DC: USGPO, 1976). For an update of this work, see Harvey Brenner, "Political Economy," in Benjamin C. Amick III, Sol Levine, Alvin Tarlov, and Diana Chapman Walsh, *Society and Health* (New York: Oxford University Press, 1995), pp. 211–46.

39. Gar Alperovitz and Jeff Faux, *Rebuilding America: A Blueprint for the New Economy* (New York: Pantheon, 1984), pp. 142–43.

40. Robert J. Samuelson, "Down-Sizing for Growth," *Newsweek,* 25 March 1996, p. 45.

41. *Ibid.*

42. Richard W. Stevenson, "Greenspan Is Upbeat on Economy," *New York Times,* 22 January 1997, p. D1.

43. Paul Krugman, *The Age of Diminished Expectations: U.S. Economic Policy in the 1990s* (Cambridge, MA: MIT Press, 1990), p. 32.

44. Michael H. Shuman, "American: Lobby or Lose It," *Global Communities,* Autumn 1991.

45. Frank Shafroth, Director of Policy and Federal Relations for the National League of Cities, Personal Communication, 2 September 1997.

46. Nicholas Lemann, "The Myth of Community Development," *New York Times Magazine,* 9 January 1994, p. 27.

47. *Ibid.,* p. 29.

48. Witold Rybezynski, "Downsizing Cities," *Atlantic Monthly,* October 1995, p. 46.

49. *Ibid.*

50. *Ibid.*

51. Rosabeth Moss Kanter, "AT&T, Call Home," *Washington Post Outlook,* 14 January 1996, p. C1.

52. *Ibid.*

53. *Ibid.*

54. Kanter, *supra* note 4, p. 28.

55. Teresa Amott, "Eliminating Poverty," in Richard Caplan and John Feffer, eds., *State of the Union* (Boulder, CO: Westview, 1994), p. 166.

56. Andrew L. Shapiro, *We're Number One* (New York: Vintage, 1992), p. 53; Christopher Jencks, *The Homeless* (Cambridge, MA: Harvard University Press, 1994), pp. 8–20; and Erik Eckholm, ed., *Solving America's Health-Care Crisis* (New York: Times Books, 1993), p. 5.

57. Shapiro, *ibid.,* pp. 53, 80, 105, 119, 126, 142, and 153.

58. Juliet Schor, *The Overworked American: The Unexpected Decline of Leisure* (New York: Basic Books, 1991).

59. The Harwood Group, "Yearning for Balance" (executive summary) (Takoma Park, MD: Merck Family Fund, July 1995), pp. 1–2.

60. *Ibid.*

61. World Commission on Environment and Development, *Our Common Future* (Oxford: Oxford University Press, 1987), p. 8.

62. President's Council on Sustainable Development, *Sustainable America: A New Consensus for Prosperity, Opportunity, and a Healthy Environment for the Future* (Washington, DC: USGPO, February 1996).

63. *Ibid.,* p. 5.

64. *Ibid.,* p. 101.

65. *Ibid.,* p. 85.

66. *Ibid.,* p. 86.

67. See, for example: Alexander Cockburn and Ken Silverstein, *Washington Babylon* (New York: Verso, 1996), pp. 189–247.

68. A notable exception is "A Just and Sustainable Trade and Development Initiative for the Western Hemisphere," crafted in 1994 by leading thinkers and activists in Canada (Action Canada Network), Mexico (Mexican Action Network on Free Trade), and the United States (Citizens Trade Campaign and the Alliance for Responsible Trade). Available from the Institute for Policy Studies in Washington, D.C.

Chapter 1. Place Matters

1. Kettering Foundation, *Citizens and Politics: A View from Main Street America* (Bethesda, MD: Kettering Foundation, 1991), p. 47.

2. Amy Gutmann, "Communitarian Critics of Liberalism," *Philosophy and Public Policy,* Summer 1985, pp. 308–22.

3. Joe Klein, "The True Disadvantage," *New Republic,* 28 October 1996, p. 34.

4. *Ibid.,* p. 36.

5. Lester Thurow, "Preface," in Todd Schafer and Jeff Faux, *Reclaiming Prosperity: A Blueprint for Economic Reform* (Armonk, New York: M. E. Sharpe, 1996), p. xi.

6. William Spriggs and John Schmitt, "The Minimum Wage: Blocking the Low-Wage Path," in *ibid.,* pp. 164–65.

7. Michael Sandel, "Morality and the Liberal Ideal," *New Republic,* 7 May 1984, p. 17.

8. *Ibid.*

9. Amitai Etzioni, *The Spirit of Community: Rights, Responsibilities, and the Communitarian Agenda* (New York: Crown, 1993).

10. Robert D. Putnam, *Making Democracy Work* (Princeton, NJ: Princeton University Press, 1993).

11. Robert D. Putnam, "The Prosperous Community: Social Capital and Public Life," *American Prospect,* Spring 1993, p. 36.

12. *Ibid.,* p. 37.

13. *Ibid.*

14. Robert D. Putnam, "Bowling Alone: America's Declining Social Capital," *Journal of Democracy,* January 1995, p. 65.

15. Robert D. Putnam, "Bowling Alone, Revisited," *Responsive Community,* Spring 1995, pp. 18–33.

16. *Ibid.,* p. 24.

17. Nicholas Lemann, "Kicking in Groups," *Atlantic Monthly,* April 1996, pp. 22–26.

18. Katha Pollitt, "For Whom the Ball Rolls," *Nation,* 15 April 1996, p. 9.

19. Sam Smith, "Building a Civil Society: Let Them Eat Discourse," *Progressive Review,* February 1997, p. 1.

20. Paul A. Samuelson and William D. Nordhaus, *Economics,* 12th ed. (New York: McGraw–Hill, 1985), p. 4.

21. Robert Gilpin, *The Political Economy of International Relations* (Princeton, NJ: Princeton University Press, 1987), p. 192; and William R. Cline, *Trade Policy in the 1980s* (Washington, DC: Institute for International Economics, 1983), p. 5.

22. Paul Krugman, *Peddling Prosperity: Economic Sense and Nonsense in the Age of Diminished Expectations* (New York: Norton, 1994), p. 241. With typical braggadocio, Krugman adds: "Yet in fact the economists are mostly right in their attitude."

23. A minority of economists also have emphasized the role of historical accident, cumulative learning, and "path dependency" in explaining why certain nations have selected one specialized industry and not another. See Paul Krugman,

Rethinking International Trade (Cambridge, MA: MIT Press, 1990); and Paul Krugman, ed., *Strategic Trade Policy and the New International Economics* (Cambridge, MA: MIT Press, 1986).

24. Samuelson and Nordhaus, *supra* note 20, p. 836.

25. *Ibid.,* p. 865.

26. George Leland Bach, *Economics: An Introduction to Analysis and Policy,* 7th ed. (Englewood Cliffs, NJ: Prentice–Hall, 1971), p. 627.

27. Gar Alperovitz and Jeff Faux, *Rebuilding America: A Blueprint for the New Economy* (New York: Pantheon, 1984), p. 149.

28. Gar Alperovitz argues that "distribution of income has worsened, step by step (as it is doing now) throughout most of the 20th Century—*except* when interrupted by significant war, postwar boom, or depression collapse" in "The Era of Fundamental Stalemate . . . and the Possibility of a Long 'Reconstructive' Revolution in America" (unpublished paper, 1992).

29. Kevin Phillips, *The Politics of Rich and Poor* (New York: Random House, 1990), p. 13 (Chart 2).

30. Paul Krugman, "The Right, the Rich, and the Facts," *American Prospect,* Fall 1992, p. 22.

31. *Ibid.,* pp. 24–25.

32. Herman E. Daly and John B. Cobb, Jr., *For the Common Good* (Boston, MA: Beacon, 1989), pp. 209–35.

33. David Ricardo, *Principles of Political Taxation and Economy,* reprinted in J. R. McCulloch, *The Works of David Ricardo* (London: John Murray, 1888), p. 77.

34. Lawrence Mishel and Jared Bernstein, *The State of Working America (1994–95)* (Armonk, NY: M. E. Sharpe, 1994), p. 359 (Table 8.20).

35. Paul R. Krugman and Robert Z. Lawrence, "Trade, Jobs and Wages," *Scientific American,* April 1994, pp. 44–49.

36. Doug Henwood, "Does Globalization Matter?" *In These Times,* 31 March 1997, p. 16.

37. Richard J. Barnet and John Cavanagh, *Global Dreams: Imperial Corporations and the New World Order* (New York: Simon & Schuster, 1994).

38. Karl Polanyi, *The Great Transformation* (Boston, MA: Beacon Press, 1944).

39. *Ibid.* pp. 154–55.

40. Johan Galtung, "Towards a New Economics: On the Theory and Practice of Self-Reliance," excerpted in Paul Ekins, ed., *The Living Economy: A New Economics in the Making* (London: Routledge, 1986), p. 101.

41. Kirkpatrick Sale, "Self-Sufficiency," in Jonathan Greenberg and William Kistler, eds., *Buying America Back* (Tulsa, OK: Council Oaks Press, 1992), p. 558.

42. *Ibid.*

43. See, e.g., Jacques Ellul, *The Technological Society* (New York: Knopf, 1964).

Chapter 2. Needs-Driven Industries

1. J. M. Roberts, *History of the World* (London: Penguin, 1976), p. 45.

2. Daniel Imhoff, "Community Supported Agriculture," in Jerry Mander and Edward Goldsmith, eds., *The Case Against the Global Economy* (San Francisco, CA: Sierra Club Books, 1996), p. 425.

3. Joseph J. Romm and Charles B. Curtis, "Mideast Oil Forever?" *Atlantic Monthly,* April 1996, p. 57.

4. *Ibid.,* p. 60.

5. Amory B. and L. Hunter Lovins, *Brittle Power: Energy Strategy for National Security* (Andover, MA: Brick House Publishers, 1982), p. 122; and Amory B. and L. Hunter Lovins, "The Fragility of Domestic Energy," *Atlantic Monthly,* November 1983, pp. 118–26.

6. Amory B. and L. Hunter Lovins, *Brittle Power, supra,* note 5, pp. 51–67; and Tim Golden, "Blackout May Be Caution Sign on Road to Utility Deregulation," *New York Times,* 19 August 1996, p. A14.

7. Joseph Persky, David Ranney, and Wim Wiewel, "Import Substitution and Local Economic Development," *Economic Development Quarterly,* February 1993, p. 18.

8. Jane Jacobs, *The Economy of Cities* (New York: Vintage, 1969), pp. 145–79.

9. *Ibid.,* p. 157.

10. Persky, Ranney, and Wiewel, *supra* note 7, p. 19.

11. Thomas Michael Power, *Environmental Protection and Economic Well-Being* (Armonk, NY: M. E. Sharpe, 1996), pp. 155–80.

12. *Ibid.,* p. 155.

13. *Ibid.,* p. 194.

14. Jacobs, *supra* note 8, p. 161.

15. Persky, Ranney, and Wiewel, *supra* note 7, p. 19.

16. In 1992, the U.S. Bureau of the Census estimated that the country had roughly 3,000 counties, 19,300 municipalities, 16,700 townships, 14,400 school districts, and 31,600 special districts. The term "local government" here includes municipalities and townships. *Statistical Abstract of the United States* (Washington, DC: USGPO, 1996), p. 295 (Table 468).

17. Richard Douthwaite, *Short Circuit* (Devon: Resurgence, 1996), pp. 228–29.

18. Gar Alperovitz and Jeff Faux, *Rebuilding America* (New York: Pantheon, 1984), p. 196.

19. Karen Lehman and Al Krebs, "Control of the World's Food Supply," in Mander and Goldsmith, *supra* note 2, p. 127.

20. Stewart Smith, "Sustainable Agriculture and Public Policy," *Maine Policy Review,* April 1993, pp. 69–70.

21. Stewart Smith, "Farming Activities and Family Farms: Getting the Concepts Right," in *Symposium: Agricultural Industrialization and Family Farms: The Role of Federal Policy,* Hearing before the Joint Economic Committee of the United States, 21 October 1992, 57-929 (Washington, DC: USGPO, 1994), pp. 117–33.

22. Imhoff, *supra* note 2, p. 429.

23. United Nations Development Programme, *Urban Agriculture: Food, Jobs and Sustainable Cities* (New York: UNDP, 1996).

24. *Ibid.,* pp. 26 and 27.

25. *Ibid.,* p. 47.

26. *Ibid.,* p. 46.

27. Elizabeth Keen, Researcher for CSA of North America, Personal Communication, 21 August 1997.

28. Imhoff, *supra* note 2, pp. 429–30.

29. Douthwaite, *supra* note 17, pp. 315–18.

30. "Adding Value to Our Food System: An Economic Analysis of Sustainable Community Food Systems" (monograph) (Everson, WA: Integrity Systems Cooperative Co., February 1997).

31. This analysis is drawn from Richard Douthwaite, *supra,* note 17, pp. 251–331.

32. *Ibid.,* pp. 270–71.

33. Cary Fowler and Pat Mooney, *Shattering: Food, Politics, and the Loss of Genetic Diversity* (Tucson, AZ: University of Arizona Press, 1990), p. 218.

34. Amory B. Lovins and Robert Sardinsky, "The State of the Art: Lighting" (monograph) (Snowmass, CO: Rocky Mountain Institute/Competitek, March 1988). RMI believes that between 70 percent and 90 percent of all lighting energy could theoretically be saved, displacing 120 large power plants. Actual experience suggests that between 50 percent and 75 percent savings are more realistic.

35. Amory B. Lovins et al., "The State of the Art: Drivepower" (monograph) (Snowmass, CO: Rocky Mountain Institute/Competitek, April 1989). Additional improvements to equipment driven by the motors could probably save about half the remaining electricity being used.

36. Howard Geller et al., "The Role of Federal Research and Development in Advancing Energy Efficiency: A $50 Billion Contribution to the U.S. Economy," *Annual Review of Energy*, Vol. 12 (Palo Alto, CA: Annual Reviews, Inc., 1987), pp.

357–95. One reason, of course, why Western Europeans are more energy–efficient is that they live in denser settlement patterns that facilitate shorter commutes, more mass transit, and district heating. They also are more energy–efficient because their governments have imposed higher taxes on gasoline, oil, natural gas, and coal. But U.S. policymakers could replicate the Europeans' success were they more conscientious about energy efficiency in their efforts at regional planning and resource taxation.

37. Hal Harvey, Director of the Energy Foundation, Personal Communication, 12 March 1997.

38. Jessica S. Lefevre, "The Energy Services Industry: Revolutionizing Energy Use in the United States" (monograph) (Washington, DC: NAESCO, 1996), p. 5.

39. *Ibid.*, p. 15.

40. Christopher Flavin, "Wind Power Growth Accelerates," in Lester R. Brown, Christopher Flavin, and Hal Kane, *Vital Signs 1996* (New York: Norton, 1996), pp. 56–57.

41. Lester R. Brown, Nicholas Lenssen, and Hal Kane, *Vital Signs 1995* (New York: Norton, 1995), p. 54.

42. Romm and Curtis, *supra* note 3, p. 64.

43. John J. Berger, *Charging Ahead: The Business of Renewable Energy and What It Means for America* (New York: Henry Holt, 1997), p. 55.

44. *Ibid.*, p. 5.

45. Romm and Curtis, *supra* note 3, p. 64.

46. Berger, *supra* note 43, p. 56.

47. Brown, Lenssen, and Kane, *supra* note 41, pp. 56–57.

48. Berger, *supra* note 43, pp. 57–58.

49. *Ibid.*, p. 73.

50. *Ibid.*, p. 55.

51. John Berger, Personal Communication, 16 June 1997.

52. Berger, *supra* note 43, p. 133.

53. Romm and Curtis, *supra* note 3, p. 64.

54. National Renewable Energy Laboratory, *Biofuels for Transportation: The Road from Research to the Marketplace,* NREL/SP-420-5439 (Washington, DC: U.S. Department of Energy, January 1995).

55. Berger, *supra* note 43, p. 194.

56. Douthwaite, *supra* note 17, p. 212.

57. *Ibid.*, p. 213.

58. *Ibid.*

59. Berger, *supra* note 43, p. 202.

60. *Ibid.*

61. Douthwaite, *supra* note 17, p. 225.

62. Romm and Curtis, *supra* note 3, p. 60. Another alternative to oil is synthetic fuel derived from shale oil or coal. President Jimmy Carter enthusiastically backed a crash program to develop this technology during the late 1970s until the economics proved dismal. Even if technological breakthroughs were to revive a national synfuels program, the associated environmental costs would make it an unwise alternative to either efficiency or biofuels. See Doug Bandow, "Synfuels, NoWinFuels," *New York Times,* 1 September 1983, p. 27A.

63. Romm and Curtis, *ibid.,* p. 63.

64. William K. Stevens, "Scientists Say Earth's Warming Could Set Off Wide Disruptions," *New York Times,* 16 September 1995, pp. A1 and A8; "Turning Up the Heat," *Consumer Reports,* September 1996, p. 38.

65. Paul Hawken, *The Ecology of Commerce* (New York: HarperCollins, 1993), p. 3.

66. Sandra Postel, "Increasing Water Efficiency," in Lester R. Brown et al., *State of the World—1986* (New York: Norton, 1986), p. 57.

67. *Ibid.,* p. 54.

68. *Ibid.,* p. 55.

69. *Ibid.,* p. 24.

70. *Ibid.,* p. 50.

71. *Ibid.,* pp. 42–43.

72. Sandra Postel and Lori Heise, "Reforesting the Earth," Worldwatch Paper 83 (Washington, DC: Worldwatch Institute, April 1988), p. 7.

73. *Ibid.,* p. 15.

74. *Ibid.,* p. 37.

75. Paul Hawken, *supra* note 65, p. 89.

76. U. S. Bureau of the Census, *supra* note 16, p. 687 (Table 1125).

77. Alan Thein Durning, "Redesigning the Forest Economy," in Lester R. Brown et al., *State of the World—1994* (New York: Norton, 1994), p. 30.

78. *Ibid.,* p. 34.

79. *Ibid.*

80. *Ibid.,* p. 28.

81. Paul Hawken, *supra* note 65, p. 37. The World Resources Institute estimates that 187,000 pounds of resources per year are necessary to maintain the lifestyle of one American. *Resource Flows: The Material Basis of Industrial Economies* (Washington, DC: World Resources Institute, 1997).

82. *Ibid.,* p. 47.

83. *Ibid.*

84. Brenda Platt and David Morris, "The Economic Benefits of Recycling" (monograph) (Washington, DC: Institute for Local Self-Reliance, January 1993), p. 1.

85. *Ibid.,* p. 9.

86. David Morris and Irshad Ahmed, "The Carbohydrate Economy: Making Chemicals and Industrial Materials from Plant Matter" (summary) (Washington, DC: Institute for Local Self-Reliance, 1992), p. 1.

87. David Morris, *Self-Reliant Cities* (San Francisco, CA: Sierra Club, 1982), p. 212.

88. David Morris and Irshad Ahmed, "Rural Development, Biorefineries, and the Carbohydrate Economy" (monograph) (Washington, DC: Institute for Local Self-Reliance, September 1993), p. 2.

89. Morris and Ahmed, "The Carbohydrate Economy," *supra* note 86, p. 7.

90. *Ibid.,* p. 8.

91. Morris and Ahmed, "Rural Development," *supra* note 88, p. 5.

92. *Ibid.,* p. 3.

93. Eric D. Larson, "Trends in the Consumption of Energy-Intensive Basic Materials in Industrialized Countries and Implications for Developing Regions," (unpublished paper for the International Symposium on Environmentally Sound Energy Technologies in Milan, Italy, 21–25 October 1991).

94. *Ibid.,* p. 2.

95. Paul Krugman, *Pop Internationalism* (Cambridge, MA: MIT Press, 1997), pp. 211–12.

96. *Ibid.,* p. 213.

97. Susan Meeker-Lowry, "Flexible Manufacturing Networks," *In Business,* September/October 1992, p. 38.

98. The Appalachian Center for Economic Networks, "Integrating Business Incubators with Community Economic Development Strategies" (unpublished paper, 1992), p. 1.

99. Bennett Harrison, *Lean and Mean* (New York: Basic Books, 1994), p. 220.

100. *Ibid.,* p. 222.

101. Michael Porter, *The Competitive Advantage of Nations* (New York: Free Press, 1990).

102. The Appalachian Center for Economic Networks, *supra* note 98, p. 1.

103. Harrison, *supra* note 99, p. 221.

104. *Ibid.,* p. 32.

Chapter 3. Community Corporations

1. Richard L. Grossman and Frank T. Adams, "Taking Care of Business: Citizenship and the Charter of Incorporation" (pamphlet) (Cambridge, MA: Charter Inc., 1993).

2. David Korten, *When Corporations Rule the World* (West Oxford, CT: Kumarian Press, 1995).

3. Jerry Mander, "The Rules of Corporate Behavior," in Jerry Mander and Edward Goldsmith, *The Case Against the Global Economy* (San Francisco, CA: Sierra Club Books, 1996), pp. 321–22.

4. Robert Fitch, "In Bologna, Small Is Beautiful," *Nation,* 13 May 1996, p. 19.

5. David Morris, *The Mondragon System: Cooperation at Work* (Washington, DC: Institute for Local Self-Reliance, May 1992), p. 2.

6. *Ibid.,* p. 3.

7. *Ibid.,* p. 30.

8. Robert H. A. Ashford, "The Binary Economics of Louis Kelso," in John H. Miller, ed., *Curing World Poverty: The New Role of Property* (St. Louis, MO: Social Justice Review Press, 1994), p. 106.

9. *Ibid.,* pp. 212–13.

10. Gar Alperovitz, "The Reconstruction of Community Meaning," *Tikkun,* May–June 1996, p. 15.

11. Burton A. Weisbrod, *The Nonprofit Sector* (Cambridge, MA: Harvard University Press, 1988), p. 172 (Table A.5).

12. David L. Imbroscio, *Reconstructing City Politics* (Thousand Oaks, CA: Sage, 1997), p. 112. Avis Vidal notes that estimates of number of CDCs in the country range from 1,000 to 5,000. *Rebuilding Communities: A National Study of Urban Community Development Corporations* (New York: New School Community Development Research Center, 1992), p. 24.

13. Hany Khalil, "Top 10 Policy Hits of the 1980s and 1990s: Pushing the Envelope" (unpublished paper) (Washington, DC: Grassroots Policy Project, October 1993), p. 4.

14. David Osborne and Ted Gaebler, *Reinventing Government: How the Entrepreneurial Spirit Is Transforming the Public Sector* (Reading, MA: Addison–Wesley, 1992), pp. 195–218.

15. Roy Morrison, *We Build the Road as We Travel* (Philadelphia, PA: New Society Press, 1991), p. 48.

16. David Morris, "The Mondragon Cooperative Corporation" (monograph) (Washington, DC: Institute for Local Self-Reliance, July 1992), p. 13.

17. Jane Jacobs, *Systems of Survival* (New York: Vintage, 1994).

18. The term "parastatal" refers to corporations or partnerships owned, controlled, or heavily subsidized by a national government.

19. See Harry E. Berndt, *New Rules in the Ghetto: The CDC and Urban Poverty* (Westport, CT: Greenwood Press, 1977).

20. Christopher Gunn and Hazel Dayton Gunn, *Reclaiming Capital: Democratic Initiatives and Community Development* (Ithaca, NY: Cornell University Press, 1991), p. 94.

21. Jonathan Rowe, "Reinventing the Corporation," *Washington Monthly,* April 1996, p. 16.

22. Lee Conrad, Personal Communication, 27 August 1997. One of the reasons for the generosity, of course, was to convince the work force not to entertain becoming unionized.

23. Lester B. Lave and H. Scott Matthews, "It's Easier to Say Green than to Be Green," *Technology Review,* November/December 1996, pp. 68–69.

24. Hanna Rosin, "The Evil Empire," *New Republic,* 11 September 1995, pp. 23–24.

25. *Ibid.*

26. David Moberg, "Skin Deep," *In These Times,* 19 September 1994, pp. 13–14.

27. *Ibid.,* p. 14.

28. *Ibid.,* p. 15.

29. Rosin, *supra* note 24, p. 25.

30. *Ibid.*

31. Moberg, *supra* note 26, p. 16.

32. Len Krimerman and Frank Lindenfeld, eds., *When Workers Decide* (Philadelphia, PA: New Society Press, 1992), p. 5.

33. Jed Emerson, ed., *New Social Entrepreneurs: The Success, Challenges and Lessons of Non-Profit Enterprise Creation* (San Francisco, CA: Roberts Foundation, 1996).

34. *Ibid.,* p. 244 (emphasis in original).

35. *Ibid.,* p. 247.

36. See, e.g., John D. Donahue, *The Privatization Decision* (New York: Basic Books, 1989).

37. Amory B. and L. Hunter Lovins, *Energy/War: Breaking the Nuclear Link* (San Francisco, CA: Friends of the Earth, 1980), p. 76.

38. Ellen R. Shaffer and Paul D. Wellstone, "Providing Comprehensive Coverage," in Richard Caplan and John Feffer, eds., *State of the Union 1994* (Boulder, CO: Westview, 1994), pp. 151–65.

39. The principle that no shareholder can own more than 1 percent of a company implies at least 100 shareholders, and a majority vote requiring the approval of at least 51 of them.

40. See, e.g.: Del. Code Ann., Title 8, Sect. 202(c)(4); Fla. Stat. Chap. 607.0627(4)(d); Ga. Code Ann. Sect. 14-2-627(d)(4); Tex. Bus. Corp. Act Ann. Art. 2.22 (D)(4); Wash. Rev. Code Sect. 23B.06.270(4)(d); Model Business Corp. Code Ann. Sect. 6.27(d)(4).

41. If a corporation is closely held, even these meager limitations might not apply. A corporation is usually considered closely held if there is only one class of shareholders, if fewer than 35 shareholders hold the stock, and if all the shareholders are individuals, estates, or trusts.

42. David L. Ratner, "The Government of Business Corporations: Critical Reflections on the Role of 'One Share, One Vote,'" *Cornell Law Review,* Vol. 56-1, 1970.

43. See, e.g., *Ling and Company v. Trinity Savings and Loan Association,* 482 S.W. 2d 841 (Sup. Ct. of Tex. 1972); *Cimo v. National Motor Club of Louisiana, Inc.,* 237 So.2d 408 (La. Ct. App. 1970); *In re West Waterway Company,* 367 P.2d 807, 811–12 (Wash. Sup. Ct. en banc 1962).

   Two peculiar exceptions prove the rule: In one case, *Hill v. Warner, Berman & Spitz,* two shareholders made the following agreement with each other: "We cannot sell, pledge or do anything with our stock in any corporation we both have an interest in without both partners agreeing." 484 A.2d 344 (N.J. Super. Ct. App. Div. 1984). This "consent-type" restraint was held invalid because it "has no limitation as to time, does not provide that the consent to act by the other shareholder will not be unreasonably withheld and does not promote the interest of the corporation."

   Another case, from Texas in 1948, invalidated a corporate bylaw that allowed a director of a corporation to stop a transfer of stock deemed to be "in furtherance of any scheme to defraud. . . ." See *Pelton v. Nevada Oil Co.,* 209 S.W.2d 645 (Tex. Ct. App. 1948). In other words, giving the board permission for unlimited discretion to make a case-by-case decision on when transfer is permissible is unreasonable. A clear rule on when transfer can or cannot take place, however, would be a different story.

44. *Bruns v. Rennebohm Drug Stores, Inc.,* 442 N.W. 2d 591, 594 (Wis. App. 1989).

45. Susan Meeker-Lowry, *Invested in the Common Good* (Philadelphia, PA: New Society Press, 1995), p. 58.

46. *Ibid.*

47. Jay Walljasper, "Burlington, Northern Light," *Nation,* 19 May 1997, pp. 18–23.

48. Steven D. Soifer, "The Burlington Community Land Trust: A Socialist Approach to Affordable Housing?," *Journal of Urban Affairs,* Vol. 12-3, p. 240.

49. Leon Sullivan, *Build Brother Build* (Philadelphia, PA: Macrae Smith Co., 1969), p. 168.

50. *Ibid.,* p. 166.

51. *Ibid.,* p. 177.

Chapter 4. Financing the Future

1. Sam Smith, "Saving the City from the Experts" (unpublished paper) (Washington, DC: Progressive Review, 1995), p. 13.

2. Jerry Knight, "U.S., Chevy Chase FSB Discussing Bias Probe," *Washington Post,* 20 August 1994, p. F1.

3. David Morris, *The New City-States* (Washington, DC: Institute for Local Self-Reliance, 1982), p. 6.

4. Christopher Gunn and Hazel Dayton Gunn, *Reclaiming Capital: Democratic Initiatives and Community Development* (Ithaca, NY: Cornell University, 1991), pp. 27–30.

5. Richard Douthwaite, *Short Circuit* (Devon, UK: Resurgence, 1996), pp. 3–26.

6. *Ibid.,* p. 121.

7. James Head and Kelly Mogle, "Race, Poverty, and Lending," *Clearinghouse Review,* Vol. 10, 1993, p. 362.

8. John P. Caskey, "Bank Representation in Low-Income and Minority Communities," *Urban Affairs Quarterly,* Vol. 29, 1994, p. 617.

9. Julia Ann Parzen and Michael Hall Kieschnick, *Credit Where It's Due* (Philadelphia, PA: Temple University Press, 1992), p. 44.

10. *Ibid.,* pp. 43–44.

11. Gabrielle Kirkpatrick, Personal Communication, National Association of Credit Unions, 25 August 1997.

12. Douthwaite, *supra* note 5, p. 125.

13. Tom Schlesinger and Regina Markey, "America's Restructured Financial System," (unpublished paper to Industrial Heartland Labor Investment Forum, 14–15 June 1996) (Philamont, VA: Financial Markets Center, 1996), pp. 2–3.

14. *Ibid.,* Table 7.

15. 12 U.S.C. Sects. 2901–2906.

16. Virginia M. Mayer, Marina Sampanes, and James Carras, *Local Officials Guide to the Community Reinvestment Act* (Washington, DC: National League of Cities, 1991). See also Anthony D. Taibi, "Banking, Finance, and Community Economic Empowerment: Structural Economic Theory, Procedural Civil Rights, and Substantive Racial Justice," *Harvard Law Review,* Vol. 107, 1994, p. 1463.

17. Allen J. Fishbein, "The Community Reinvestment Act After Fifteen Years: It Works, but Strengthened Federal Enforcement Is Needed," *Fordham Urban Law Journal,* Vol. 20-2, 1993, p. 294.

18. *Ibid.,* p. 296.

19. *Ibid.,* p. 298.

20. Parzen and Kieschnick, *supra* note 9, p. 11.

21. *Ibid.*

22. Michel Negenman, General Manager of the ASN Bank, Personal Communication, 30 July 1997 and 27 August 1997; Ton Bervoets, former General Manager of the ASN Bank, Personal Communication, 1 September 1995. ASN also oversees two socially responsible investment funds with assets over $110 million.

23. Douthwaite, *supra* note 5, pp. 150–53.

24. David Skidmore, "Clinton Signs Measure Aimed at Spurring Credit in Poor Areas," *Boston Globe,* 24 September 1994, p. 63.

25. 12 U.S.C. Sect. 4701.

26. Skidmore, *supra* note 24.

27. Douthwaite, *supra* note 5, pp. 133–35.

28. "WSEP Fact Sheet," May 1996.

29. Barbara B. Buchholz, "Giving Credit," *Chicago Tribune,* 28 April 1996, Section 13, p. 8.

30. Francine Knowles, "Guiding Women Out of Welfare," *Chicago Sun-Times,* 12 March 1995, p. 40.

31. For further information, contact Working Capital, 99 Bishop Allen Drive, Cambridge, MA 02139, or at 617-576-8620.

32. Douthwaite, *supra* note 5, pp. 136–49.

33. Federal Deposit Insurance Corporation, "Statement of Policy Regarding Applications for Deposit Insurance," *Federal Register,* Vol. 57, 13 April 1992, p. 12822.

34. Tom Schlesinger, "Nationwide Banking: An Analysis of the Treasury Proposal" (monograph) (Philamont, VA: Southern Finance Project, March 1991); David Morris, "Bill with Steel National Asset: Community-based Banking," *St. Paul Pioneer,* 29 July 1991, p. 9A.

35. Doreen Carvajal, "Housing Firm Builds Success on Unusual Methods," *Los Angeles Times,* 6 December 1993, p. A3.

36. Douthwaite, *supra* note 5, pp. 100–105.

37. *Ibid.,* p. 340.

38. Schlesinger and Markey, *supra* note 13, Table 1.

39. "The Last Mile—U.S. Communities and South Africa," *Global Communities,* Winter 1991–1992.

40. *Ibid.,* at 2.

41. "Nuclear Free Zones with Legislation Regarding Nuclear Free Investment and/or Contracting" (Baltimore, MD: Nuclear Free America, November 1987).

42. Susan Meeker-Lowry, *Invested in the Common Good* (Philadelphia, PA: New Society Press, 1995), p. 49.

43. Phil Young, Social Security Administration, Personal Communication, 2 September 1997; Krzysztof M. Ostaszewski, "Privatizing the Social Security Trust Fund? Don't Let the Government Invest," SSP No. 6 (monograph) (Washington, DC: Cato Institute, 14 January 1997); Anthony Ellsworth Scoville, "A Proposal for a Commission on the Investment of Social Security Trust Funds" (unpublished paper, 10 October 1992), p. 3.

44. Scoville, *ibid.,* pp. 3 and 8.

Chapter 5. Pro-Community Local Governance

1. *New State Ice Co. v. Liebman,* 285 U.S. 262 (1932) (Brandeis, J., dissenting).

2. Kettering Foundation, *Citizens and Politics: A View from Main Street America* (Bethesda, MD: Kettering Foundation, 1991), p. 48.

3. Alexis de Tocqueville, *Democracy in America* (New York: Perennial, 1988), p. 68.

4. Greg LeRoy, "No More Candystore" (monograph) (Washington, DC: Grassroots Policy Project/Federation for Industrial Retention and Renewal, 1994), p. 9.

5. Hany Khalil, "Top 10 Policy Hits of the 1980s and 1990s: Pushing the Envelope" (unpublished paper) (Washington, DC: Grassroots Policy Project, October 1993), p. 4.

6. *Charter Township of Ypsilanti v. General Motors Corporation,* 506 N.W. 2d 556 (1993).

7. The Federal Worker Adjustment, Retraining, and Notification Act requires companies with more than 100 or more employees to give at least two months' notice of a plant shutdown or major layoff.

8. Khalil, *supra* note 5, p. 5.

9. *Ibid.,* p. 5.

10. *Smaller Mfrs. v. Council of City of Pittsburgh,* 485 A.2d 73.

11. Khalil, *supra* note 5, p. 4.

12. *Ibid.*

13. *Ibid.*

14. *Ibid.* City officials believe that Gulf and Western was using Morse as a cash cow and bleeding off its assets. The threat to take over the plant proved to be too little, too late. After Gulf and Western sold the company, it never recovered. Since 1992, the U.S. Environmental Protection Agency has spent a small fortune carting away asbestos, cyanide vats, and other hazardous wastes left behind by the disloyal firm. David Kennedy, City Planner for the City of New Bedford, Personal Communication, 6 August 1997.

15. Khalil, *ibid.,* p. 5. Similar bills have been passed in Louisiana, Ohio, and Texas, as well as in several municipalities. Arthur S. Hayes, "Companies Are Finding It Hard to Move Out of Town," *Wall Street Journal,* 1 March 1993, p. B8.

16. Khalil, *supra* note 5, p. 5.

17. *Ibid.,* p. 6.

18. BNA *Labor Relations Reporter,* 10 January 1994, p. 24.

19. Joseph Persky, David Ranney, and Wim Wiewel, "Import Substitution and Local Economic Development," *Economic Development Quarterly,* February 1993, p. 25.

20. Jane Jacobs, *Systems of Survival* (New York: Vintage, 1992), pp. 167–70.

21. Persky, Ranney, and Wiewel, *supra* note 19, p. 21.

22. Eugene Moehring, Professor of History, University of Nevada at Las Vegas, Personal Communication, 25 August 1997.

23. Mike Wilson, Nevada Attorney General's Office, Personal Communication, 15 August 1997.

24. Susan Meeker-Lowry, "The Potential of Local Currency," *Z Magazine,* July/August 1995, p. 16.

25. Richard Douthwaite, *Short Circuit* (Devon, UK: Resurgence, 1996), p. 86.

26. Paul Glover, "Creating Ecological Economies with Local Currency," *Whole Earth Review,* Fall 1995, p. 24.

27. 18 U.S.C. Sect. 486 (1988) and Sect. 491 (1995).

28. Lewis D. Solomon, *Rethinking Our Centralized Monetary System* (Westport, CT: Praeger, 1996), p. 127.

29. Steven Levy, "The End of Money," *Newsweek,* 30 October 1995, p. 64.

30. Joseph J. Romm and Charles B. Curtis, "Mideast Oil Forever?" *Atlantic Monthly,* April 1996, p. 58.

31. Mickey Kaus, *The End of Equality* (New York: Basic Books, 1992), pp. 121–35.

32. William Raspberry, "Time Dollars: A Concept for Caring," *Washington Post,* 19 January 1996, p. A27.

33. Edgar S. Cahn, "Time Dollars, Welfare and Co-Production," Testimony before the Washington, DC, City Council, 30 September 1996, p. 2.

34. Olaf Egeberg, "An Exchange Directory for Every Neighborhood," *Whole Earth Review,* Fall 1995, p. 26.

35. Saskia Sassen, *The Global City* (Princeton, NJ: Princeton University Press, 1993).

36. Alice M. Rivlin, *Reviving the American Dream: The Economy, the States, and the Federal Government* (Washington, DC: Brookings, 1992), p. 128 (Figure 8–1).

37. Henry George, *Progress and Poverty* (New York: Random House, 1879).

38. Gurney Breckenfeld, "Higher Taxes that Promote Development," *Fortune,* 8 August 1983, pp. 68–71. Had Pittsburgh's property tax not been diluted by traditional taxes assessed by the school district and the county, the ratio would have been five to one.

39. A tally is kept by the Center for the Study of Economics in Columbia, Maryland.

40. Rivlin, *supra* note 36, p. 128 (Figure 8–1).

41. David Morris, "Green Taxes" (monograph) (Washington, DC: Institute for Local Self-Reliance, July 1994), p. 1.

42. Peter T. Kilborn, "When Wal-Mart Pulls Out, What's Left?" *New York Times,* Business Section, 5 March 1995, p. 1.

43. *Ibid.*

44. *Ibid.,* p. 6.

45. Scott Cech, "Picking Up Speed: State's Electric Car Industry Not Stalled by Regulation Changes," *San Francisco Examiner,* 5 May 1996.

Chapter 6. Bringing Home Power, Not Bacon

1. Alice Rivlin, *Reviving the American Dream: The Economy, the States, and the Federal Government* (Washington, DC: Brookings, 1992), p. 98.

2. *California v. Federal Energy Regulatory Commission,* 495 U.S. 290 (1990).

3. *Ibid.,* p. 497, citing 16 U.S.C. Sect. 821 (1982).

4. *Ibid.,* p. 506.

5. William Julius Wilson, "Research and *The Truly Disadvantaged,*" in Christopher Jencks and Paul E. Peterson, eds., *The Urban Underclass* (Washington, DC: Brookings, 1991), p. 464.

6. Robert Morlan, "Municipal vs. National Election Voter Turnout: Europe and the United States," *Political Science Quarterly,* Fall 1984, p. 469.

7. *Ibid.*

8. *Exxon Corp. v. Governor of Maryland,* 437 U.S. 117 (1978).

9. See, e.g., *Raymond Motor Transportation, Inc. v. Rice,* 434 U.S. 429 (1978); and *Kassel v. Consolidated Freightways Corp.,* 450 U.S. 662 (1981).

10. *Pike v. Bruce Church,* 397 U.S. 137, 143 (1970), citing *Parker v. Brown,* 317 U.S. 341 (1943).

11. *Pike v. Bruce Church, ibid.,* citing *Pacific States Box and Basket Co. v. White,* 296 U.S. 176 (1935).

12. *Hunt v. Washington Apple Advertising Comm'n,* 432 U.S. 333, 350 (1977), citing *Florida Lime & Avocado Growers, Inc., v. Paul,* 373 U.S. 132, 146 (1963).

13. *Ibid.,* at 473.

14. *Lincoln Federal Labor Union v. Northwestern Iron & Metal Co.,* 335 U.S. 525, 536 (1978).

15. Agreement on SPS, Sections 6 and 9.

16. Agreement on TBT, Sect. 1.3.

17. Codex meetings held between 1989 and 1991 involved more than 2,500 participants; approximately 25 percent came from industry and only 1 percent came from public interest groups. Eighty-one percent of the "nongovernmental" representatives on national delegations also came from industry. Reported in Tim Lang and Colin Hines, *The New Protectionism: Protecting the Future Against Free Trade* (New York: The New Press, 1993), p. 101.

18. Agreement on SCM, Art. 1.1(a)(1) and (2).

19. *Ibid.,* Art. 5.1.

20. *Ibid.,* Arts. 6.1 and 6.3.

21. *Ibid.,* Art. 1, 1.1 (a)(1)(i).

22. Agreement on Government Procurement—Addendum, GPR/74/Add. 1, 6 January 1994.

23. Lori Sherman, U.S.T.R. Office, Personal Communication, 17 March 1994.

24. Agreement on TBT, Preamble.

25. *Ibid.,* Art. 2.1.

26. GATS, Art. 17, Sect. 1. This provision is limited to "sectors inscribed in [a signatory nation's] schedule."

27. Alan Tonelson and Lori Wallach, "We Told You So: The WTO's First Trade Decision Vindicates the Warnings of Critics," *Washington Post,* 5 May 1996, p. C4.

28. 276 C.A.2d 221.

29. Charles Komanoff and Margaret Sikowitz, *Crossroads: Highway-Finance Subsidies in New Jersey* (New York: Komanoff Energy Associates, April 1995), p. 1.

30. James MacKenzie, Roger Dower, and Donald D. T. Chen, "The Going Rate: What It Really Costs to Drive" (monograph) (Washington, DC: World Resources Institute, 1992), cited in David Morris, "Communities: Building Authority, Responsibility, and Capacity," in Richard Caplan and John Feffer, eds., *State of the Union 1994* (Boulder, CO: Westview, 1994), p. 225.

31. Tom Kenworthy, " 'Green Scissors' Coalition Seeks $33 Billion in Cuts," *Washington Post,* 31 January 1995, p. A13.

32. Robert Kuttner, "Rewarding Corporations That Really Invest in America," *Business Week,* 26 February 1996, p. 22.

33. Pamela Gilbert and Susannah Goodman, "Banking Regulation," in Mark Green, ed., *Changing America: Blueprints for the New Administration* (New York: Newmarket Press, 1992).

34. Tom Schlesinger, "Reinvestment Reform in an Era of Financial Change" (monograph) (Philamont, VA: Southern Finance Project, April 1995), Table 17.

35. *Ibid.,* p. 6.

36. *Ibid.*

37. *Ibid.,* p. 44.

38. Norman G. Kurland and Michael D. Greaney, "The Third Way: America's True Legacy to the New Republics," in John H. Miller, ed., *Curing World Poverty: The New Role of Property* (St. Louis, MO: Social Justice Review, 1994), pp. 269–80.

39. Schlesinger, *supra* note 34, Table 17.

40. *Ibid.,* p. 15.

41. For evidence on the success of corporate lobbying, see Jeffrey H. Birnbaum, *The Lobbyists: How Influence Peddlers Work Their Way in Washington* (New York: Times Books, 1992), and Kenneth H. Bacon, "For Citicorp, Which Has Largest Lobbying Force in Banking Industry, Victories Are Won Quietly," *Wall Street Journal,* 14 December 1993, p. A18.

42. "Main Street U.S.A.—Lobby or Lose It," *Global Communities,* Autumn 1991.

43. *Ibid.,* p. 5.

44. The National League of Cities' resolution of support for the North American Free Trade Agreement (NAFTA), which simply assumes that free trade is in the interest of communities, is typical. Resolution 94–7, 5 December 1993.

Chapter 7. Making History

1. Richard Flacks, *Making History: The American Left and the American Mind* (New York: Columbia, 1988).

2. Ralph Estes, *Tyranny of the Bottom Line: Why Corporations Make Good People Do Bad Things* (San Francisco: Berrett-Koehler, 1996), pp. 220–31. See also Thad Williamson, "The Content of Ethical Impact Reports: A Two-Tiered Proposal," *Tikkun,* Vol. 12-4, pp. 36–40.

3. Wess Roberts, *Victory Secrets of Attila the Hun* (New York: Dell Trade, 1993), p. 59.

4. John P. Kretzmann and John L. McKnight, *Building Communities from the Inside Out* (Evanston, IL: Center for Urban Affairs and Policy Research, 1993).

5. Elizabeth Kline, "Sustainable Community Indicators" (monograph) (Medford, MA: Consortium for Regional Sustainability, 1995), and Elizabeth Kline, "Defining a Sustainable Community" (monograph) (Medford, MA: Consortium for Regional Sustainability, 1993).

6. Richard Douthwaite, *Short Circuit* (Devon, UK: Resurgence, 1996), p. 336.

7. *Ibid.,* p. 337.

8. Alex MacGillivray and Simon Zadek, "Accounting for Change" (monograph) (London: New Economics Foundation, October 1995), p. 26.

9. A nice summary of these studies can be found in Christopher Gunn and Hazel Dayton Gunn, *Reclaiming Capital: Democratic Initiatives and Community Development* (Ithaca, NY: Cornell University Press, 1991), pp. 37–53.

10. Michael E. Porter, "New Strategies for Inner-City Economic Development," *Economic Development Quarterly,* February 1997, p. 14.

11. John J. Berger, *Charging Ahead: The Business of Renewable Energy and What It Means for America* (New York: Henry Holt, 1997), p. 61.

12. Brenda Platt, Senior Researcher for the Institute for Local Self-Reliance, Personal Communication, 16 April 1997.

13. *Ibid.*

14. Kenneth Boulding, *Stable Peace* (Austin, TX: University of Texas Press, 1981), p. 93.

15. Jane Jacobs, *Cities and the Wealth of Nations* (New York: Vintage, 1984), p. 42 (emphasis in original).

16. Lewis Mumford, *The Transformation of Man* (New York: Harper, 1956).

17. Douthwaite, *supra* note 6, p. 334.

18. Brian Headd, Advocacy Officer in the U.S. Small Business Administration, Personal Communication, July 1997.

19. Sherman Kreiner and Kenneth Delaney, "Labour-Sponsored Investment Funds in Canada" (monograph) (Winnipeg, Canada: Crocus Fund, 1996).

20. Patrick McVeigh, "Study SRI No More," *Investing for a Better World,* 15 October 1996, p. 1. See also Estes, *supra* note 2, p. 238.

21. Robert L. Morlan, "Municipal vs. National Election Voter Turnout: Europe and the United States," *Political Science Quarterly,* Fall 1984, p. 462 (Table 1).

22. *Ibid.,* pp. 462–65.

23. William Greider, *Who Will Tell the People: The Betrayal of American Democracy* (New York: Simon & Schuster, 1992), p. 22.

24. *Buckley v. Valeo,* 424 U.S. 1 (1976).

25. Examples in this section are drawn from Michael H. Shuman, *Toward A Global Village: International Community Development Initiatives* (London: Pluto Press, 1994).

26. Robert Keohane and Joseph Nye, Jr., *Power and Interdependence,* 2nd ed. (Glenview, IL: Scott, Foresman, 1989).

27. Shuman, *supra* note 25, pp. 30–31.

Index

Abortion, 20, 126
Absolute advantage, 43
Adams, Frank T., 83
Agriculture
    community-supported agriculture
      (CSA), 61, 82, 220–221
    monoculture, 62–63
    sustainable, 63, 262–263
    urban, 59–61, 268–269
    wastes, 68–70, 76
Aid to Families with Dependent
    Children (AFDC), 60
Alabama, 10
Alaska, 55
Albuquerque, New Mexico, 111
Algae, 69, 70
American Association of Retired People
    (AARP), 36
American Cast Iron Pipe, 86
American Enterprise Institute, 137
American Federation of Labor-Congress
    of Industrial Organizations (AFL-
    CIO), 23
American Federation of State, County,
    and Municipal Employees, 93
American Water and Energy Savers, 73
Anacostia, Washington, D.C., 106–107
Anaheim, California, 11
Antifederalists, 154
Apartheid, 120–121
Apple Computer, 81
Arco, 14
Arendt, Hannah, 91
Arizona, 55, 72, 87
Arkansas, 158
Armendiarrieta, Don José Mariá, 84,
    118, 188
Arthur D. Little Corporation, 86

Articles of Confederation, 124, 154
ASN, Netherlands, 110–111
Association of Community Organizations
    for Reform Now (ACORN), 109
Atlanta, Georgia, 14, 108
Atlantic Monthly, 18
Atlantis Energy, 68
AT&T Company, 18, 19
Audubon Society, 24
Australia, 135
Austria, 138, 197
Avis, 86

Bach, George Leland, 40, 41
Baltimore, Maryland, 1
Bangladesh, 112
Banks, 26, 106–122, 164, 189–191,
    207–208
    bankers vs. communities, 107–111
    community-development financial
      institutions (CDFIs), 111–115,
      122, 172, 214–215
    deregulation, 171–172
    locally owned equity, 117–120
    pension reinvestment, 120–121
    public policy role and, 121–122
    unconventional loans, 115–117
Barber, Benjamin, 33
Barnet, Richard, 44
Barry, Marion, 89
Barter system, 116, 134–137, 208
Base Realignment and Closure
    Commission, 169
Bellah, Robert, 33
Ben & Jerry's, 26, 91–92, 98
Bennett, Bill, 32
Bentham, Jeremy, 38
Berkeley, California, 187, 195

Berkshire Farm Preserve Notes, 116, 121
*Bethlehem Steel v. Board of
    Commissioners* (1971), 164
Big City Forest, New York, 186–187
Bingaman, Jeff, 170
Biochemicals, 76
Biomass wastes, 68–69
Bioregionalism, 25, 125, 209
Birmingham, England, 69
Bloomington, Indiana, 9–10
Bluestone, Barry, 9
BMW, 10
Body Shop, The, 26, 88, 92, 98
Boeing, 14, 18
Bologna, Italy, 84, 89, 90, 98
Bonoir, David, 178
Boston, Massachúsetts, 19, 60
Boston Company, 57
Boulding, Kenneth, 187
"Bowling Alone" (Putnam), 35
Boycotts, 163, 209–210
Bradley Foundation, 137
Brandeis, Louis, 127
Brazil, 12, 90, 148
Bremen, Germany, 197
Brenner, Harvey, 13
British Columbia, 134, 135
Browning-Ferris Industries, 23
Brundtland, Gro Harlem, 22
Buchanan, Patrick, 15
Buckley v. Valeo (1976), 194
*Building Communities from the Inside
    Out* (Kretzmann and McKnight),
    184
Burma, 121, 163
Business schools, community-friendly,
    188–189
Butler, William, 2
Buy American Acts, 164

Cable television co-ops, 86
Cahn, Edgar, 142, 143
California, 11, 19, 44, 54, 60, 64, 66, 71,
    76, 79, 81, 87, 115, 131, 140, 148,
    150–151, 155–156, 164, 186, 195
Cambridge, Massachusetts, 113
Campaign finance reform, 193, 194,
    210–211
Canadian International Development
    Agency, 197

Capital punishment, 126
Carbohydrate economy, 76–77, 211
Carbon emissions, 70–71
CARE, 94
Caskey, John, 108
Cato Institute, 168
Cavanagh, John, 44
Celeste, Richard, 2
Center for a New American Dream, 21
Center for Energy and Environmental
    Studies, Princeton University, 79
Chain stores, 14, 98, 132, 149
Chattanooga, Tennessee, 60, 183
Checks and balances, 125
Chester, Pennsylvania, 186
Chevron Corporation, 23
Chicago, Illinois, 54, 89, 111–113, 115,
    130, 132, 142, 154
Child labor, 11, 21
China, 12, 59, 166, 200–201
Chrysler Corporation, 9
Church attendance, 36
Ciba-Geigy, 23
Cities and the Wealth of Nations
    (Jacobs), 46
City council meetings, 35
Civic Center Barrio Corporation, Santa
    Ana, California, 115
Civic participation, 35–36
Civil rights, 154, 155
Civil War, 154
Cleveland, Ohio, 1–3, 6, 19, 44
Cleveland Browns, 3
Cleveland World Trade Association, 2
Climate Alliance, 197
Clinton, Bill, 17, 32, 91, 106, 111, 147,
    148, 168–169, 177
Clinton, Hillary, 91
Clustering, 81–82
Cobb, John, Jr., 42, 46
Coca-Cola Company, 14
Coffee, 56, 199–200
Cold War, 154, 169
Collective bargaining, 21
Commerce Clause, 157, 165
Communitarianism, 33–36, 211–212
Community
    breakdown of, 32–37
    defined, 32–33
Community-based family farming, 58

Community Bill of Rights, 181–183
Community Capital Bank, New York
City, 111
Community corporations, 6–7, 27, 49,
50, 83–105, 212. *See also* Local
government
community loyalty, 97–99
community usefulness, 88–90
efficiency, 94–97
empowerment through ownership,
104–105
new models, 98–104
responsible production methods,
90–94
Community currency, 133–138,
191–192, 238
Community Development Block Grants,
17
Community-development corporations
(CDCs), 26, 87, 89, 90, 212–213
Community-development financial institutions (CDFIs), 111–115, 122,
172, 214–215
Community-development loan funds,
111
Community-friendly business schools,
188–189
Community loyalty, 97–99
Community Reinvestment Act (CRA) of
1977, 109–110, 122, 189,
219–220
Community Rights Acts, 156
Community-scale agriculture, 58
Community self-reliance, 46–50
banks, 26, 106–122, 164, 189–191,
208–209
bankers vs. communities, 107–111
community-development financial
institutions (CDFIs), 111–115,
122, 172, 214–215
locally owned equity, 117–120
pension reinvestment, 120–121
public policy role and, 121–122
unconventional loans, 115–117
community corporations, 83–105, 212
community loyalty, 97–99
community usefulness, 88–90
efficiency, 94–97
empowerment through ownership, 104–105

new models, 98–104
responsible production methods,
90–94
in history, 51
local government, 123–151
hiring, 140–144
purchasing, 132–138
reinvestment, 128–132
selective privatization, 138–140
subsidiarity, 125–128
taxation, 144–149
needs-driven economy, 51–81, 109
energy industries, 64–71, 254–256
food industries, 58–63
import replacement, 52–58, 78
materials industries, 74–77
natural-resources industries, 71–74
ten steps toward, 180–198
anchor corporations, 186–188
Community Bill of Rights,
181–183
community currency, 191–192
community-friendly business
schools, 188–189
community-friendly city hall,
192–193
interlocalism, 196–198
lobbying for localism, 195–196
localized banking, 189–191
political reform, 193–195
State of the City Report, 184–186
Community Service Block Grants, 17
Community-supported agriculture
(CSA), 61, 82, 220–221
Community usefulness of corporations,
88–90
Comox Valley, British Columbia, 134,
135
Comparative advantage, 39, 43
Comprehensive Anti-Apartheid Act of
1986, 120–121
Concord Commission, 177
Connecticut, 60
Conservation
energy, 64, 66
water, 72–73, 147
Conservatives, 5, 8, 33, 125, 144, 154, 170
Consolidated Edison Company, 53
Constitution of the United States, 126,
131, 154, 155, 157, 158, 165, 194

Consumer co-ops, 86
Consumer credit unions (CCUs), 103
Consumer product safety, 155
Consumer Reports, 182
Consumers' Water Company, Portland,
    Maine, 73
Contract with America (1994), 125, 155,
    178
Cooperative Home Care Associates of
    the Bronx, 86
Cooperatives, 84, 86, 88–89, 98, 99,
    102, 118–119, 180, 183, 221–222
Corporate mobility, 7–15, 22, 23, 25, 164
Corporate structure, 85–88
Corporate taxes, 144–145, 167–168
Corruption, 89–90, 99, 130, 179
Co-Steel, Inc., 10
Craxi, Bettino, 90
Credit. *See* Banks
Credit unions, 86, 108, 111, 114, 173,
    174, 190, 213–214
Crime, 13, 20
Curitaba, Brazil, 148
Currency systems, 133–138, 191–192, 238

Dad-Redalia, Debra, 92
Daley, Richard, Sr., 89
Daly, Herman, 42, 46
D'Amato, Alfonse, 11
Daschle, Tom, 170
Defective products, 11
Deforestation, 197–198
Delaware, 101
Deli Dollars, 115–116, 121
Delta Airlines, 14
Democratic party, 125, 155, 194–195
Denmark, 69, 200
Deregulation, 43–44, 64–65, 171–172
Desert Sands Unified School District
    (DSUSD), Indio, California, 66
Detroit, Michigan, 60, 157
Devolution, 157, 225
Diamond Star Motors, 9
Dingell, John, 93
Divorce, 20
Dofasco, Inc., 10
Dole, Bob, 32, 177
Domestic violence, 13
Douthwaite, Richard, 46, 62, 134, 135
Dow Chemical, 91

Dow Chemical Corporation, 23
Drexel Burnham Lambert, 57
Drug consumption, 20
Durham, North Carolina, 111, 115

E.F. Schumacher Society, 6, 115, 137
Economic Circle, Switzerland, 116–117,
    122, 190, 250
Economic conversion, 153
Economic Development Assistance
    Grants, 17
Economic multiplier, 50, 77, 132
Economic Revitalization, 17
Economic segregation, 3
Economics (Samuelson and Nordhaus),
    37–40
Economies of scale, 57, 81
Economy of Cities, The (Jacobs), 46, 54
Edgar, Jim, 11
Education, 96, 97, 188–189
Efficiency, 94–97
    science of, 37–39
Egeberg, Olaf, 143–144
Ekins, Paul, 46
Electric Power Research Institute, 67
Electric utilities, 53, 64–68, 96, 99, 201,
    202
Eminent domain, 131
Employee Stock Ownership Plans
    (ESOPs), 86
Endangered species, 13, 22
Energy conservation, 64, 66
Energy industries, 53, 64–71, 254–256
Energy-service companies (ESCOs),
    65–68, 72, 82, 226
Engels, Friedrich, 38
Enron Corporation, 23, 68
Enumerated powers, 154
Environmental Defense Fund, 23, 24
Environmental justice, 25, 226–227
Environmental protection, 11, 13, 22,
    37, 44, 91–94, 155, 162–163,
    197–198
*Environmental Protection and Economic
    Well-Being* (Power), 46
EPIC Healthcare, 86
Equity banking, 117–120
Estes, Ralph, 182
Etzioni, Amitai, 34
Eugene, Oregon, 132

European Economic Community (EEC), 119, 125
Euthanasia, 126
Export-Import Bank, 167
Export-led theory of development, 55–56
Exxon Corporation, 14, 158–159

Fair trade movement, 199–200, 227–228
Farm Chemurgic Council, 75
Farmers' markets, 60–61
Farming. *See* Agriculture
Farm Service Agency, 174
Farrakhan, Louis, 46
Fast-food restaurants, 107
Federal Credit Union Act of 1934, 103
Federal Deposit Insurance Corporation (FDIC), 171
Federal Energy Regulatory Commission (FERC), 155
Federal government, 17, 152–176
    banking and, 171–174
    community lobbying, 174–176
    new approach to trade and, 158–167
    treatment of corporations, 167–170
Federal Housing Administration, 174
Federalism, 127, 154, 196
Federal Power Act, 155–156
Federal Reserve Board, 137, 173–174, 192
Feuerstein, Aaron, 91
First Amendment to the Constitution, 194
Florence, Italy, 107
Florida, 19, 75, 76, 185
Food industries, 58–63
Food Research and Action Center, 60
Ford, Gerald, 17
Ford, Henry, 75
Ford Foundation, 87
Forest resources, 73–74, 266–267
For the Common Good (Daly and Cobb), 42, 46
Fowler, Cary, 63
Fox, Arkansas, 158
France, 97, 198
Free Society of Traders, 102
Free trade, 38–45, 164
Friedman, Milton, 7, 16
Friends of the Earth, 169

Gaebler, Ted, 87
Galbraith, John Kenneth, 38
Galston, William, 33
Galtung, Johan, 47, 49
Gap, The, 26, 88
Garbage, 74–75, 148
Garn-St. Germain Act of 1982, 171
Gasoline cleanliness, 162–163
General Agreement on Tariffs and Trade (GATT), 14, 25, 38, 45, 159–164
General Motors Corporation, 7, 10, 23, 130
General Revenue Sharing, 17, 153
George, Henry, 145–146
Georgia, 14, 108
Georgia-Pacific, 23
Geothermal energy, 67
Gephardt, Richard, 177
Germany, 72, 197, 200
Gigot, Paul, 5
Gingrich, Newt, 178
Glass-Steagall Act of 1933, 171
Glendon, Mary Ann, 33
Global Dreams (Barnet and Cavanagh), 44
Global economy, 8, 9, 23
Global Green Bank, 200
Global warming, 70–71, 197
Glover, Paul, 135–136, 182
Goodman, Paul, 6
Grameen Bank, Bangladesh, 112
Grassroots organizing, 229–230
Graybar Electric Company, 86
Great Barrington, Massachusetts, 115–116
Great Depression, 133, 171
Greater Cleveland World Trade Alliance, 2
Great Leap Forward, 200–201
Great Transformation, The (Polanyi), 45–46
Green Bay, Wisconsin, 3–6
Green Bay Packers, 3–6, 87
Green money, 134–135
Green politics, 25
Green purchasing, 121
Green Scissors Coalition, 169
Greenseal, 182
Greenspan, Alan, 16

Green taxes, 146–149, 156–157, 168, 230–231
Greider, William, 194
Gross Domestic Product, 21
Grossman, Richard, 83
Groundwater Protection Act (Iowa), 148
Guatemala, 199
Guerard, John, Jr., 191
Gulf and Western Corporation, 131
Gun control, 90
Gunn, Christopher, 90, 107
Gunn, Hazel Dayton, 90, 107

Hamilton, Alexander, 154
Harkin, Tom, 177
Harrison, Bennett, 80–82
Hartford, Connecticut, 60
Harwood, Richard, 32, 127–128
Harwood Group, 21
Hawken, Paul, 74, 148
Hazardous materials monitoring, 231–232
Head, James, 108
Health care, 20, 96–98, 178, 251
Henderson, Hazel, 46
Henwood, Doug, 43
Heritage Foundation, 137
Herkimer, New York, 40–41
Hiring, local, 140–144
Home Depot, 3, 86
Homelessness, 20
Hong Kong, 59
Hoover, Herbert, 160
Hope LAS Horticulture Corps, 60
Housing co-ops, 86
Houston, Texas, 14
Human Scale (Sale), 46
Hyster, 10

IBM Corporation, 91
Illinois, 9–11, 54, 89, 111–113, 115, 131, 132, 142, 154
Illiteracy, 20
Illych, Ivan, 6
Import substitution, 50, 52–58
Income and wealth, distribution of, 41–42
Income taxes, 146, 147, 233
India, 12

Indiana, 9–10
Indonesia, 12
Industrial-development bonds, 128, 129
Industrial ecology, 25
Infant mortality, 20
Inflation, 15, 16, 34, 37
Institute for Community Economics, 6, 103
Institute for Local Self-Reliance (ILSR), 6, 76, 107
Insurance company co-ops, 86
Intel, 81
Intentional communities, 235
Intergovernmental Panel on Climate Change, 70
Interlocalism, 196–198, 235–236
Internal Revenue Code, Section 501 (c)(3) of, 86
Internal Revenue Service, 95
International Board for Plant Genetic Resources, 62
International Council of Local Environmental Initiatives (ICLEI), 198
International Monetary Fund, 200
International Trade Commission, 13
International Union of Local Authorities (IULA), 198
Internet, 8, 138
In These Times (weekly), 92
Inventories workbooks, 236
Iowa, 148
Ireland, 134
Irish potato famine, 62
Irrigation, 72–73
Isolation, 196, 198
Italy, 80, 84, 89, 90, 98, 107
Ithaca, New York, 135–137
Ithaca HOURS, 135–137, 191
Ithaca Money (newspaper), 136, 182
Izaak Walton League, 24

Jackson, Jesse, 32
Jacksonville, Florida, 185
Jacobs, Jane, 6, 46, 54, 56, 89, 183, 188
Japan, 165–166
Jennings, Peter, 91
Jericho, 51
Job security, 15–16
Johnson, Lyndon B., 87
Journal of Democracy, The, 35